TO STAND AT THE POLE

Also by William R. Hunt:
  North of 53°
  Alaska: A Bicentennial History
  Arctic Passage
  Vilhjalmur Stefansson
  Dictionary of Rogues

TO STAND AT THE POLE

The Dr. Cook-Admiral Peary North Pole Controversy

WILLIAM R. HUNT

STEIN AND DAY/*Publishers*/New York

Photographs of Dr. Frederick Cook in 1909, Cook's Eskimo companions, his diary at the Pole, his map of his polar journey, his companions at the Pole, and of Peary's Eskimo mistress and their child from Cook's book *My Attainment of the Pole,* 1913 edition. Newspaper article "Prof. Parker Lays Bare Mt. McKinley Fake of Dr. Cook" from the *New York Evening Telegram,* September 8, 1909. Cook's summit photograph, Belmore Browne's, Bradford Washburn's, and Adams Carter's photographs of the "fake peak" courtesy of the *American Alpine Journal,* 1958, and Bradford Washburn and Adams Carter. The title page and photograph of Peary's ship, the *Roosevelt,* from a Peary Arctic Club brochure, and the cover of *Hampton's Magazine,* courtesy of the Center for Polar Archives, National Archives (Peary Collection). Newspaper article "Peary to Tell Contemporary Club of His Dashes to the North Pole" from the *New York World,* January 8, 1908. Portrait of Roald Amundsen courtesy of the Scott Polar Research Institute.

First published in 1981
Copyright © 1981 by William R. Hunt
All rights reserved
Designed by Judith E. Dalzell
Printed in the United States of America
STEIN AND DAY/Publishers
Scarborough House
Briarcliff Manor, N.Y. 10510

Library of Congress Cataloging in Publication Data

Hunt, William R.
   To stand at the Pole.

   Bibliography: p.
   Includes index.
   1. Cook, Frederick Albert, 1865–1940.   2. Peary,
Robert Edwin, 1856–1920.   3. North Pole.   4. Explorers—
United States—Biography. I. Title
G635.C66H86   910'.091632   80-6156
ISBN 0-8128-2773-2   AACR2

To my children:
Chris,
Tom,
Maria,
and Alexander.

ACKNOWLEDGMENTS

Researchers into polar subjects have reason to be grateful to the Center for Polar Archives Division of the National Archives. It is a great treasury of Arctic-Antarctic knowledge that is capably tended by helpful experts, including Franklin Burch, Alison Wilson, and Gerald Pagano. Other federal research centers important to this book include the Library of Congress Archives Division and the Federal Records Center in Fort Worth, where the Cook oil fraud trial record is housed.

In connection with research for this book and another on the explorer Vilhjalmur Stefansson, I have also benefited from the use of the Baker Library at Dartmouth College and the help of Erika Parmi, formerly curator of the Stefansson Collection there.

My thanks to the staff of the Elmer E. Rasmuson Library of the University of Alaska—Fairbanks; the Scott Polar Research Institute of Cambridge, England; the University of Virginia Library; and the University of Santa Clara Library. And to Commander Edward P. Stafford and Dennis Rawlins for permission to use the Peary and Henshaw Ward collections at the National Archives.

Individuals who have either read the manuscript or answered queries include Richard S. Finnie, Terris and Katrina Moore, Dennis Rawlins, Keith Van Cleve, Claus-M. Naske, Terrence Cole, Robert Bates, Bradford Washburn, H. Adams Carter, Einar Nilsson, and Irmgard Hunt.

Bob Carlson and Chick Hartman of the Institute of Water Resources of the University of Alaska gave me particular encouragement and help over several years.

CONTENTS

ILLUSTRATIONS

(Between pages 142 and 143)

Dr. Frederick Cook in 1909
Newspaper Account Alleging Mount McKinley Fraud
Cook's Summit Photograph
Belmore Browne's 1910 Photograph of "Fake Peak"
Bradford Washburn's 1956 Photograph of "Fake Peak"
H. Adams Carter's 1957 Photograph of "Fake Peak"
Title Page of a Peary Arctic Club Brochure
Robert E. Peary's Ship, the *Roosevelt*
Peary Announces His Plans in January 1908
First Report of Cook's Progress to the Pole
Cook's Eskimo Companions
Cook's Diary at the Pole
Cook's Map of His Polar Journey
Cook's Photograph of His Companions at the Pole
News of Cook's Success
Peary's Announcement
Peary Claims the Pole
Mrs. Cook Denies Peary's Charges
Peary's Eskimo Mistress and Their Child
Hampton's Magazine Cover Blazoning "Cook's Confession"
Roald Amundsen

PREFACE

Dr. Frederick Cook remains one of the most controversial figures in American history. He claimed the first ascent of Mount McKinley in 1906 and the first journey to the North Pole in 1908. Vociferous critics, led by the explorer Robert E. Peary, disputed both claims. The international news coverage of the controversy in 1909–1910 was voluminous. Few private individuals have ever received so much attention. Cook's veracity was thoroughly discredited, yet he made a remarkable comeback campaign after disappearing for a year in November 1909. And, in the last few years, a number of books have been published which present vindications of him.

Why do the claims of Dr. Cook retain their vitality? An obvious answer is that the explorer's career makes a good story. Cook was not an ordinary faker. Indeed, he was a man of varied accomplishments, and one who won the respect of many others. If we widen our consideration of the Cook mystery, its appeal becomes clear. The mystery is not simply whether or not Cook accomplished what he claimed, although that issue retains the power to arouse emotions. The wider mystery is the receptivity of people to arguments they wish to believe. Our gullibility is expressed on many levels. We are not always overwhelmed by rational explanations. So in examining Cook's record, I have focused on other individuals who have been concerned with him over the last seventy years. Some of these individuals favored Cook; others deplored him. Some thought themselves polar experts; others did not. All shared a passion. Was it a passion for truth—the ultimate mystery? It seems to me that anyone engaging himself in the Cook controversy is committed to a search for truth. If all the evidence bearing on the controversy is available —and I believe it is—then disagreement should end. Yet I don't really expect this to happen. Thus the mystery remains: the mystery of Cook himself and of others who seek truth through him.

Don't look in this book for the definitive analysis of evidence for or against Cook's Mount McKinley and polar claims. Both feats were probably physically possible, but surrounding circumstances have created suspicion. All the arguments have been exercised by the partisans, but by focusing on the people who believed or doubted Cook we gain another perspective. It is the involvement of others besides Cook and Peary over a long period of time that has transformed an athletic event into a great human drama, the most compelling event of the early twentieth century.

I

THE NORTH POLE

1

THE PRIZE

"In skating over thin ice, our safety is in our speed."
— *Ralph Waldo Emerson*

The three men rested within striking distance of the North Pole, the great prize of explorers for four hundred years. They camped on the smooth ice of the polar sea, terribly fatigued but enthused by the proximity of their goal. It was the morning of April 20, 1908; the sun glowed on the ice pack, giving it a purple hue. Dr. Frederick Cook eased his cramped legs and told his two Eskimo companions to forget about boiling water for tea. Melted snow and pemmican pounded from a frozen bulk with an ax would sustain them. Before they finished their meal they fell asleep, dead to their strange surroundings for eight hours.

After waking they fed their hardworking dogs. But for the sturdy animals, the explorers could never have accomplished their goal. Earlier explorers had experimented with other pack animals or tried to haul their own sledges over the ice, but dogs served the purpose far better than any other means.

The dogs ate greedily and lay down to sleep. Cook took time to brew tea. There was plenty of light at all hours. No need to hurry now with just one march ahead. Let the Eskimo boys sing and relax, thought Cook, they had earned it.

3

At midnight Cook told Etukishook and Ahwelah to harness the dogs. In a few minutes all was ready. Whips cracked over the two sledges in the light of the midnight sun and the howling dogs dashed off. Cook ran with the sledges, stopping sometimes to check his navigational instruments. Swiftly they advanced to the top of the world. Cook felt feverish in his impatience; his heart filled with a strange rapture of conquest.

Suddenly he ordered a halt. They were there! At last Cook had achieved his fondest dream. He looked about at the expanse of ice extending beyond the eye's reach. In physical appearance there was nothing singular about the point they had reached. The Eskimos felt Cook's excitement without understanding clearly why the North Pole was important.

The doctor's imagination danced with colorful imagery. He seemed to see silver and crystal palaces, unlike any ever built by man. From an imaginary castle, imaginary flags flapped in the polar breeze. He felt the presence of ghosts and saw mirages of dead armies, magnified and transfigured, huge and spectral, moving along the horizon, bearing the wind-tossed phantoms of golden, bloodstained banners. Somehow these mirages represented the men who had dared to attempt in former ages what Cook had so gloriously accomplished. Their ghostly presence paid tribute to Cook's success. All this was imagined, yet it was real enough in the doctor's bedazzled mind.

The wind throbbed, suggesting martial music. "Bewildered, I realized all that I had suffered, all the pain of fasting, all the anguish of long weariness, and I felt that this was my reward. I had scaled the world, and I stood at the Pole!"[1]

Putting aside his romantic musings, Cook ordered the boys to pitch the tent and build an igloo. For all his sensitivity and imagination, Cook remained a practical man, a scientist. Bedazzled dreamers cannot achieve what he achieved. He had built upon his dream of polar conquest with sound planning. Essentially the task had involved logistical skills: a precise determination of the necessary stores; a fine calculation of each day's march; the right choices of equipment, dogs, men, and navigational instruments. Physical strength and endurance were important, but skillful planning and experience separated the winners from the losers in polar exploration.

Planning—and the indefinable drive that makes one an explorer. Such men are driven by ambition and ego. They dream and dare; most men only dream. Some special restlessness urges adventurers like Cook on beyond the point where others would succumb to discouragement. Somehow adventurers manage to impose an iron discipline upon their emotions. Initially they must conquer themselves, subdue any tendencies to diversion, and shape themselves toward a single, all-consuming purpose.

Pride sustains them. But it need not be a wholly selfish pride. As Cook looked at the American flag flying from the tent pole, he expressed a love for his nation: "The prize of an international marathon was ours. Pinning the stars and stripes to a tent-pole, I asserted the achievement in the name of the ninety millions of countrymen who swear fealty to that flag. And I felt a pride as I gazed at the white-and-crimson barred pinion, a pride which the claim of no second victor has ever taken from me."[2]

But Cook had to put aside such patriotic sentiments, too, and make careful calculations of his position. His sextant observations gave a latitude of a few seconds below 90°. Unknown refraction and some uncertainty about the precision of his timepiece allowed him assurance that he stood as close to 90° as could be geographically determined. He had traveled as closely as possible along the ninety-seventh meridian. At noon the sun was 11° 55′ above the magnetic northern horizon. His 6-foot-high tent pole cast a shadow 28 feet long. The seawater temperature beneath the ice was 37.7° F; the air temperature was –36° F; the barometer read 29.83 and falling.

The sky was almost clear, of a dark purple-blue with some white and colored streaks. Although the ice surface was fairly smooth, there were signs of ceaseless activity in new cracks and young ice healing over previous breaks. The ice of the 2-square-mile section on which the explorers camped measured 16 feet thick.

Two days of blissful rest followed the April 21 discovery. The dogs received double rations of pemmican and the leisure to sleep when they liked. On the march their rations had been short and their workdays had been long.

The men's celebratory meal consisted of ice water, which Cook found more delicious than any wine; hot pemmican soup, flavored with musk-ox tenderloins; strips of frozen musk-ox meat; blocks of pemmican; and musk-ox suet for dessert. Then refreshing tea. What a feast! On the long walk they had seldom bothered with a hot meal.

Cook remained edgy over the two days' sojourn at the Pole. He continued to calculate his position, realizing the importance of fixing it as accurately as his instruments allowed. An explorer must prove to himself beyond a reasonable doubt that he has reached his geographical goal. Cook moved around, making sextant observations of the sun from various places until he was satisfied. He knew that even the most painstaking observations could be open to question. All he could do was repeat his observations with the sextant and the artificial horizon, while noting the times registered on his pocket chronometers, and supplement his figures with close visual observations of sky and ice. To the best of his ability, he exercised every safeguard for accuracy. His Eskimo companions wondered at his persistence and expressed their disappointment that no such "Big Nail," as had been described to them, actually existed on the icy sea.

Now Cook turned his attention to getting back to land safely. It was no light matter. The Arctic shore was 500 miles distant over shifting, perilous sea ice, and hummocks of ice were forced upward wherever moving floes collided. Only half of the party's original twenty-six dogs remained; the others had been fed to the survivors. For a month dogs and men had existed on three-quarter rations. Food supplies had diminished alarmingly. Eventual starvation was a daily prospect.

Days of monotonous travel back to shore forced further reductions in food rations. Half-fed men and beasts felt the cold severely, even though the air grew warmer as the season advanced. Cook worried about madness, his own or the boys'. The desolation of their icebound world, the uncertainty of the location of land, and the absence of any living creatures save themselves created anxiety. Weakened men were prey to despair.

On June 10, Cook announced a celebration to offset depression. It was his birthday—reason enough for boosting morale. By this stratagem he masked his own hopelessness. Let the Eskimos believe that all was well. He presented pocket knives as gifts and served an extra cup of hot tea with a double slab of pemmican. The little party cheered the men. Even the dogs sensed something favorable, some change in their masters that boded well. They sniffed the air and howled, either in joy or because they wanted more food.

On the morning of June 11, the men arose in better spirits and worked harder, helping the dogs pull the sledges over hummocks. Several days later the cloud cover cleared to reveal land in the distance. The explorers shouted their excitement. Ignoring their fatigue, they drove on, sometimes stumbling with weakness. Where the sea ice rafted against the shore, the hummocks stood like fortifications. The men hacked, pulled, and scrambled for several hours to cross the last barrier to terra firma, then dropped exhausted on the gritty sand.

Land embraced them, but they needed food desperately. Cook had only a vague notion of where he had landed. Unless they found game soon, they could perish on the desolate shore. There were probably no Eskimo communities within 600 miles.

Cook examined his companions with compassion as he distributed 4 ounces of dried meat and tallow for each man and dog. Both Eskimos, twenty years old, appeared wilted and aged, their faces wrinkled and colored like winter-dried russet apples. Still, they looked tough enough to endure if only food could be found soon. Cook did not need a mirror to know his own gauntness, nor another physician to tell him how wasted the months of exertion had left him.

He surveyed their meager possessions: a badly worn tent of shantung silk; two sledges of hickory, still in good shape; two rifles, a Remington .22 and an ancient Sharpe; a precious 100 rounds of ammunition between the two weapons; and few cans of pemmican—enough for a few days of sparing distribution; dishes; knives; matches; a canvas boat; and some mending materials.

They set off for a hunt, returning empty-handed hours later to their wretched camp. They packed up the sledges the next morning and pushed inland. A dog died of exhaustion. Lemming tracks cheered them; they saw a bird, then an old bear track. Any sign of life thundered with hope.

A gale struck them. They huddled in the shelter of rocks, not daring to raise their rotting tent to the tempest's fury. Men and dogs cuddled together for mutual warmth. For twenty-four hours they waited out the storm as snow drifted over them. When the storm was over, they pushed on. Following an old bear track, they spotted the king of beasts of the North, a polar bear as hungry as themselves. The bear charged at the men, ignoring the snarling, hysterical dogs until a well-placed bullet brought him down.

Now all seemed well. They feasted on raw bear meat with relish, slept, and feasted again. The danger of starvation passed for a time. They packed up every portion of the animal and set out to the east. By this time Cook had figured out his location to be near Grinnell Peninsula. They had to cross icy Penny Strait. Some 600 miles to the east their Greenland camp awaited them, but with luck they might meet summer whalers in Lancaster Sound.

They had no luck in meeting whalers. Winter caught them well short of their destination. Starvation threatened once again. Months of agony and anxiety passed before another spring released the explorers from their travails. When Cook finally reached safety and an outpost of civilization, his friends had given him up for dead.

On April 18, 1909, Cook arrived at his base camp of Annoatok. Harry Whitney, a New York sportsman, and two of explorer Robert E. Peary's men, Denis Murphy and Billy Pritchard, greeted him.

Whitney prepared a hot bath for Cook, the first such luxury he had enjoyed in over a year. As Cook soaked and scrubbed away layers of grime, he confided to Whitney (and swore him to secrecy): He had reached the Pole!

2

FROM HEALER
TO EXPLORER

"Except as an emplorer I am no good at anything."
                    —Sir Ernest Shackleton

What do we know of men like Cook? No other explorer tried harder than Frederick Cook to explain his motivation. As he stood alone on the deck of the ship carrying him north in 1907 and watched the midnight sun over Melville Bay, he described his deep absorption with the "spell" of the North. It was a mystical experience. The sun, like "some monstrous perpetual light to some implacable, frozen, wasted deity," burned on the horizon. "The golden colors suffused my mind, and I swam in a sea of molten glitter." A yearning filled and intoxicated him, an unquenchable desire to go where no man had ever been. Why should he have this ambition? "Perhaps," he answered, "it is the human desire to excel others, to prove, because of the innate egotism of the human unit, that one possesses qualities of brain and muscle which no other possesses." But he was not really sure if this was what "has crazed men to perform . . . the most difficult physical test in the world."[1]

In considering those who had made earlier explorations, Cook recalled that their tales had flushed him with excitement "and inspired me with the same mad ambition." Their noble, indefatigable efforts and their heartsickening failures had been shared vicariously, and he felt "their awful, goading determination . . . to subdue the forces of nature . . . to reach the silvershining vacantness which men called the North Pole."[2]

In some respects Cook's explanation of his motivations was refreshing. He uttered no cant about yearning to benefit science. It was simply a battle. "I never regarded the feat as of any great scientific value. The real victory would lie, not in reaching the goal itself, but in overcoming the obstacles which exist in the way of it." Incentive enough existed in the excitement and danger and in the taxing of mental and physical resources. Cook insisted that he was equally unmoved by hope of glory or gain in any extraordinary sense. He likened himself to an athlete seeking preeminence in a sport by "a feat of brain and muscle in which I should, if successful, signally surpass other men."[3]

Such statements are certainly straightforward, yet, as Cook recognized, they did not really express his drive toward the Pole. He knew only that the glamour of the North had gripped him for years; he could explain it as imperfectly as a poet or musician might explain his creative work. He had found his life's ambition in the conquest of the Pole. Nothing life had to offer could equal the exultation the achievement promised.

Cook's conception of his ultimate victory was that of a romantic triumph. After struggling over land and sea he would pierce those white and terrible spaces, assailing all obstacles with success, although a mere dark mite in the region's vastness. Then, alone, he would stand upon the world's pinnacle. Being alone in this victory was important. Of course there were the Eskimos, but he would be the one white man.

Frederick A. Cook was born in 1865 in rural New York State. His father, a country doctor, died five years later, and the widow and five children moved to Brooklyn. Maintaining the family was not easy. Mrs. Cook made dresses for neighbors, and all the children worked at various jobs when they were old enough.

Frederick held down a night job in Manhattan's Fulton Market while still continuing his public school education. Ambition stirred him to unusual efforts. His father, whom he had hardly known, had been a doctor, and he would be one as well.

Medical training was expensive and Cook had to hustle. He managed to buy a small, secondhand printing press to meet the advertising needs of Brooklyn businesses and to produce greeting cards. While in college, he ran his own milk delivery service, working in the early morning hours before attending classes at Columbia University. In the spring of 1889 Cook took his medical degree from New York University, gave up his milk route, married, and set up practice in Manhattan.

Until this point Cook's life was not unusual. He showed more initiative and energy than most young men but expressed these powers in conventional ways.

Tragedy struck Cook hardly a year after his marriage. His young wife died shortly after giving birth to a child, and the baby died too. With these losses Cook also lost self-satisfaction in the achievement of ordinary goals. What else was there in life? he asked himself.

Cook began reading the narratives of polar exploration. He found Elisha Kent Kane and Charles Francis Hall most fascinating. Both were Americans who had attracted a tremendous following in the States. And he could identify with these polar heroes: Kane had been a medical doctor until a thirst for travel and adventure swept him into exploration; Hall had been a printer before he gave up his shop and with scanty means set forth to solve the mystery of Sir John Franklin's expedition. Both men had disdained established careers in becoming explorers. Frederick Cook wondered if he dared do the same.

Over breakfast on a January morning, Dr. Cook read a notice that altered his life irrevocably. Robert E. Peary planned to explore North Greenland in 1891–92 and needed scientists. Cook trembled with anticipation. This was it! He knew at once that he had been called. It was as if a prison cell had suddenly opened.

That morning he did not hold office hours. Instead, after getting Peary's address from *The New York Herald,* he caught the train for Philadelphia.

Cook met Peary at his home. They quickly reached an agreement: A medical doctor was an asset to any expedition. This meeting dramatically altered the course of the lives of both men. Cook gained a new interest in life that was to develop into an obsession; Peary, already obsessed by the Pole, awakened the monster in Cook that was capable of destroying his benefactor. Men cannot read the future. Somewhere, soothsayers might have read horrible portents in the heavens, but Peary and Cook, each well pleased with the other, shook hands, smiled, and parted.

Cook performed well on Peary's Greenland expedition and earned the leader's praise as a physician and ethnologist. Though without training in ethnology, Cook observed the Eskimos with curiosity and took notes on their customs. Previous explorers had used Eskimos for labor but had generally ignored them otherwise, so Cook's interest gained him some scholarly credit, though his observations were superficial.

Although customarily parsimonious in praising others, Robert Peary uttered a published compliment of Cook's work on his 1891–92 Greenland expedition: "I personally owe much to his professional skill and unruffled coolness in an emergency." Cook merited Peary's approval as an "indefatigable worker," and "earnest student of the peculiar people among whom we lived." But Peary's puffing of Cook's "record of the tribe [as] unapproachable in ethnological archives"[4] was nonsense. Peary even published the doctor's amazing gaffe: an assertion that Eskimo women only give birth in the spring.

Cook's 1891–92 service in Greenland proved to be adventurous. The expedition party had not even reached its Greenland base when Peary broke his leg aboard ship. Dr. Cook set the leg skillfully, and there was ample time for the healing process that summer and fall.

In mid-February, Peary, Cook, and Eivind Astrup, a young Norwegian, made a trial journey on the great Greenland ice cap that almost ended disastrously. Peary made the near-fatal blunder of camping overnight in a poorly built snowhouse. A blizzard weakened the snowhouse roof, causing a cave-in as the men slept. Peary woke up in time, roused Cook, and both men dug Astrup out of the snow.

The men had to wait out the blizzard without shelter or even clothes, huddled in their sleeping bags. Cook suffered greatly from the cold despite Peary's efforts to dig a hole for the doctor's sleeping bag and to place himself in a sheltering position at the windward edge of the hill.

When the wind died down in the morning, the men were able to dig their clothes from beneath the drifting snow and return to their base.

Peary was not yet the veteran traveler and master of meticulous detail that he became through subsequent explorations, but he was learning the hard way.

On May 3, Peary, Cook, Astrup, Matt Henson, and Langdon Gibson started a major ski and dogsled journey to explore the northern reaches of Greenland. Peary's luck was bad. Storms slowed their progress. Several dogs died. At one point a storm forced them to hole up for forty-eight hours. Peary sent Henson back to base after a few days, then on May 24 he sent Cook and Gibson back, forging on with Astrup.

The going was tough because of the grade, soft snow, crevasses, and wind. Once out of the soft snow, they encountered steep, slippery surfaces which caused bad falls. At times the men had to pull the reluctant dogs to keep them moving. Peary's diary showed his discouragement:

Feel less like writing than for last three or four days even. It was almost sure my dream of years is ended. This cursed land is forcing more and more to the east and south. I have not yet been to the eighty-second meridian. But I will do all that man may do.

It is now twenty-seven hours since I turned out and during twenty-three of these have been traveling over the roughest kind of ice and ground, all the time with a troubled mind, part of it is bitterness of spirit. The combination has nearly done me up.[5]

Peary cheered up soon after reaching this low point, thanks to a successful musk-ox hunt. Men and dogs feasted happily, then traveled a short distance to reach a high plateau. From there Peary looked down on what he thought was a snow-filled channel separating Greenland from undiscovered land to the north. Actually the northern tip of Greenland was 100 miles to the north. Peary erred in believing that he had determined the insularity and northern extent of Greenland at what he named Independence Bay, between the eighty-first and eighty-second parallels.

A cautious man might not have jumped to geographic conclusions as readily. But Peary felt compelled to report his "discovery" despite the casualness of his investigation. An explorer needed to return with some trophies if he hoped to lecture successfully the following winter and raise funds for a new expedition.

Cook agreed to join the expedition planned for 1893, and Peary was pleased to sign him on again as a volunteer physician. However, Peary sternly refused to permit Cook's publication of an article on Eskimo health in a medical journal. Contracts limiting publication to expedition leaders for a year or so after expedition return were common practice. Cook had signed one but expected Peary to make an exception for a noncommercial, scholarly article. Peary, an unbending man, did not favor exceptions to rules, even for those who served him well without pay. Cook's expectation was disappointed. The doctor resigned.

In 1893 and 1894, Cook led touring expeditions to the North on the strength of his modest reputation as an explorer. Although the party planned some scientific work, their brief field sojourn did not permit much more than sightseeing. Cook's leadership probably assured him free passage. The captain of the 1893 charter was reluctant to take his ship into icy waters, so the tourists saw little of the Arctic. The next year a bolder captain smashed his *Miranda* into an iceberg, forcing the early return of the damaged ship. But good fellowship flourished on the 1894 cruise of the

Miranda nonetheless; the members formed the Arctic Club in New York, a society of business and professional men enthusiastic about exploration. The association lasted for a few years.

Peary's explorations in 1893–95 did not achieve notable results, but he did perfect the travel methods that made his later successes possible. He had learned to rely upon Eskimo dogs, and to use some of the dogs as food for the others. He also learned to utilize Eskimo and white support parties to implement rapid, lightweight, long-range surface travel. And he developed techniques for better provisioning and to ensure that he was better equipped. In short, he adapted his methods to the polar environment, building on a tradition begun several decades before by the American, Charles Francis Hall, and after Peary, culminated brilliantly by Vilhjalmur Stefansson.

Dr. Cook's interest in the practice of medicine faded even more during that period, and in 1898 he made a major commitment to exploration by joining the Belgian Antarctic Expedition. This expedition won distinction as the first whose ship wintered in Antarctica. Cook's contribution was highly praised by his comrades; Belgium conferred a medal; and Cook published a narrative of the adventure, a well-written book that gave him a reputation for modest, accurate reporting.

The Antarctic venture came close to being a complete disaster. By Christmas Day, 1898, the *Belgica* had been frozen fast in the ice for almost a year. Prospects for release with the season's change were by no means certain.

The crew tried to celebrate the feast with good cheer, but their enthusiasm was forced. "At worst," Cook noted, "we were not in a feasting mood, and the doubt of our future was pictured on every face."[6]

Earlier, in October and November, conditions had appeared more promising. The ice surrounding the ship had broken up in places, leaving wide-open leads, some a mile wide, winding through the ice pack for great distances. If the *Belgica* could be moved into one such lead, perhaps it might allow free passage to the open sea. But the ice clinging near the ship did not open. There was no way to push the ship the necessary 2,000 yards to reach an open lead.

Weeks of anxiety passed. In January they were no better off than in October. As summer in the southern hemisphere moved along, it looked like a second winter in the ice was a distinct possibility. Provisions would run out during a second winter, and even if the crew stretched rations to survive, the ice might hold them as fast the second summer.

Cook urged the officers to action. He suggested that the crew dig trenches through the ice pack to the nearest open lead. He hoped that the current penetrating the two narrow trenches leading from the bow and stern would aid the sun in weakening the ice.

For three days the men worked with picks, axes, and shovels to dig the trenches. But it was no use. The sun's heat was not sufficient to affect the ice measurably. Temperatures dropped at night and new ice formed to offset the day's melting.

Cook refused to be discouraged. If the crew could cut ditches, why couldn't they cut a canal wide enough to allow the ship's movement? Earlier they had tried to blast a passage with explosives and had failed, but manpower might be more effective.

It took all of Cook's persuasive powers to get the project going. Every crew member and scientist set to work on January 11. Sawing went on around the clock in three eight-hour shifts. It was 2,200 feet to open water. Two cuts had to be made so the total distance to be cut was about a mile.

After removing 1-to-2-foot-deep surface layers of ice and snow, the depth of solid ice below was 3 to 4 feet thick. The sixteen men worked desperately. Only three months' food remained in the ship's stores, but they had plenty of seal and penguin meat. Penguin steaks were fishy but nourishing, and the seals made hunting easy by swimming into the canals as they were cut.

Cook described the work in scoutmasterly terms. No regard was given to distinctions of rank. All worked cheerfully with "superhuman" vigor. Everyone had a sore back, but it was "capital exercise" and the men developed "ponderous muscles." Sunburn caused discomfort, and it did not pay the men to wash their painfully cracked hands.[7] They ate seven meals a day to keep their energy high.

By February 1 they had extended the canal 100 feet. This was some progress, but now the ice was 6 to 7 feet in depth and hard enough to defy their saws. "In one spot we sawed eight hours and cut less than five feet."[8]

As if things didn't look grim enough, the wind shifted and drove neighboring ice floes directly into the canal. Worse yet, the ice put heavy pressure on the *Belgica,* threatening to crush the ship in its relentless grasp. All hands had to quit sawing on the canal and work on the pressuring ice. It was

February 13 before they relieved the pressure on the ship. By then new ice had completely closed their hard-won canal.

Then, as the men's spirits drooped to despair, the wind shifted again. This time nature favored them. The ice pack expanded suddenly, leaving open leads on all sides. The canal opened, too, and the ship was free to steam forward into open water.

Within two days the *Belgica* voyaged 30 miles through the loose, shifting ice pack. Then, within sight of the open sea, the wind brought the pack around the ship once more. This time the men just watched and waited. Even Dr. Cook did not urge another sawing project. Again their luck turned. Just thirty days after being caught, when another winter in the ice seemed a certainty, a southerly wind drove the ship and the enclosing ice into the open sea. Finally they were free.

A reader of Cook's text, *Through the First Antarctic Night,* would never guess that the expedition failed in its purposes. They had hoped to land scientists near the magnetic South Pole for observation, and to go farther south by ship then anyone before them. Adrien De Gerlache, the expedition leader, spent six weeks surveying the coast of Tierra del Fuego before steaming south, meeting the ice, and becoming caught. By that mischance the expedition did make a record as the first whose ship wintered in Antarctic waters.

The experience was not a happy one, yet Cook performed very well. He won the gratitude of Roald Amundsen, first officer of the *Belgica,* who later won fame for voyaging through the Northwest Passage and as the discoverer of the South Pole. Others aboard praised Cook's good cheer, resourcefulness, and courage. Years later, when Cook lived under a cloud of disgrace, Amundsen recalled how Cook acted over the thirteen fearful months of imprisonment in the ice: "He, of all the ship's company, was the one man of unfaltering courage, unfailing hope, endless cheerfulness and unwearied kindness. When anyone was . . . disheartened, he was there to encourage and inspire."[9]

Cook's modesty shines throughout his narrative. He described his role in a manner that invites admiration for his humanity, good humor, and good sense. Clearly he was a team player, helping wherever he could, a perfect model of manliness and professionalism to the others.

Cook revealed a fine writer's talent for descriptive passages stressing the contrasting effects of nature. He orchestrated his scenes with a good balance. Above all, he was tasteful in avoiding exaggerated effects. In his first book, unlike his later ones, he did not charge his descriptions with intense, mystical experiences suggestive of an overwrought poet. He wrote as a man of thought and impressions, yet his feelings did not break down his control. He wanted the reader to see what can be seen, not what the fevered imagination might conceive.

After returning from Antarctica, publishing his *Through the First Antarctic Night,* and traveling to Belgium to receive a medal from the king in 1900, Cook might have been reasonably content to practice medicine for a time. But in 1901 he took the occasion offered by Peary's sponsors to return briefly to the Arctic. Dr. Cook joined Herbert L. Bridgman, Peary's friend and financial backer, who usually functioned as press agent because of his newspaper connections, on a relief voyage to Cape Sabine. Peary was physically in terrible shape. Before resigning over personal differences, Dr. Thomas S. Dedrick, Peary's physician, had amputated the explorer's badly frozen toes—the result of Peary's latest, unsuccessful attempt to sledge to the Pole. Cook treated Peary's feet and also diagnosed pernicious anemia. But Peary only rested over one winter before trying again in 1902, once more without success.

Meanwhile, Cook, whose fate decreed that he continue to encounter Peary, remarried in June 1902. Marie Fidele Hunt, a widow, had some money, and thus Cook's material outlook improved. He loved autos and happily replaced his horse and buggy with a car. He also invested in an X-ray machine for his medical work and, reportedly, his practice thrived. Patients liked Dr. Cook. He was kind and inspired confidence in his capacity to alleviate distress.

But the good doctor still yearned for something else. His taste for exploration did not wane. The classic goal of the North Pole still remained to be reached, and other adventures were calling.

For some reason the ascent of Mount McKinley commanded Cook's attention. The recently named Alaskan mountain had not been climbed to the summit, yet it was recognized as North America's highest peak. In 1903 Cook organized a party consisting of Robert Dunn, a journalist; Ralph Shainwald, a friend whose loyalty to Cook was never to falter; Walter Miller, a Seattle photographer; and Fred Prinz, a Montana horse packer. Dunn and Shainwald paid their own expenses. Cook financed all other costs with an advance from *Harper's Monthly* in anticipation of an article.

The party made a very tough trip around the base of Mount McKinley that summer without finding a means of reaching the summit. Cook waited three years, then organized another attempt in 1906. The 1906 Mount McKinley venture marked the commencement of the extraordinary period of Cook's career. By then he was forty-one years old, of respected reputation in exploration circles, and also respected as a physician. But he longed for something more than a modest reputation as an explorer. Ambition drove him toward his remarkable destiny.

Some note should be made of the 1903 Mount McKinley climb. No controversy ensued, but accounts of it tell us of Cook's behavior and character on the eve of his major claims to fame. Cook's *To the Top of the Continent*, primarily concerned with the 1906 climb, contains a summary of the 1903 venture, but more documentation exists in a book published by the expedition member Robert Dunn.

Dunn wrote a curious, debunking book, dispelling the image of camaraderie around the campfire, shattering the images of heartiness and psychological wholesomeness associated with sturdy outdoorsmen. His revelations were as contrary to sporting traditions as shooting the fox after the dog ran it down. Every explorer, hunter, fisherman, and hiker insists that there is an inherent virtue in wilderness life. Never mind the laborious exertions and the rain, the mosquitoes, the blackflies and gnats, the boggy tundra and the danger of drowning at river crossings, the frustrations and disappointments, the lousy meals and sour stomachs: According to the established mythology, nature ennobles men who flee the anxieties of the city for the wilderness.

Biographers who are cautioned to describe their subject "warts and all" should read Dunn's picture of the 1903 Mount McKinley expedition: It is all warts. The men quibbled endlessly about blanket drying, food preparation, route, climate, and time of day. One packer stopped speaking to Dunn and Cook because of fancied grievances. Another packer complained of Cook's choice of pack horses: "The man hasn't the least idea of a horse's needs, nor of Alaskan travel." Dunn asked Cook to inspect the horses, but Cook was too busy. "What do you think of that? His pack train is going to the devil, and he doesn't pay the least attention. Still just packs and unpacks his instruments. I wonder if he can use a theodite, after all." Other members of the party marveled that for all of Cook's concern with instruments for measuring elevation, he seemed not to understand their use. Against such grumbling and general lack of confidence, Cook "shows his gold front tooth as he smiles so slowly," and tries to calm everyone. As Dunn and the others brooded and watched, Cook emphasized his self-possession. Dunn raged: "I no longer ask him to show quality; I wish he'd show something. He's too silent; hopeful without being cheerful; slow-witted." Cook wooed his companions, particularly those with Alaskan experience, by displaying an expertise they could not match: "The Professor," as Dunn called the doctor, "is lisping about eating seal and penguin and killing pelican in the Antarctic."[10]

Dunn's only sympathies went to the poor horses, who were driven to exhaustion. Seeing a packer beat the beasts enraged him and he threatened to knock some sense into the packer's head for not knowing about horses and not wanting to know. Cook, ever patient, turned aside this wrath: " 'Dunn, it doesn't do any good to talk like that,' he said quietly." Dunn apologized and Cook only remarked: "You talk too much and too loud all the time."[11]

Dunn nagged the leader to take them into his confidence more. Cook agreed to tell his plans at the start of each day. But nothing could really soothe his restive men. The work was hard and their goals were too mundane and ill formed. Cook must have reflected privately on the disparity between himself and the others. It had been just the same on the Antarctic expedition, although Cook made no mention of the discord in his book. His Antarctic comrades never forgot his sweet temper in the face of all vicissitudes; he spent himself to comfort the others. On the Mount McKinley trek he tried to close his ears to the incessant muttering, a scourge worse than blackflies. He was a pilgrim embarked on a significant spiritual mission; the others reacted to obstacles as if betrayed by some enemy. Cook urged the heaviest complainer to turn back. No wonder. Poor Cook! What could the leader of such a crew accomplish?

As it turned out, nothing. The 1903 attempt on Mount McKinley gave Dunn a series of articles and a book, which pained the members as much as Dunn's company on the march; otherwise, there was no profit for all the time and money spent. Cook learned certain things, however, and did not abandon his hopes.

A leader has to put on a bright face if he hopes to find sponsors in the future. In his own narrative, Cook obscured the bickering endemic to such a joint enterprise. He followed a firmly established precedent. After all, who really wanted to read a carping narrative like Dunn's? Cook wrote effusively: "In this northland, where dusk and dawn run together, men get into the real swing of nature and close to each other's hearts at the campfire."[12] After reading Dunn, this pleasant assertion makes us smile, yet

Cook was right in believing that the wilderness *should* temper aggressive men somewhat, and perhaps at times the serenity of nature soothed the weary men.

Of course, Cook idealized the venture. He was a city man. To him the wilds always looked positive, and for his readers it was good form to contrast the falseness of city manners with the honesty of the trail: "There is something about the crackle of the fire, the inspiration of the blaze, and the long frosty nights of twilight, which bares the breast of each camper to the scrutiny of his companions."[13]

Cook went on to perpetuate the idyllic myth: "At the club a man may be a good fellow superficially, with the veneer of a make-believe spirit of human brotherhood over a selfish center of commonplace discord, but in the sub-arctic wilderness this is impossible." Why? Because sitting around without clothes leaves men unable to conceal false fellowship. Clothes have been stripped for drying, and in "naked manliness" men sit together at the evening roundup "with the aroma of the spruce and the music of the forest wilds."[14]

Cook was too aware of Dunn's previously published anecdotes to leave readers with a totally false image of general harmony around the campfire. There were exceptions, as there was a serpent in the Garden of Eden. A man who was a true artist, "with system and order in the daily routine of his home life," contributed "bits of light that dispel the fatigue of the hard day and trail" and earned the admiration of his companions, but one without these advantages was different. "The haphazard chap who has run the life of a literary hack bewails his misfortunes, makes copy, secretes his observations of interesting things, and makes life tiresome by his egotism." Cook did not name Dunn, but he was the only journalist of the party. Dunn earned Cook's closing thrust: "As a discloser of manly character the campfire surpasses the confession booth."[15]

THE TOP OF
THE CONTINENT

"Travellers ne'er did lie,
Though fools at home condemn 'em."
—William Shakespeare

We know virtually nothing of Cook's activities between 1903 and 1906, when he set out for Alaska once more. This time he joined with Professor Herschel Parker of Columbia University as coleader of the expedition. Other members had talent and training: Belmore Browne, an artist, had mountaineering experience; and Russell W. Porter, a young scientist and skilled topographer, was a veteran of the Ziegler expeditions to the Arctic. Parker, a physicist, assumed responsibility for scientific work within his expertise, such as the determination of altitudes. S. P. Beecher joined as cook, and Fred Prinz, the packer in 1903, was joined by a Montana blacksmith, Edward N. Barrill. With help again from *Harper's Monthly,* Cook and Parker covered most of the expedition costs.

From Cook Inlet (named for Captain James Cook) the Mount McKinley party voyaged up the Susitna River to approach the mountain. Once in the rugged upland country they worked hard, but after several weeks they were forced to give up. They had not been able to find a likely route for ascent. After agreeing with Cook that they would try again in 1907, Herschel Parker took a ship to Seattle and returned to New York. Other party members also went their separate ways.

As it turned out, Cook had apparently not given up despite the disbanding of the party. When he followed Parker to Seattle some weeks later, he had already declared himself the conquerer of Mount McKinley.

Cook and Barrill's challenge to Mount McKinley tested their endurance and courage. A three-day trek from Cook Inlet brought them to a glacier that seemed to offer a better chance of ascent than any route previously surveyed. Yet the hazards were obvious. Two men could not carry much food. If storms halted their progress, they would exhaust their provisions.

Avalanches were a constant menace. Cook scarcely slept at night for fear of being swept away. The distant thunder of rock slides was a continuing reminder of this danger. And fierce winds roared their warnings, too.

Out of black clouds "from the invisible upper world . . . there rushed with the noise of a thousand cannons and the hiss of a burning volcano indescribable quantities of rock and ice mixed with snow and wind. The tumble from cliff to cliff, from glacier to glacier down the seemingly endless fall was soul-stirring to the verge of desperation." Under them the glacier cracked, "the whole earth about quivered as from an earthquake, and as we tossed in our bags the snow squeaked with a metallic ring. That third night we felt as if we were at the gates of Hades."[1]

After this restless night they pushed up the glacier at dawn, avoiding gaping crevasses and rough ice barriers. Avalanches coursed down to either side as they picked their way upward through the misty cloud-world to reach the rim of an amphitheater. At noon they rested and ate some pemmican. Despite their thirst, they could not delay to melt snow. By nightfall they had to reach a ridge 2,000 feet above them to establish a safe camp. For each yard's progress of the perilous ascent, they had to hack steps in the ice.

With aching muscles they reached the ridge safely. Winds tore at them, now from the east, then from the west. "We were on the battle ground and in the firing line of clouds from the tropic and the arctic."[2] As the wind shifted there was a fall of snow and a rush of drift.

Where was there a safe place to camp for the night? Cook improvised, drawing on his polar experience. He cut out blocks of densely packed snow to build an Eskimo snowhouse that provided a snug shelter. Pemmican, tea, and biscuits provided their supper. And twelve hours' sleep refreshed their bodies.

In the morning they started upward again, hacking another staircase rising 2,000 feet more. To one side they saw a sickening drop of 10,000 feet. But they struggled on "into the mystery of a lower arctic world. . . . With eternity but an easy step below every moment of this climb we went from hanging glacier to snow slopes, from blue grottoes to pink pinnacles, from security to insecurity, with the thundering rush of avalanches on both sides."[3]

Nightfall caught them on the steep face of the ice. They had reached the limit of their endurance. Within the little distance they could see ahead there was no secure resting place. And none below them either. To the sides there were snow slopes, but they were swept by avalanches. With a desperate effort in the dusk they cut their way upward to reach a steep, snow-sheeted ridge. They had to stop there and dig a place into the precipitous icy slope.

Their night was not pleasant. They wrapped themselves and their gear into bundles that they lashed to their embedded ice axes. Hanging precariously in this fashion, hardly daring to move, they lasted out the night.

All night they discussed their plight, agreeing to descend if they survived until morning. But the break of day gave them fresh courage. "Its fetching polar glory" dispelled their gloom. "Now our determination to retreat resolved itself into a resolution to go to the top."[4]

The next day they climbed on. Each crest ahead seemed to be the summit, and each turned out to be only a spur. Climbing was easier. They did not have to cut steps in the ice, but the effects of a sleepless night weighted their limbs. As night fell they were delighted to find snow suitable for another snowhouse and a secure amphitheater to camp in.

On the following morning—the sixth day of their climb—the men crawled out of their sleeping bags for their final effort. It was very cold. Below them clouds formed eerie patterns. Stars still glistened above in the dark gray-blue sky as the sun emerged to make snow and rocks glitter. Feeling the stiffness and fatigue in their limbs, they moved on from the 16,300-foot level. But not too swiftly. At that altitude breathing was a problem. They had to stop frequently to rest.

When the day's light faded, they had only huffed and puffed their way to the 18,400-foot mark. They pitched their tent and turned in, only half-conscious of their surroundings.

Sleep did not come. Their overtaxed bodies could not relax. They rested through the night in a semireclining position, lungs heaving and hearts pumping against the conditions of thin air and cold. Cook recalled with amusement Mark Twain's fictional hero's arrival at the North Pole, where his words froze and tumbled around him up to his knees.

Morning came at last. They saw the summit towering 2,000 feet above their camp. Now for the ultimate stage! They were numb with cold and not fit to enjoy the spectacular unfolding of nature's grandeur as golden sunshine pierced the night's gloom.

They climbed, halted after twenty steps, gasping for breath, climbed again. Just below the summit they collapsed in exhaustion on an icy ledge. But their goal summoned them. With magnificent courage they rose again and staggered on. "We edged up along a steep snowy ridge and over the heaven-scraped granite to the top. AT LAST! The soul-stirring task was crowned with victory; the top of the continent was under our feet."[5]

Victory was theirs!

Cook claimed that he climbed Mount McKinley. He then wrote magazine articles and a book, *To the Top of the Continent,* his narrative recounting the terrific struggle he and Barrill endured to reach their goal. From near the highest point in North America he saw "a magnificent spread of an otherworld glory." It was awe-inspiring: "A weird world in white, with stars fading in gloomy blackness." The climbers could see the Pacific Ocean and "fifty thousand square miles of our arctic wonderland," and, more amazing still, they saw the Arctic Circle. "After several long breaths the ghastly *unreality* of our position began to excite my frosted senses."[6]

Let Cook's words stand for the romantic version of the first climb of the lofty peak. The overwhelming evidence indicates that Cook faked the climb. Why would someone attempt such a monumental fraud? Perhaps Cook can only be understood if we trace his steps and try to imagine what might have been running through his mind. What follows is my effort to reconstruct the actual event and to show a plausible explanation.

Cook took Barrill off on a river voyage without declaring his true intentions. As the little gasoline launch pushed upriver against the current of the Susitna, he asked himself, Why not? Audacity was the key and it was now or never. As the little *Bolshoy* chugged along, he weighed his chances. If he returned to Cook Inlet after an appropriate time, met the now-scattered members of his Mount McKinley climbing party, and told them that he and Barrill had succeeded because they discovered a new route to the summit, who could doubt him? He would own a page of history: First atop Mount McKinley! All he would need would be Barrill's confirmation. And not even that, actually, just his silence. Looking at the powerful Montana blacksmith sitting placidly in the stern, he figured that his companion's acquiescence could easily be gained. Barrill was none too bright, a straightforward western type—a workingman who did what he was told without questioning or grumbling. Secretly Barrill probably held the city men he packed for in contempt; their willingness to spend money and endure discomfort to climb the continent's highest mountain made no sense to him, but they paid him to help and he needed work.

Frederick Cook pondered the risks as the launch eased through the murky, glacier-fed waters of the river. Birch and spruce lined the shore, and already autumn shades of yellow, brown, and red interrupted the green expanse. Fall came early to interior Alaska, but the days were still warm and long. Before many more weeks elapsed, the Susitna River would be iced over. He would be back in New York by that time enjoying some celebrity as the first successful climber of Mount McKinley. Mountain climbing didn't interest people as much as exploration, but the modest acclaim would benefit him in the small world of exploration patronage.

Planning to deceive the public about Mount McKinley gave him no pleasure; it was simply necessary. Unless he got support soon for an expedition to win the North Pole—a truly significant feat—it would be too late. Peary was preparing another attempt on the Pole. Robert E. Peary: The thought of the arrogant, mean-spirited explorer made Cook involuntarily clench his teeth. Once he had respected Peary and had been grateful when Peary accepted his medical services on an earlier Greenland expedition. But working with Peary disenchanted him. There was little camaraderie or sense of a joint purpose among Peary's men. Everyone existed as a cog in the wheel of Peary's machine, a small and virtually unacknowledged crutch to the leader's relentless ambition.

Cook knew people. In Antarctica he had learned the value of morale and fine leadership. Had he had Peary's opportunities, Cook knew he would have reached the Pole long ago. He would have been generous and comradely to his companions and they would have outstripped themselves in the cause. Peary, a martinet, demanded obedience and unswerving loyalty to the point of obeisance, and gave little gratitude in return. A small measure of graciousness was beyond the naval engineer who made a subsidized career of independent exploration. It still rankled Cook to think of Peary's offhand refusal to authorize the publication of a medical paper, as if an obscure printing of Cook's technical notes on Eskimo health would rob Peary of his fame. And Cook knew of nastier cuts, such as Peary's sending superfluous men home from Greenland, then hinting at disloyalty in public rather than admitting that a shortage of provisions occasioned the dismissals.

As far as Dr. Cook was concerned, Peary had forfeited any right to greatness by his petty conduct and egomania. Someone else should beat Peary to the Pole, and who else could do it but Cook? He would know how to act in his moment of triumph. Subsequently, he would heap praise on his backers and companions and accept honor modestly as only one man among many who helped unveil one of the world's last great geographic mysteries. Peary, on the other hand, would ignore his predecessors and barely mention his helpers. If the world groveled at his feet, he would accept it as his due. Probably he would demand that the President make him Admiral of the Fleet.

Yes, there was justice in a bit of fudging just now. Cook must find money to beat Peary to the Pole. Exaggerating about Mount McKinley was no significant deceit. It would harm no one and would give him the necessary means.

From the Susitna the *Bolshoy* chugged into the Chulitna, another brown-hued glacier stream. Shallow water stranded them briefly until they dragged the boat to a deeper channel. Now they were in higher country. Snow-streaked mountains loomed ahead: One of them, seldom visible through mists and clouds, was Mount McKinley. From the Chulitna they headed up the Tokositna to meet headwaters emerging from the Ruth Glacier. At this point they would walk and leave behind a prospector who had voyaged from Cook Inlet with them. Now it was up to Cook and Barrill alone. Cook gazed at Barrill as they packed their gear. Could he depend upon him? How much should he confide? Probably the less said the better. Just get a commitment from Barrill and let it go at that. Hint that more money for packing than agreed upon would be forthcoming—*if* all went well.

Shouldering a 65-pound pack and starting up the glacier, Barrill thought they were only scouting for a route that Cook and Herschel Parker, coleader of the disbanded expedition, might try the following year. Already it was September 9, too late in the season to consider serious climbing. The trek promised to be enjoyable. Cook was always amiable, and in a larger party there were always soreheads and grumblers. Earlier they had had a devil of a time: men refusing to do their fair share of work, the strain of swift stream crossings with frightened packhorses, and rain, rain, rain.

Now, with the sun on his back, the pack was nothing to a 6-foot-2-inch, 200-pound blacksmith. A picnic, in fact!

Cook talked to Barrill about his diary at the start. Write only what I tell you, he said. Barrill wrote what the doctor ordered without comment, watched Cook take photographs at various places, and posed holding an American flag on top of a small peak. He guessed what Cook was up to but was not greatly worried. Soon he would return to Montana where his wife and five kids waited. Back to work and money worries. If Cook paid him promptly and well, that was all he asked. He didn't care what the doctor did, although it was becoming obvious that Cook was hatching faked evidence. So long as he didn't have to look any man in the eye and lie, he didn't give a damn. Let New Yorkers think the doctor was a great man if they liked. No skin off him. After Barrill posed with the flag, Cook seemed very pleased, commenting that the point would make a good top for Mount McKinley. Barrill did as he was told: The less said the better, he thought.

Barrill did his part and Cook was pleased. As Cook expected, no one questioned him much upon return to Cook Inlet. He sent the news outside by wire from Tyonek, then took Barrill with him to Seward. His lawsuit against the rogues who had cheated him with bum packhorses was to be heard in October, and Barrill was needed as a witness. Alaskan justice prevailed: The judge decided for the local man over the supposedly rich sportsman. Regretting the wasted time, Cook and Barrill took a ship to Seattle. From Seattle he saw Barrill off for Montana with promises of prompt payment. He had no money to pay Barrill or his other packer, Fred Prinz, on the spot. It was probably just as well to keep them hungry—and quiet. Barrill seemed trustworthy, but it would be a safer bet if he realized that no money would come if he opened his mouth.

In Seattle Cook got good treatment from the press and was feted by the local mountaineering club. It was all right, but he was impatient to get back east. By spring he had to raise enough money to launch an assault on the Pole. The Mount McKinley honors would help him attract backers, and a few articles and lectures would allow him to pay off pressing debts. His wife's income did not reach nearly far enough. Exploration was an expensive business.

As the eastbound train carried him home, Cook went over his plans. At worst Barrill could tell a nosy newsman that the climb had not been made. But, meanwhile, the people who count in the East would have accepted

Cook's story and no one would pay much attention to an uneducated Montana blacksmith. Cook could brazen it out; his reputation was excellent. No problems. Anyway, Barrill had no reason to talk and expose himself as a rogue or a fool. The only documentation Barrill could show were diary entries in his own hand that attested to Cook's story.

Besides, with luck, in about a year's time, Cook would be returning to New York from the North with the grandest prize of all. Who would care about Mount McKinley after he had conquered the Pole? That rotten Peary had a club of millionaires waiting on him, building him his own ship, and crowing of the Great Day; all Cook required was a head start and minimal backing. A irreligious would-be French king once concluded that attaining control of France was worth attending the required coronation Mass; Cook understood this sentiment. The deception about McKinley was his Mass, his small sacrifice of principle, and the North Pole would be his France. The thing was done; there was no looking back. No one could mock him if he won the Pole, and he had the will to achieve it. One thing was surpassingly clear: If he were once able to start for the prize, he would not return without it. Let others follow whatever course pleased them. Most men slog along without any sense of destiny, following rutted paths to their obscure ends. But not Frederick Cook, who, by his own will and talents, had been marked for grand purposes. By some divine process not clear to men, he had been selected to rise among his fellows, to reach what was unattainable to ordinary mortals. The train's wheels beat out a tattoo he had heard many times before: He-would-not-fail; he-would-not-fail. Yes, the very steel of the inanimate rails pulsed with the message. He would not fail.

Mountaineering did not approach exploration as a sensation with the public. Newspapers reported climbing feats with respect and low-keyed interest. The drama of exploration was lacking, and even the news of a successful climb of a major peak like Mount McKinley did not burn up international telegraph circuits the way an unsuccessful polar attempt did. Like amateur sportsmen and combatants in small wars, mountaineers played on a remote stage to a primarily local audience.

The Seattle press customarily gave Alaskan matters ample coverage. Cook's first Mount McKinley expedition in 1903 received good notice. *The Seattle Post-Intelligencer* interviewed Cook, who was confident that his climb would be successful, though he allowed: "During my experience with the Peary expeditions I have had a good deal of experience at glacial climbing, but have not done much in the mountains."[7]

As the 1906 expedition got underway, Seattle newspapers gave Cook fuller coverage, and when he returned to the city with word of his attainment, his story was featured. *The Post-Intelligencer* described Cook as a tall, deep-chested, wide-shouldered man with powerful lungs, a man who "thoroughly looks the great part he is playing in contemporary exploration." Although "quiet" and "modest," he told a story equal to the tales of the Vikings or the ancient Greeks.[8]

In his mild-mannered way, Cook laid it on rather heavily in describing altitude sickness, which caused the climbers' ears, eyes, and noses to bleed and brought them close to death. His "hazel eyes twinkling," Cook told of reaching the top with one companion, seeing the Pacific, and planting the flag. Few provisions remained in the climbers' packs at the summit, "yet, although Dr. Cook does not look like a man of sentiment, yet in all the desperate struggle he stuck to the Stars and Stripes, and on the top of a mountain for the next explorers to find, or rest eternally should the present feat remain unmatched, reposes a case in which the flag is folded and on which are inscribed the names of the members of the expedition."[9]

This pretty story of patriotic sentiment conformed to mandatory standards for explorers of the day. It would be unthinkable for Cook to be without a flag and equally unthinkable for a reporter to forbear some gushing over the ceremony! Patriotism and exploration, even fringe exploration like mountaineering, went hand in hand. No one would ever accuse Cook of resorting to the last refuge of a scoundrel in covering his venture with the flag, because such expression of patriotic sentiment was universally expected.

The flag anecdote provoked great consternation in Cook's companions (later to be called deserters by his partisans), because they had wondered why he left them behind, disavowing any intent to seek the summit, and then he ended up there with a conveniently packed flag. A small matter, however. The worst that could be said against him was that he did not care to share honors with anyone. He needed one helper and chose a packer rather than a scientist. A scientist would deserve a greater share of the limelight. So, rightfully, Herschel Parker, Belmore Browne, and Russell Porter grumbled about Cook's selfishness, just as others complained later of Peary's leaving all his white companions behind on his final dash to the Pole. Under pressure in an interrogation, Peary even admitted his selfish reasons. Explorers have never been remarkable for selflessness.

In Seattle, though, Cook revealed more than reluctance to share his glory, and his slip raised some questions—or would have if the *Post-Intelligencer* story had been more generally publicized. Cook altered the account of his undertaking to fit the circumstances under which such a climb would have been made. Rather than telling the truth about disbanding his party on Cook Inlet and wandering off with one companion to do some reconnaissance and to look at a nearby glacier, he described a much more orderly attack: "As the party climbed higher and higher, and as one by one stayed behind on the communication line, and as the path grew harder and harder, the amount carried had to be decreased." Two men climbed, with "the others waiting in camps below the 12,000-foot line."[10] All humbug, of course. There was no such communication line. However, Cook did not repeat this in his published narratives. Apparently he let it slip out to the Seattle newsman or was misquoted. No one taxed him with this incredible version of events, so a denial did not become necessary.

Professor Herschel Parker first read the news of Cook's Mount McKinley climb in *The New York Times* on October 3, 1906. Some facts were garbled. Mount McKinley's height was given as 22,800 feet, and Cook was quoted as reporting that his two barometers for measuring height failed to work. The story made the front page, indicating that something praiseworthy had been accomplished. No immediate follow-up appeared in the papers; the event did not command that much interest.

But on October 7 a long story with photos of the people involved appeared in the *Times*. It was Parker's red-hot response to the original announcement. The article, featured in the magazine section, was bannered: HAS DR. COOK SCALED AMERICA'S HIGHEST PEAK? TRUTH DOUBTED . . .[11]

Parker had certainly felt left out when he read the first account of Cook's feat. As a coorganizer and cocontributor to the expedition, it burned him to hear that his party, disbanded when he left Alaska, somehow had reorganized and accomplished its goal. To hear that Cook, practically alone, in unfavorable conditions, without instruments, lacking fresh pack animals and provisions, overcame all the physical difficulties to ascend Mount McKinley staggered belief. The effort had officially been abandoned! He had parted from Cook at Tyonek, Cook Inlet, on amicable terms, with the agreement that they would go together again the following year for another summit attempt. "This fact being a pledge, as it were, from Dr. Cook, alone makes it impossible to my mind, that the information from him is correct."[12]

Although boiling over, Parker kept control of himself. As the *Times* reported delicately, "Prof. Parker was not concealing a considerable feeling about the whole matter. Cook had his esteem, but 'he will have to tell me how he did it before I will believe it was done.' "[13]

Parker elaborated on his reservations. The logistics seemed all wrong: lack of food, time, and instruments capable of measuring the 20,300-foot height of the mountain, not to mention the absence of Porter, who "had all the instruments that would have made the ascent practically valuable."[14] Despite his heat Parker handled himself judiciously and fairly, avoiding mention that Cook did not understand elevation-measuring instruments and techniques well enough to gather precise data without assistance.

At some point, either before or after Cook's announcement, Parker had learned that Cook wrote to Herbert Bridgman, a friend and newsman, on August 25, promising news if there would be anything to tell of final reports. As it seemed to Parker, Cook had patently deceived his party by dispersing them and had double-crossed Parker by trying for the prize after the latter left Alaska. The professor told the *Times* about the letter without making more than oblique references to Cook's unethical tricks.

Before going to the *Times,* Parker took the matter up with the Explorers Club, or at least some members of it. The *Times* learned of an all-night meeting at the Explorers Club after Cook's telegraphic announcement. Parker wondered that Cook claimed an ascent by a route he had found impossible on the 1903 attempt. At the Explorers Club, Parker apparently tried his best to provoke suspicion of Cook's claim and indignation at Cook's deceit in cheating other party members out of participation in the victory—if indeed there was one. Yet Parker failed. The club members were gentlemen and loath to believe wrong of one of their own. Later some members, including Peary, blamed Parker for not pursuing the matter. What else could he have done? He trod dangerous ground in publicizing his suspicions and was rebuffed for his pains.

Whatever the nature of the all-night meeting at the Explorers Club, Parker did not implant his doubts deeply among the membership. Cook's standing was recognized soon afterward by his election as president of the club, a high honor and not one given to a suspected pretender! Within a short time of his return, Cook also spoke at the annual dinner of the

National Geographic Society and at the Association of American Geographers.

The next *Times* story highlighted Parker's dilemma. It quoted Robert Dunn, who had met Cook in Seldovia, Alaska, heard his story, and believed it. Dunn wondered "why the dispatch from Tyonek should ever have been questioned."[15]

Nevertheless, Parker persisted in public expression of his doubts, lecturing on November 9 to a New York club and telling its members what he told the *Times* and the Explorers Club.[16]

On November 28 the *Times* interviewed Cook in New York, where he had returned after reporting his climb to geographical societies and government bureaus in Washington, D.C. The story led off with Parker's suspicions, yet nothing indicated that reporters harried Cook on the matter. Cook described his innovations in equipment to lighten pack loads and took credit for inventions making possible the elimination of porters for the first time in mountaineering history. He admitted that the expedition had been disbanded and that the work had been ended for the season. Then, almost by chance, he had found a glacier at the base of the mountain that provided an excellent ascent.

Parker now maintained his silence and even attended functions at which Cook spoke. He could do no more than wait for Cook's publication of expedition details. In the interval he did not change his mind about Cook, particularly after hearing from his friend Belmore Browne. After encountering Cook and his great news in Alaska, Browne initially kept his own counsel. Unlike Parker, he had not contributed financially to the expedition and had less reason to be indignant, yet he thought Cook's behavior in dispersing the party and then trying for the summit rather strange.

After a hunting trip, Browne returned to Seldovia and heard rumors that Cook and Barrill had climbed Mount McKinley. He denied this, knowing that Cook had had no time for such a journey. Then, to his surprise, Cook and Barrill reached Seldovia and Cook confirmed the rumor. Browne took Barrill aside and the men took a walk along the beach. They liked each other and had shared some tough times on the mountain. Browne rather pointedly asked Barrill what he knew about Mount McKinley. Barrill hesitated before answering: "I can tell you all about the big peaks just south of the mountain, but if you want to know about Mount McKinley go and ask Cook." That was enough for Browne: He now knew the truth and was confirmed in his belief that Barrill "would tell me the truth."[17] In effect, Barrill had charged Cook with a fraud.

4

RACE TO
THE POLE

"Polar exploration, like war, breeds controversy."
—The New York Times

Once back in New York, Cook accepted honors for his Mount McKinley climb. While dodging creditors, he quietly planned a brilliant coup, an assault on the ultimate prize: the North Pole. He did not have to worry too much about Professor Herschel Parker's grumbling doubts concerning Mount McKinley once the Explorers Club and other societies laid laurels on his brow. Let Parker make another climb and fuss about, it would not matter. Whatever Cook did on Mount McKinley, he gained confidence in his abilities. The mountain did not concern him now; it had served him well enough. He earned a little money from lectures and a book advance, but not nearly enough to clear his debts. Debts plagued him. He even owed Russell Porter and others of the Mount McKinley expedition. A stern fiscal advisor would have cautioned him to settle down for a bit and arrange an extensive lecture series on Mount McKinley or practice medicine until his debts were cleared. But how could he listen? There were other pressures as well.

Once Cook seized the bold course, he could not lose time. He probably reasoned that he had to take the field before Peary. Peary, the veteran polar aspirant, intended to go north in 1907. As it turned out, Peary was forced to postpone his expedition until 1908. Peary's delay proved to be Cook's greatest advantage.

How to beat Peary? First, get the money. Cook needed backers to pay expedition costs. Ironically, he had to keep his plans somewhat secret. It was not easy to secure financial support for exploration, even with ample publicity and encouragement from the Establishment. If he announced his plans, there would be an uproar. Solemn, influential men would call and beg him to do the sporting thing, to stand aside and let the aging lion of the North make his last try. It would cause embarrassment all around, and not help his money-raising efforts either. Once Cook had the Pole, let Peary's fans cry all they wished. Then the rage and anguish would not affect him; it would be swallowed up in the universal acclaim for his daring. But now he must be wary.

Peary and his friends, Herbert Bridgman, Thomas Hubbard, and others, had been warned of Cook's plans. Men who believed that the Mount McKinley climb was a hoax insisted that Cook was capable of repeating his bold stunt with a polar claim. But Peary and the Peary Arctic Club men did not take the warning seriously. It seemed too farfetched. Even if they had, what could they do to stop Cook without making themselves look ridiculous?

Everyone liked Frederick Cook. Unlike many explorers, whose egotism and brash drives resembled those of testy prima donnas, he was mild-mannered and unassertive. Not that he showed passivity in the field—far from it; decisiveness, boldness, and leadership highlighted his earliest exploration ventures. If he changed somewhat in personality after his 1906 claim to Mount McKinley, no one remarked on it. Basically, he remained a likable fellow and looked like the kind of man you might well appreciate as your family doctor.

Despite the stereotype of the brawny adventurer, most explorers were not outsized men. Peary was a big man and so was Shackleton, but Scott, Amundsen, Stefansson, and most others ranged among the middle-sized. Cook stood about 5 feet, 10 inches, and was of wiry build, athletic enough but not rugged-looking. With his brown hair, brown eyes, and modest mustache, he could have passed as a professor, lawyer, or salesman.

Today explorers seem a strange breed. In earlier times the public had a sharper consciousness of geography. The explorer and his goals compelled intense popular admiration. They were all-season heroes. As models for manly conduct, self-sacrifice, and noble ideals, they could not be surpassed. Part of the appeal of their daring and manliness reflected an awed view of strange parts of the world. Always they pitted themselves against harsh obstacles, awful cold, terrible heat, impenetrable jungle, or arid desert. Whatever threatened in the physical world, there they were, challenging it to victory or to death.

The North Pole was just one of many geographic points defying man as the twentieth century opened. It gained its place as an ultimate triumph for an explorer as other regions became better known. The slow pace of Arctic exploration over 350 years and the high toll of lives sacrificed there stimulated interest. Some people joked about the foolishness of striving toward a point of no inherent significance and even seriously deplored the expenditure of monies and human energy toward such an end. Such carpers voiced a minority sentiment. For most people reaching the North Pole represented a human achievement of significance, one that would reflect glory beyond the attainer—to his nation, race, to all of humanity. To adventurers of the peculiar lot who called themselves explorers, the Pole was recognized as a crown jewel without parallel. Otherwise sensible men died to reach it, and for every one sacrificed, untold thousands of others yearned to try for it.

Cook had the good luck to meet a wealthy man who suited his purposes. Cook cultivated the sportsman John R. Bradley without revealing his aspirations. Once he gained Bradley's confidence, the rest was easy. Bradley was a professional gambler who, with his brother, owned the most exclusive casino in America, the Beach Club of Palm Beach, Florida. Bradley started his fortune as a faro dealer in New Orleans. According to legend, he cleaned out every game in town during one remarkable stint. Then he and his brother opened the Bacchus Club in El Paso, did well there, and, at the bequest of Henry M. Flagler, railroad and real estate tycoon, founded the Beach Club. For recreation Bradley took up big game hunting. It was after his return from an Asian hunt that he met Cook at the Explorers Club in New York. Cook, who gave the appearance of being at loose ends at the time, agreed to help Bradley gather Arctic trophies. Nothing was said about the North Pole initially, but once Cook gained Bradley's confidence, he revealed his ambitions. Bradley agreed to help; he would carry the explorer to Greenland.

In June 1907 Bradley and Cook were ready to head north. Cook's departure was quiet, even furtive, which was uncharacteristic of polar explorers, who usually embarked ceremoniously in the full, satisfying glare of the public eye. He avoided a clamorous send-off, heralded by speeches, cheers, newspaper publicity, and ensuing debate on methods of travel, equipment, route, and expectations. Usually an explorer became something of a public property by beseeching money from individuals and institutions. Even if he did not have to appeal for funds, he was engaging in a public endeavor. He was a sportsman competing for a world record, a goal that meant nothing unless generally accepted. No matter how individualistic his motivations, or how independent of supporters he might be, his enterprise was a corporate affair. The North Pole belonged to everyone, and its ravisher owed an accounting to others.

A modest man might wish to avoid the customary fanfare and sensationalism. Glory accepted in advance must be repaid in bitter personal disappointment and, possibly, in open recrimination. Better to slip off quietly, rather than be scorned as a fool or coward later on, if the once-adoring public has turned on you. Explorers, like kings, wore their crowns on uneasy heads. One slip could plunge a man from laureled throne to ignominious disgrace.

Frederick Cook was a modest man. Everyone acknowledged that. And his plans for assaulting the North Pole, he said, were tentative. Until he reached Greenland he would not determine finally whether conditions appeared advantageous for an attempt the following year. He was a careful man and first needed to check on the prosperity of Greenland's Eskimos. If they were thriving in their northern villages with plenty of food, skins for clothing, and dogs for transport, Cook could then decide whether he would undertake the hazardous journey with the Eskimos' help.

We don't know if Cook actually intended an all-out effort for the Pole on leaving New York. If his plans were tentative, there was good reason why they should have been. By the standards of the day, he was woefully unprepared for such a journey. He lacked experience, navigational expertise, and support in manpower and provisioning. Other explorers, notably Charles Francis Hall, had accomplished a good deal with similar handicaps, but not even the bold Hall tried anything comparable in daring to the long dash over drifting sea ice to the Pole.

Cook and Bradley reached Etah, Greenland without difficulty. There Eskimos were willing to join Cook and dogs were available. He gathered a party, including Bradley's cook, a twenty-nine-year-old German, Rudolph Franke, and steamed north to the village of Annoatok, where he planned to winter.

Cook spent the winter months at Annoatok making meticulous preparations. Following his designs, the Eskimos built the sledges and a collapsible boat for crossing leads. Together the men had hunted musk-oxen, walrus, and other game, which they dried for pemmican. These important provisions would supplement the stores that had been carried north with Cook on the *Bradley*. Again and again he calculated the number of marches necessary to reach the Pole, determined what food would be required for dogs and men, considered where caches should be laid for the return journey, and brooded over the probabilities of sea-ice drift and other navigational problems. On February 19, 1908, Cook and his nine Eskimo helpers, 11 sledges, and 103 dogs set out for the jumping-off point at Svartevoeg, on the northern tip of Axel Heiberg Land.

No one could doubt, in reading *My Attainment of the Pole,* that Cook's planning had been thorough and comprehensive, nor that he was strongly—perhaps mystically—motivated. More puzzling was his reference to years of discouragement and failure, because he had not made any earlier attempts to reach the Pole. Perhaps Cook made the point to blur a distinction between himself and his rival, Robert Peary. Everyone knew how long and arduously Peary had been working to achieve the Pole. Comparatively, Cook seemed like a Johnny-come-lately, a casual freelancer who entered the race at the last minute without having serious aspirations. This point of view was certainly manifest in Peary's camp, where much was made of Cook's emergence "out of nowhere" as a polar contender. If, indeed, Cook was a dark horse in the race, it was not as if he lacked polar experience. Nobody's experience equalled Peary's, which did not mean that Peary alone was capable of reaching the Pole. Disputation over comparative background entertained the public in the years following the polar race, and, like all other points of dispute, these arguments missed the point.

Perhaps Cook had all that was necessary to accomplish his purpose: Eskimos, provisions, dogs, equipment, and a plan. As for determination and motivation, the explorer was not lacking; he had the dedication and idealism of a medieval knight. We can imagine Frederick Cook kneeling reverently to receive his investiture, rising after the ceremony with a sense of veneration and mission, and, under the influence of the awesome moment, saying: "I became more intensely conscious than ever of the transfiguring influence of the sublime ideal to which I had set myself. I exulted in the thrill of an indomitable determination, that determination of human beings to essay great things—that human purpose which, throughout history, has resulted in the great deeds, the great art, of the world, and which lifts men above themselves." Cook's inspiration at the moment he described here came from on high, but not through the ministrations of feudal lord or churchman. He was fired by the leaping flamboyance of the aurora borealis, in which he felt his own apotheosis as a polar hero. "Spiritually intoxicated, I rode onward. The aurora faded, but its glow remained in my soul."[1]

But we return to the practical application of Cook's spiritual quest. Cook and his party reached the Arctic shore on March 17. At this point they were 520 miles from the Pole. Only two twenty-year-old Eskimo lads, Etukishook and Ahwelah, were chosen to accompany the explorer on the final trek, although two other Eskimos helped out on the first three days of the ice trip. Two sledges were loaded with 805 pounds of beef pemmican, 130 pounds of walrus pemmican, 50 pounds of musk-ox tenderloin, and other food and equipment for the departure from land on March 18. This food, Cook calculated, would be enough to sustain the three men and 26 dogs for eighty days—and in eighty days they could be back on land to gather food from their caches. Of course, some of the dogs who weakened along the way would be fed to those who were hardier.

Off went the daring men. They crossed a big lead on March 23, and by March 24 they had traveled 131 miles from Svartevoeg. Only 389 miles to go! Then their pace slowed drastically for a week because of storms. When the weather cleared, on March 30, Cook discovered a new land and named it after his backer, John R. Bradley. After twenty-four days' travel they were within 160 miles of the Pole and all was going well.

Critics have found it hard to trace Cook's movements with any confidence. A traveler who was uncertain of his navigation skills or was reluctant to go too far out on the sea ice would be inclined to keep land within sight. And this is what the Eskimos later reported was the situation: They were never more than two sleeps from land. As Cook explained this, however, he had engaged in a little deceit to keep the morale of his companions high: "The thought occurred to me that on our trip I could take advantage of the mirages of low clouds on the horizon and encourage a belief in a constant nearness to land." Cook's explanation was not entirely implausible; explorers had been fooled by clouds at times and had claimed nonexistent land. But to maintain such a deception for weeks, in varying atmospheric conditions, with Eskimos who had some experience in observation, would seem somewhat incredible. But at this point, we are viewing events as Cook narrated the voyage.

All was going well on the trek, but still there were hazards and discomforts. Once a lead in the ice opened up right under Cook while he rested. In the nick of time the Eskimos pulled him from the frigid water. At all times the exertion was strenuous. Each morning, they broke camp in a rush, loaded the sledges, harnessed the dogs, and set off on the run in order to warm themselves in a hurry. "The pace for dog and man is two and a half miles an hour, over good ice, on bad ice, hard snow or soft snow, or tumbling over neckbreaking irregularities. There is no stop for lunch, no riding, or rest, or anything else. It is drive—drive." The worst discomfort came from perspiration that froze in their clothes. This was dangerous as well; frostbite had to be guarded against assiduously—it could be crippling.

The way was cold and windy. Once the temperature fell to –89° F. Cook did not indicate how he measured this. An air temperature that low was unlikely, but the chill factor experienced was probably that low at times. Chill factor temperatures are determined by a formula that adds the bite of the wind to the air temperature. With a wind of 15 miles per hour it feels colder at –20° F than it would at –35° F with no wind.

At the end of each day's run, it was a pleasure to rest. Hurriedly they fed the dogs, built a snowblock shelter, undressed partially, and plunged into their fur sleeping bags up to their waists. Only then did they think of eating. "A brick of pemmican was next taken out and the teeth were set to grind on this bonelike substance. Our appetites were always keen, but a half pound of cold, withered beef and tallow changes a hungry man's thoughts effectively." Then cups of tea were brewed over a cheerful fire and their frost-encrusted upper garments were removed before they burrowed into their furs for a sound sleep.

Usually they were thirsty, often they were pained by the stinging wind and hurt by frostbite. "But there was no monotony; our tortures came from different angles, and from so many sources, that we were ever aroused to a fighting spirit." Relentlessly they drove north. "We travelled until dogs languished or legs failed. Ice hills rose and fell before us, mirages grimaced at our dashing teams with wondering faces. . . . Night was now as bright as day."

Their dash each day was not in a straight line. On April 8, after long marches on the previous nine days, Cook observed that only 96 miles had been covered over that period. "Much of our hard work had been lost in circuitous twists around troublesome pressure lines and high, irregular fields of very old ice." And also, the drift of the ice occasionally necessitated a shift in direction.

No polar traveler has described more convincingly or romantically than Cook the mood that could be induced by constant fatigue and exposure. "The sun at times flamed the clouds, while the snow glowed in burning tones. In the presence of all this we suffered the chill of death." It was as if he were on some drug-induced hallucination. "All nature exulted in a wave of hysteria. Delusions took form about us—in mirages, in the clouds. We moved in a world of delusions. The heat of the sun was a sham, its light a torment. A very curious world this, I thought dumbly, as we pushed our sleds and lashed our lagging dogs." It was as if there were no motion on their part but as if everything else, all the surrounding topographical features, were in motion without showing visible movement. "We moved with it, but ever took our landscape with us."

What kept him going?, Cook wondered. "Unseen beings . . . whose voices urged me in the wailing wind; who, in my success, themselves sought soul peace, and who, that I might obtain it, in some strange, mysterious way succored and buoyed me."

After days of agony they were within 100 miles of the Pole. Ice conditions were growing easier, but fatigue was mounting. Now they rested during the day and traveled at night over the firmer, cooler ice pack. But, despite weariness, Cook kept scrupulous records: "I never permitted myself to be careless in regard to this, for I never let myself forget the importance of such data in plotting an accurate course." Thus, from the mystical he descended to the pragmatic.

These were his assertions concerning data and its importance, but unfortunately his critics were to question whether his thirst for scientific measurement matched his psychological intensity. Of the latter, however, there could be no doubt. Often he described his feelings as he rested out on the ice: "I felt the terrible oppression of that raging, life-sucking vampire force sweeping over the desolate world. Disembodied things—the souls of those, perhaps who had perished here—roamed frenziedly calling me in the wind." Cook's sensitivity to his dead predecessors in polar exploits inspired him: "I felt the desolation of this stormy world within my shuddering soul; but, withal, I throbbed with a determination to assert the supremacy of living man over those blind, insensate forces." He would triumph. He would prove that "the living brain and palpitating muscle of a finite though conscious creature could vanquish a hostile nature which creates to kill." Frederick Cook burned "to justify those who had died here" and set their calling souls at rest by accomplishing the task they had failed at. "The storm waked in me an angry, challenging determination."

Cook faced down a disruptive crisis when his Eskimo helpers refused to go farther. He appealed to them to hang on for five more days. They protested: "On ice always is not good. The bones ache." Cook spoke of bravery, honor, parents, sweethearts, and the Great Spirit. It is a tribute to the explorer's rapport with his men that he was able to convince them, although he tended to give credit to his eloquence. "I spoke hurriedly. The two sat up and listened. Slowly they became inspired with my intoxication. Never did I speak so vehemently."

At 29 miles from the Pole, on the thirty-third day on the ice, Cook felt confident enough to relax. An extra pot of tea was brewed and a surprise of fancy biscuits was shared. The explorer tried to tell his companions about the Pole and showed them how he calculated its position with his instruments. All they understood was that in two days they could turn home, and this joyous thought set them dancing and singing for two hours.

Just after midnight of April 21, they reached the Pole. As usual, Cook suffered delusions: He "seemed to be walking in some splendid golden realms of dreamland" as the ice swam about in "circling rivers of gold."

He felt himself "lifted to the paradise of winners as we stepped over the snows of a destiny for which we had risked life and willingly suffered the tortures of an icy hell." The ice under them seemed almost sacred because of the sacrifices of other men who had sought that place. "At last we step over colored fields of sparkle, climbing walls of purple and gold—finally, under skies of crystal blue, with flaming clouds of glory, we touch the mark!" What joy at last! "The soul awakens to a definite triumph; there is sunrise within us, and all the world of night-darkened trouble fades. We are at the top of the world."

5

GARLANDS
AND HONORS

"Out of whose womb came the ice?
And the hoary frost of Heaven, Who gendered it?"
—The Book of Job

Cook's return to his base a year after reaching the North Pole has been described. After a rest and the enjoyment of meals prepared by Billy Pritchard, the cabin boy of Peary's *Roosevelt,* Cook was eager to reach civilization. Leaving his personal records in New York sportsman Harry Whitney's care, he mushed south 600 miles to Upernavik, Greenland. From there he took a ship to Egedesminde, further down the coast, and boarded the steamer *Hans Egede* bound for Copenhagen.

The *Hans Egede* halted at the Shetland Islands briefly, and from there Cook telegraphed his first newspaper statement to *The New York Herald.* He chose the *Herald* for sound reasons. Its publisher, James Gordon Bennett, favored exploration news, as everyone knew; it was Bennett who had helped Henry M. Stanley to fame for his Africa venture. An exchange of wires settled the matter: Cook received $3,000 for two thousand words. The story was bannered in the *Herald* on September 2, 1909. Once in Copenhagen, Cook wrote a series of follow-up stories for the paper.

In giving an exclusive to the *Herald,* Cook adhered to accepted practice among explorers. It was of equal benefit to the explorer and the fortunate newspaper. As with Peary's contract with *The New York Times,* such arrangements were often made in advance. Cook certainly knew enough to have done this, as he had arranged articles about Mount McKinley with a magazine earlier, but he had not wished to declare his intent before starting north.

Steaming for Copenhagen aboard the *Hans Egede,* Cook perhaps did not worry about formalities. Maybe he anticipated too keenly the honors awaiting him. He was a confident man—or at least could appear so.

An incident aboard ship must have shaken him. Perhaps he was not really ready for public scrutiny. He was privately challenged on a mistake of fact, a kind of slip that, if uttered publicly, would have provoked ridicule. With a scientist aboard, Alfred de Quervain, Cook discussed the sun's height at the Pole, insisting that the sun appeared at different heights at midnight and midday. Impossible, said de Quervain kindly, in that case you saw the sun from somewhere else. For a moment Cook stood fast, arguing for his precise measurement, and then, quite suddenly, he saw de Quervain's point. The trusting scientist explained Cook's monstrous mistake to him and suggested a psychological explanation. Didn't Cook think that memory had played tricks on him and that the sun's position as he described it was as it appeared somewhat south of the Pole? Cook agreed heartily.[1]

The ship finally nosed into Copenhagen and the commotion began. Small boats, decorated with flags of all nations, surrounded the *Hans Egede.* People waved at Cook and shouted joyful greetings. He described the reception very effectively himself: "Wave after wave of cheering rolled over the water. Horns blew, there was the sound of music, guns exploded."[2] The effect was dazzling; it would be to any man.

Amid the tumult of Copenhagen's harbor, Cook stood at the peak of the world's esteem and loved it. It had been a long road from the poverty-stricken fatherless days in upstate New York and the tedious obscurity of a Brooklyn neighborhood's desultory medical practice. He had burned and suffered for those cheers, and had doubtless never heard music of such surpassing sweetness.

Oh, some qualms assaulted him. Aiming high, he risked humiliation. Some unusually impudent and probing newsman had already threatened his ease. But probably the worst had passed. From his view the world seemed very much at his feet, and his spirits soared with each volley of cheers. Such clamor as this could drown out a handful of doubters. Be bold, keep smiling, turn a soft cheek—and all would be well.

In any game, judges determine the winner. Cook's judges howled and whistled from the dock and from the flotilla of tugs, launches, and other small vessels. That uproar said he won. His position did not differ too much from that of a battered, foggy prizefighter standing on buckling knees while a referee lifts an arm too heavy for the fighter to lift himself, coming to consciousness to find that the champion could be beaten after all. Most exploration fans had expected Robert Peary to win the Pole, yet Cook heard the roar of triumph and won fairly enough through a stroke of boldness. To the bold belongs the prize.

Exploration was a game, and one played without any rules. Cook knew much of the liberties Peary had taken with truth after earlier expeditions, and it did not seem inappropriate that he challenge the veteran polar traveler for the ultimate crown. After all, could he not be as bold as Peary? Certainly he felt himself to be the stuff of a champion and had served apprenticeship enough—near both poles. Triumph was no fantasy, although he had fantasized at times; the wave of sound was real enough. Cook stood, listened, and waved, eyes dimmed with tears, the winner in the most individualistic and rugged sport of them all.

At times Cook knew right from wrong and held to a strict, old-fashioned code. The excitement of meeting Denmark's princess, the United States minister to Denmark, and other dignitaries, and then addressing an enthusiastic crowd in some building in town before being whisked to his hotel, dead tired and genuinely dazed, caused him to do wrong. A manicurist had been summoned to the hotel to do his nails: "I had not paid or tipped her, and with the girl's image a perturbed feeling persisted, 'Here is someone I have wronged.'"[3] In this episode the punctilious, kindly Cook is clearly revealed, and only an unfair critic could doubt his sincere remorse.

Before his ship reached Copenhagen, Cook had encountered the first hostility to his claims. Philip Gibbs, an eager English reporter boarded at Elsinore, asked hard questions directly, and openly expressed dismay at the explorer's answers. Gibbs, later renowned as a brilliant international correspondent, represented *The London Daily Chronicle*. He was a veteran reporter, thirty-two years old, and not awed by instant celebrities. Apparently Gibbs had doubted Cook from the beginning. As he traveled to meet Cook, he burned to ask questions in order to test the truth of his story.

Gibbs had immediately asked Cook for evidence of his discovery. This was a fair question. Cook responded: "I bring the same proofs as every other explorer. I bring my story. Do you doubt that? When Shackleton and Peary came home you believed what they told you. Why, then, should you disbelieve me?"[4]

A defensive answer: Cook already felt somewhat persecuted. But there was some justice in his complaint. When Shackleton and Peary had made their claims on their earlier expeditions, newsmen had not badgered them for proofs. However, Cook remained calm, explained his polar observations, and told Gibbs that his records and instruments had been left in Greenland for eventual shipment to the States. Gibbs thought it curious that Cook left his evidence in Greenland. Later Cook played down the importance of the records, which were never recovered. "These field papers with their miscellaneous notes had served their purpose. . . . A few of the important calculations were kept more as a curiosity."[5] This incredible disregard for documentation was unprecedented in exploration history. Even someone less suspicious than Gibbs might have been shocked by Cook's carelessness.

Aside from explaining his calculations, Cook praised his Eskimo companions. He assured Gibbs that Eskimos were an intelligent and cultured people. This assessment surprised Gibbs. Although he had no experience with Eskimos, he shared the prejudices of his day and commented sarcastically: "I had always thought the Eskimos were the most primitive and ignorant race on earth, but Dr. Cook of course, is a high authority."[6]

If Gibbs's probing unsettled Cook, he was gratified by wires from American magazine and book publishers begging for his story. "The clamor of ovation" overwhelmed him.[7] Crown Prince Christian and other dignitaries greeted Cook with congratulations. All the excitement seemed too much for him. Cook retired to his cabin to rest, but Gibbs thought the explorer was hiding and perceived dark reasons for such conduct: "He . . . came out . . . with a livid look, almost green. I never saw guilt and fear more clearly written on any human face."[8]

In his hotel, Cook faced a news conference and acquitted himself well. His direct and frank answers turned away suspicion. Gibbs was not among the reporters at this session. He had already made up his mind and was busy writing an exposure for the *Chronicle*. On September 7 Gibbs moved from skepticism to accusation, writing that people believed Cook only because of his pleasing personality. Cook had no proofs.

On September 8 Cook lectured before the king of Denmark and the Royal Danish Geographical Society. According to Gibbs, "There were many awkward pauses, and Dr. Cook stumbled badly over his figures," His appearance confirmed the newsman's bias: "His face was flushed, and his forehead beaded with perspiration. He had the grim look of a man determined to be believed as he drove that 'big nail' home with unconvincing, flashy phrases."[9]

Gibbs made much of the lecturer's manner, which could have been the result of a commonly experienced platform fever. Clearly the newsman was moving toward a kill. How could Gibbs be so sure that Cook lied and that the lecture "proves conclusively that his claim to have reached the north pole belongs to the realms of fairy tales"?[10] Cook's quick passage to the Pole, followed by a dilatory return journey of several months' duration, pointed to falsity. Yet, for all Gibbs's certainty, his charges were no more securely based than Cook's claims. Cook's reasons for delaying his return were not obviously implausible.

At his first formal press conference in Copenhagen, Cook won over most journalists with the help of the famed correspondent W. T. Stead, who presided. No one at the meeting was capable of asking very tough questions, and he met the true issue squarely. He had no reason, he said, to hoodwink the world. "I am in this work for the love of the work, gentlemen," Cook stated boldly, with a tired, patient smile. "I am not in it for money. And I have brought back just exactly the sort of records and proofs that every Arctic explorer brings back."

Things became easier as questions grew more ridiculous: Did he like to eat fox? Was he a Christian? Had he planted the Stars and Stripes at the Pole? Yes, yes, yes, and in fact he had photographed the flag at the Pole.

The next day Cook read the European press notices with satisfaction and guessed without seeing American papers that many headlines announced: STARS AND STRIPES PLANTED AT POLE. European newsmen had liked his manner: "calm and imperturbable"; "answering with directness and frankness"; "sincere manner made profound impression." And Stead summed it up well: "Some believed in Dr. Cook at first; all believe in him now."[12]

Now he felt ready to face the Danish scientists. Members of the Royal Geographical Society as well as officials of the University of Copenhagen, led by Rector Torp, questioned him gently. Torp was a man after Cook's own heart. After Torp told the press about "an exhaustive series of mathematical questions" that Cook answered to "our full satisfaction" without nervousness or excitement, Cook's admiration for Torp's discernment abounded.[13] At some point Cook knew he would have to submit data to a scientific body: He decided that the University of Copenhagen would serve well enough. Obviously the Danes loved and accepted him, and Torp had committed himself. Why not offer that university his records? There was no rush; he had explained that some data had been left in Greenland and were presumably enroute to the States. Working up the data and returning them for the University of Copenhagen's consideration would take time. Meanwhile, he would be spared any importunate calls for evidence at home. Risking this offer to the Danes seemed a brilliant stroke, yet Cook blundered terribly.

Blunder is perhaps the wrong word to use. In the normal course of things, the university or any other scientific group might have scanned his records cursorily and praised his work—had it not been for the diversion created by his rival. Electrifying news arrived at a banquet given for Cook and for foreign correspondents on his third day in Copenhagen. It had promised to be a wonderful evening for Cook—fine dining and drinking, pleasant talk, and a comfortable place in the limelight—a forecast of many such nights at home and elsewhere in the world. Then a messenger interrupted the festivities with a telegram that was read aloud by Stead. The simple message, "In a wire from Indian Harbor, Labrador, dated September 6, 1909, Peary says: Stars and Stripes nailed to the Pole," unsettled everyone. Was it a hoax? The unflappable explorer was not to be ruffled. Playing it perfectly, Cook stood up to announce his pride "that a fellow American has reached the Pole." Hitting just the right note, he quoted his friend Rear Admiral Winfield Schley, who had declared at Santiago as the American forces demolished Spain's, "There is glory enough for us all." Cook called Peary a brave man and directed his listeners to the best way of thinking about the news: "If the reports are true his observations will confirm mine and set at rest all doubts."[14] A good thought that, and the newsmen scurried off to duty, more sober than they cared to be. Cook went back to his hotel looking benign and composed, yet feeling as if he had been kicked in the stomach and wishing that this had come at a more advantageous time.

Then on September 9 the drama quickened. Peary announced that Cook's claims were false. Peary's men had questioned Cook's Eskimo companions and concluded that the party could not have reached the Pole. *The New York Times* made much of Peary's story, yet the report did not really prove anything against Cook. Of Peary's interrogators, only Matt Henson spoke Eskimo; other experts agreed that such leading questions as were probably asked could produce only uncertain results. Peary did not convince the Danes, because their Arctic hero, Knud Rasmussen, an Eskimo expert, had been satisfied with his talks with the tribesmen of

Cook's Eskimo companions. But now the fat was in the fire. The *Times* pushed Peary's claim vigorously and continued to publish Gibbs's stories. Other papers followed suit, featuring interviews with authorities who doubted Cook. On September 10 Peary sent the famous telegram in which he accused Cook of handing the public "a gold brick," a denunciation that hurt Peary's reputation and damaged Cook as well.

Thus in early September 1909, a sensation was developing that reflected adversely on Cook's integrity. The timing could not have been more devastating to Cook's reputation. In February 1908, when Cook was about to march away from Greenland toward the Pole, an account of his adventure of the previous year had been published. *To the Top of the Continent* recounted a Cook first: the conquest of North America's highest mountain, the towering Mount McKinley in south central Alaska. To return home with polar victory the same year would surely have confirmed the explorer's fame. But this was 1909. Meanwhile, Peary had appeared on the scene.

Now Cook would have to tackle New York under glowering clouds of suspicion. However, nothing had really changed if Peary's accusations were only jealousy and vindictiveness. Let Peary insist that he was the second man to reach the Pole. After all, only one man could be first at the Pole. Cook had forestalled his rival by nine months.

New Yorkers and all Americans were waiting for him. A restful sea voyage would fit him well for the ardors of the lecture series his agent was arranging. No one could stop him now. Frederick Cook had grasped the Grail first! Yet such affirmations could not turn the forces which were growing in New York and the charges that he was a liar, imposter, and coward. Unknown to Cook, the shadow of Mount McKinley loomed as well. His Alaskan adventure had not been forgotten: The erupting polar dispute stimulated a reexamination of his mountaineering record.

PEARY'S PASSION

"To strive, to seek, to find, and not to yield."
—Alfred Tennyson

Robert E. Peary's career as a polar explorer exposes both bright and dark sides of the venture. He did not lack heroic qualities: courage, determination, and skill. But he amply showed the imbalance in character that the demands of exploration forced upon the leading actors. His ambition and ego caused him to be petty to underlings and jealous of rivals. His frustrations and the terrible demands of fundraising put his honesty to trial. Admitting mistakes became impossible; claiming victories not actually won became easy. This tall, powerful man of magnificent personal qualities was flawed by vanity and meanness and was marked to be the tragic hero of American exploration.

In his youth Peary aspired to great things. He reveled in outdoor life and sports in Maine and built a muscular body. At Bowdoin College he excelled in his studies. After graduation he became a career engineer in the United States Navy. Once he was smitten by the polar passion, the Navy generously permitted him to focus on his exploration ambitions.

From 1886, when he voyaged to Greenland for the first time, he shaped himself for great deeds. He explored north Greenland in 1891–92, again in 1893–96, and in 1897 announced his plans for conquering the North Pole. From 1898 to 1902 he hurled himself at his goal. The prize was denied him, but he did return home with much experience and long-considered schemes for ultimate success.

51

Peary's assignment to the naval dockyards in New York improved his possibilities. As the rising star among the nation's explorers, he attracted the attention of wealthy and influential men who loved the cause of geographic discovery. These exploration fans were willing to back their enthusiasm with money, and in 1904 the Peary Arctic Club raised $100,000 for a ship built to Peary's specifications.

Now Peary was confident of his plans and the means to attain the Pole. The ship *Roosevelt* would be an ideal base for his assault. Although at fifty years he was rather old for an explorer, he steamed off in July 1905 tasting victory.

Over the years Peary had worked out a technique for success. He employed numbers of Eskimos as dog drivers and seamstresses. His large party would help blaze the trail and establish food caches, and then divisions of it would return to shore when no longer needed. The idea was to husband the strength and capacity of the party designated for the final dash to the Pole.

Yet Peary failed. Low temperatures reduced his speed; provisions were used up. Peary did manage, with a tremendous effort, to set a new farthest-north record.

He would win yet. His wealthy backers did not desert his cause. The *Roosevelt* needed extensive repairs, which prevented him from trying again in 1907. But in July 1908, the *Roosevelt* and Peary were ready. Everyone realized it would be his last attempt; he was fifty-three years old. This time he must succeed.

Before Peary left New York with Captain Bob Bartlett, the *Roosevelt*'s skipper and a veteran ice pilot; Matt Henson, a skillful, sturdy Negro dog driver whom Peary usually identified as his body servant; Donald B. MacMillan; and others, he was concerned about Cook's rivalry. By Peary's egotistical standards (which were common among explorers), Cook had violated the gentlemanly code of the game. It was not right that Cook planned a march along a route similar to the one Peary had pioneered, nor that he might engage Eskimos trained earlier by Peary. Others would disagree and argue that an explorer could not claim priority over an object not yet achieved. At any rate, the matter was not an issue except in the view of Peary and his most dedicated supporters.

Robert E. Peary had every reason to feel that the victory denied to him for so long was within his grasp. He felt particularly pleased because his progress northward to the Pole conformed to his precise schedule. An explorer's chances of success—and survival—owed less to fortune, or even to weather, than to logistics. Preparation was the paramount factor. In theory, if a plan were well laid, its execution to completion should go on as a matter of course. You learn from previous failures, Peary reflected, and no one in exploration history persisted as long and relentlessly as did he.

Peary had sailed for the Arctic in July 1908. At Etah, in northwest Greenland, he added 50 Eskimos and 250 dogs to the expedition and made meticulous preparations. Before winter he established his advance base at Cape Columbia. In February 1909 Peary and his party started north in separate divisions, establishing bases along the coast and on the ice to support the advance and return journeys.

Travel was slow during March. Low temperatures, heavy winds, and open leads in the sea ice were obstacles to progress. The determined men required patience while waiting for ice to close over impassable leads of open water.

Peary knew how to drive his men, and he had tough division leaders in Bob Bartlett, Donald MacMillan, George Borup, Dr. J. W. Goodsell, and veteran Matt Henson.

By April 1 Peary broke his own northward record, reaching 87° 47′ N. The work of his four advance parties had been accomplished. They had already returned to the *Roosevelt* with the surplus dogs. Now Peary sent the fifth division under Bob Bartlett back to base. Bartlett, the tough Newfoundlander who skippered the *Roosevelt,* hated to go. But Peary was unmoved by Bartlett's hopes to make the final drive. It would not do to share polar honors with a British subject.

Peary, Matt Henson, and four Eskimos readied for the final dash. The Pole was only 133 miles distant. Men and dogs were in good shape.

Peary reckoned on five marches of at least 25 miles each to gain the Pole. He could count on ten hours of sunlight for each day's work. If the weather remained fine, if pressure ridges (hummocks of ice thrown up by shifting ice floes) did not delay his progress too much, and if impassable open leads were not encountered, he had nothing to fear.

Certainly a sudden gale could disrupt everything. In a severe storm, he could not travel. And even after the weather cleared, he might find that the storm had opened wide water leads to the north or had raised pressure ridges he could not cross.

Just three years previously, on April 1, 1906, Peary had been defeated by temperatures of –60°F which had slowed progress on the first stages of his march to one-half of what he projected. Then he knew making the Pole was impossible, but in a desperate drive he forged on far enough to set a new northward record. Peary's risk paid off. By returning with a farthest-north record that eclipsed that of European explorers, he kept his backers happy.

But in April 1909, Peary's position was anything but desperate. Schedules had been met. All prospects were overwhelmingly favorable. "This was the time," he wrote, "for which I had reserved all my energies, the time for which I had lived the simple life and trained myself as for a race. In spite of my years, I felt fit for the demands of the coming days and was eager to be on the trail. As for my party, my equipment, and my supplies, they were perfect beyond my most sanguine dreams of earlier years."[1]

The explorer's confidence induced pleasant, ego-building reflections. Henson was a great ice traveler. The Eskimos were excellent, too. But Peary was indisputably the leader. They looked to him. If he faltered, they would be lost. For all the good qualities of his companions, he felt that their racial inheritance limited them in daring and initiative.

The first day's run covered about 30 miles, taking the party well over the eighty-eighth parallel. Peary got a scare near the end of the day's march in coming upon a lead which was just opening. The lead was 10 yards wide, but to the east the water gaps were still insignificant. Peary led his men to the east and found a passage, jumping from one solid ice floe to another, picking a way to safety.

Twice on that first day's stretch Peary plunged into thigh-deep water that had flowed over the ice. His clothing was watertight. As the water froze on his fur trousers, he had only to scrape off the ice.

No little mishap could daunt him. "The joy of again being in the lead affected me like wine. The years seemed to drop from me, and I felt as I had felt those days fifteen years before, when I headed my little party across the great ice-cap of Greenland, leaving twenty or twenty-five miles behind my snowshoes day after day, and on a spurt stretching it to thirty or forty."

On April 3 the weather remained clear and calm. They encountered broad pressure ridges in the morning and had to labor with pickaxes to clear gaps for the dogs and their two 12-foot sledges. In ten hours they made only 20 miles.

Ice conditions were better on April 4, and the weather was fine. They covered 25 miles without strain, although Peary's foot was injured slightly when a sledge runner ran over it.

In the evening they reached a lead of 100 yards covered by a thin coat of ice. Peary guided the dogs across cautiously. "I was obliged to slide my feet and travel wide, bear style, in order to distribute my weight, while the men let the sledges and dogs come over by themselves, gliding across where they could. The last two men came over on all fours."

Peary anxiously watched the others cross. He could see the ice bend under the weight of sledges and men. One sledge's runner cut clean through the thin ice just before it reached a firmer surface. It was a close call.

That night the men rested very near the eighty-ninth parallel. "Give me three more days of this weather!" Peary wrote in his diary. It was cold, −40° F, but the cold and calm stabilized the sea ice. It was time to separate the healthier dogs from the weaker. As provisions were used up, Peary had planned for the use of only one sledge. The surviving dogs would be fed with the weaker dogs' flesh.

There was some discomfort because of the cold. The bitter wind burned the travelers' faces until their flesh cracked, causing extreme pain, especially at night as the weary men tried to sleep. The Eskimos even complained that their noses hurt, a complaint Peary had never heard before. But Peary had no complaints. Signs were too favorable. He could stand almost any measure of mere discomfort.

Not that Peary was free of anxiety. So far they had not encountered an impassable lead, but they could run onto one at any time. "At every pressure ridge I found myself hurrying breathlessly forward, fearing there might be a lead just beyond it, and when I arrived at the summit I would catch my breath with relief—only to find myself hurrying on in the same way at the next ridge."

On April 5 Peary let his men sleep longer than usual. Everyone was very tired. His latitude sight showed a position of 89° 25′—only 35 miles from the Pole.

They started out again in the evening dusk. Peary wanted to reach the Pole during daylight so that he could determine his position with more certainty.

The party moved rapidly for 15 miles, rested, fed, then moved on at a good clip for another 15 miles. Conditions were still perfect and the march had gone exactly as planned.

On April 6 the Pole was within Peary's grasp:

We were now at the end of the last long march of the upward journey. Yet with the Pole actually in sight I was too weary to take the last few steps. The accumulated weariness of all those days and nights of forced marches and insufficient sleep, constant peril and anxiety, seemed to roll across me all at once. I was actually too exhausted to realize at the moment that my life's purpose had been achieved. As soon as our igloos had been completed, and we had eaten our dinner and doubled-rationed the dogs, I turned in for a few hours of absolutely necessary sleep, Henson and the Eskimos having unloaded the sledges and got them in readiness for such repairs as were necessary. But, weary though I was, I could not sleep long. It was, therefore, only a few hours later when I woke. The first thing I did after awakening was to write these words in my diary: "The Pole at last. The prize of three centuries. My dream and goal for twenty years. Mine at last! I cannot bring myself to realize it. It seems all so simple and commonplace."

Everything was in readiness for an observation at 6 P.M., Columbia meridian time, in case the sky should be clear, but at that hour it was, unfortunately, still overcast. But as there were indications that it would clear before long, two of the Eskimos and myself made ready a light sledge carrying only the instruments, a tin of pemmican, and one or two other skins; and drawn by a double team of dogs, we pushed on an estimated distance of ten miles. While we travelled, the sky cleared, and at the end of the journey, I was able to get a satisfactory series of observations at Columbia meridian midnight. These observations indicated that our position was then beyond the Pole.

Nearly everything in the circumstances which then surrounded us seemed too strange to be thoroughly realized, but one of the strangest of those circumstances seemed to me to be the fact that, in a march of only a few hours, I had passed from the western to the eastern hemisphere and had verified my position at the summit of the world.

Peary's actions at the Pole showed his concern for form: "After I had planted the American flag in the ice, I told Henson to time the Eskimos for three rousing cheers, which they gave with the greatest enthusiasm. Thereupon, I shook hands with each member of the party—surely a sufficiently unceremonious affair to meet with the approval of the most democratic." Peary also left a glass bottle recording his success—a useless gesture on the shifting sea ice, but part of the polar tradition. He also did not fail to note the names and races of his five companions: All were men of color. There was only one white man astride the Pole. Peary always made that point clearly.

Later, after resting, Peary had enough ease to muse on his experience. "For more than a score of years that point on the earth's surface had been the object of my every effort. To its attainment my whole being, physical, mental and moral, had been dedicated." How could such a man fail after twenty-three years of arduous striving? How could he be beaten to the Pole?

In describing his return journey, Peary tried to clarify for the readers of his *North Pole* what the twenty-three years of struggle and disappointment were all about, what it meant to place "the flag of my country at the goal of the world's desire. It is not easy to write about, but I know that we were going back to civilization with the last of the great adventure stories—a story the world had been waiting to hear for nearly four hundred years, a story which was to be told at last under the folds of the Stars and Stripes."

Peary returned safely and speedily to the *Roosevelt,* arriving on April 26, only two days after Bartlett. In July Peary steamed south along the Greenland coast and stopped at Etah. There he heard alarming news: Cook had told the Eskimos he had reached the Pole the previous year. Peary's anguish can be easily imagined. Cook's companions were interrogated by Peary's men. According to what they reported, Cook had never left sight of land. This testimony confirmed Peary's suspicions.

Peary headed home, stopping at Indian Harbor, Labrador, to send telegrams announcing his victory. He also wired United Press on September 8: "Cook's story shouldn't be taken too seriously. The two Eskimos who accompanied him say he went no distance north and not out of sight of land. Other members of the tribe corroborate their story."[2]

In a longer telegram to *The New York Times* he advised editors not to trouble with Cook's story: "He had not been to the Pole on April 21, 1908, or at any other time. He has simply handed the public a gold brick."[3]

When this news reached the press, a bitter battle commenced between Cook and Peary partisans. It is still going on more than seventy years later.

THE SEEDS
OF DOUBT

*"His success . . . may prevent other
fools from going there."*
　　　　—George Melville

What must it feel like for a son of New York to enter the great city's harbor to a roaring fanfare of acclaim, a hearty, loving tribute from one's own people? A hero: Fred Cook of upstate New York and Brooklyn, Dr. Frederick Cook of Brooklyn and New York City. What do the horns and whistles, the band music, the bunting and flags, the outstretched hands and the cheers really mean to the individual so honored? It touches deeply; and the more sensitive and inward a man, the more dreamer he has been, the more he is moved by such expressions of public devotion. *Devotion* is the right word. Hero-makers elevate themselves and humankind in conferring honors. Like prayer, praise is reciprocal; it enhances and raises those who give as well as those who receive. Such occasions are love feasts, unions of felicitation and brotherhood, precious occasions on which we divine that one has lifted himself above us through fine character and genius.

A heady affair for Cook. Richer in sensation by far than the similar greeting in Copenhagen because it came from countrymen. And the family was there, proud and grateful; wife and daughters glowing in the happy tumult. Mrs. Cook, too tense perhaps, too uncomfortable in the public eye to enjoy herself; but the girls rose to the delirium without strain.

Cook appeared tired but fit, and, as always, calmly dignified. He possessed the wonderful restraint and control that many public figures strive for in vain. He seemed just right; not self-conscious; certainly not arrogant; a man content with himself.

Thousands of jubilant fans thronged the dock and many joined the automobile parade after debarkation; 300 cars in all wound up South Fifth Street, ending at the Bushwick Club, where Cook shook hands until lamed, sat down to a banquet, and heard tribute after tribute to the native son who took the world's glittering exploration prize. Afterward reporters got to ask questions, respectfully couched questions, yet some queries revealed that clouds hovered over Cook even on this glorious September day. The pressure was muted. Cook answered most questions with ease and turned aside a few. He was in command. All could be explained. There was no doubt in his mind, he said, that he could absolutely show that he won the Pole. It was as if the good doctor had to assure Americans that they need not be anxious; his manner proved he was not. The explorer's patience and kindness impressed most observers; they were taken with him.

Cook did not realize his vulnerability on September 21. The conflict, just smoking a bit above the surface like an underground fire hiding intense heat below, could not really be squelched by a nice manner and manly presence. Who, standing on the brink of as passionate an imbroglio as ever aroused Americans, could know the hidden forces of defamation?

Nothing too much to worry about, Cook thought. His claim was good enough to prevail. Priority was no problem: His was the first polar claim made. Who could contest his right? In all New York, few people possessed any experience of the Arctic. His word should be good enough for New York—and for the world. Peary reached the Pole, too, and Cook did not begrudge him whatever honors were left in the exploration enterprise.

And there was much to do after installing the family, with some flair, in a suite of the splendid Waldorf-Astoria Hotel. He would meet the press daily at the Waldorf, or elsewhere around the country as he lectured. The more lectures the better, he told his eager agent. In lecturing he brought his case directly to the people. Ordinary people would flock to hear Cook—and believe him. They did not owe allegiance to exploration cliques. What better response could he make to the doubts expressed in papers that played up Peary's slanders. Lecturing, although tiring, was lucrative. His appearance in Saint Louis at the Exposition earned a huge sum, although the report of a $20,000 fee may have been exaggerated.

No need to fear the slanders levied against him, it seemed, as long as he could be heard personally by innumerable audiences throughout the land and could reach millions more through newspapers and magazines. *The New York Herald* led the field with a series of exclusive articles; other papers followed along. He was modest but not reticent and had ample outlets for his own side of things. On the platform he skillfully brought the Pole closer to people's consciousness. Thousands of Americans knew nothing of the Arctic beyond what Dr. Cook told them. From the platform, he was close to them in spirit—and they listened and applauded. Dr. Cook was close; the Pole was far away. But, unfortunately, the mountain, Mount McKinley, was nearer. A mountain cannot stalk a man, but mountaineers can. Two former Cook companions, Herschel Parker and Belmore Browne, were stalking Cook, although he did not realize it yet.

On September 23, 1909, the Arctic Club honored Cook with a banquet. Testimonial speakers praised his polar feat as if no question existed concerning it. Tributes to Cook appeared in papers around the country and in Canada. Newsmen were anxious to interview anyone who knew Cook and found acquaintances willing to evaluate the explorer. An Arctic veteran who worked with Cook and Peary affirmed that "Dr. Cook is a splendid character. He is a gentleman clean through; brave, generous to a fault, always thinking of the comfort of others and never for one moment sparing himself." His companions were invariably impressed by Cook's coolness: "Never for one moment did he ever lose his temper; no circumstance, however trying, ever seemed to ruffle his genial spirit." He gave his professional services to the Eskimos without stint, pulling teeth, dispensing drugs "without thought of reward or recompense." And did such former Cook companions think he had reached the Pole? Why not? they responded. "He was physically as fit as any man who ever went north; he knew Arctic conditions as thoroughly as Peary or any other man; he had dogs, Eskimos, game, plenty of supplies, and more than that, he had the pluck to make the dash."[1]

Such stories as these helped balance the suspicions raised by some in the press. Cook saw himself very much in the running against assaults on his honor. To doubters he offered the surest defense a man could present (aside from technical proofs that would be evaluated at a later date): his good reputation. It appeared that Dr. Cook, relying on his good name, had time to still criticism through his personal efforts and those of his friends. Many supporters had rallied to him, and Peary's truculence tended to intensify the loyalty of Cook's fans. As a public-relations tactician, Peary, a bristling, stern, dogmatic figure, was no match for Cook. In a test of personalities alone, Peary would be driven from the field like a whipped puppy. Soon after Peary's return to the States, he shut up about Cook in public. Although his biographers have insisted that his silence showed his dignity and confidence, it was really a tactic urged by press-wise advisers. They knew how unsympathetically he came across to the public, and wished to control the public debate.

Actually Cook's days of glory were numbered. Peary and Hubbard might have relaxed had they divined the pace of events. For exactly sixty-one days from his return to America, Cook successfully resisted the pressure. He needed money, and having been offered a deluge of requests for lectures, he had a great opportunity to earn it. One of the high points was an event sponsored by Brooklyn's Danish-Americans. Had Cook wished so, the proud Danes would have marched with him against his critics. The association between Cook and Denmark made Danish-Americans proud that their little country had the chance to honor Cook first.

Even in *The New York Times,* a newspaper committed to Peary's cause by virtue of a contractual arrangement for an exclusive, the public read much about Cook that was favorable or at least neutral. On September 24 the *Times* reported the Arctic Club banquet and published an interview with an acquaintance defending Cook's veracity and an account of all the publishers and lecture agents besieging the celebrated explorer. Three days later Columbia University's Professor J. E. Spingarn backed Cook in a *Times* interview; on September 29 Cook was featured on Peary's lack of proof for his charges, while the enthusiastic audience at Cook's Philadelphia lecture was mentioned.[2]

October news stories reported Cook's appearance before a large Boston crowd as well as his answers to questions raised by journalist George Kennan; Cook's plans to give his records to the University of Copenhagen before any other authority; plans for an official reception in Washington; a proposed western lecture tour; a projected $500,000 income from his book and lectures; Cook's change of mind on the presentation of his records (he would submit to Copenhagen and to an American group simultaneously); the official reception in Washington; Cook's charges that Peary misused supplies; Cook's wire to Copenhagen University stating that he would indeed submit records to them first; a warm reception in Pittsburgh; New York City aldermen's plans to honor Cook; severe cold threatening to curtail his lecturing; Cook's welcome in Saint Louis, the "cheering crowds" of centennial visitors there, and the ovation after his lecture; Britain's Queen Alexandra's profession of belief in Cook; Cook's charges that Peary and his men distorted the testimony of Cook's Eskimo companions concerning their route; Cook's lecture at Atlantic City and his statement that he would answer Kennan's critical articles later; Captain Joseph Bernier's insistence that Eskimo testimony solicited by Peary against Cook should not be believed; and the presentation of the Freedom of the City award by New York aldermen on October 15.

In this three-week period, Peary's charges against Cook, based upon what was allegedly learned from Cook's Eskimo companions, received a good deal of attention. Headlines also proclaimed doubts about Cook raised by polar authorities. Altogether, the *Times* and other papers gave the polar matter huge coverage from September 2, when the *Herald* first announced Cook's journey, through October 15. As a continuing story it was every editor's dream, one that broke with a sensation and was buoyantly sustained by an unbroken series of newsworthy incidents after Peary's initial story on September 7.

II

THEY ALSO
SOUGHT GLORY

KANE AND HALL

"The ice was here, the ice was there,
The ice was all around."
—Samuel Taylor Coleridge

S ome background on polar exploration before Cook and Peary highlights the nature of the endeavor and its hazards. Exploration hazards went beyond the physical dangers encountered in the field. With its elements of sporting contest and public event, the explorer's venture was a complicated pursuit.

Before Cook and Peary entered the field, the principal American Arctic explorers of the nineteenth century were Elisha Kent Kane, Charles Francis Hall, George Washington De Long, George Melville, ship's engineer under De Long, and Adolphus W. Greely. These men differed a good deal in personality and accomplishments, but all possessed eccentricities and drives characteristic of explorers.

Kane was a United States Navy medical doctor with an obsessive urge to travel and gather scientific data. He had traveled in the Orient and Africa before joining the First Grinnell Expedition in 1850. Lieutenant E. J. DeHaven commanded this search for the missing British explorer Sir John Franklin; the search was sponsored by the American shipping entrepreneur Henry Grinnell. This was the first American Arctic exploration venture. On Beechey Island, near the entrance to Barrow Strait, De Haven found the campsite where Franklin spent his first winter. And Kane became smitten with the North.

The sponsor put Kane in charge of the Second Grinnell Expedition, which set out in 1853. Kane took his *Advance* up the west coast of Greenland, halting enroute to buy dogs and retain an Eskimo hunter. All of Kane's American successors in the field followed the same practice of using dogs and Eskimos, while the British, with few exceptions, maintained their ironbound tradition of man-hauled sleds and nondependence upon hunting right into the twentieth century.

Kane wintered over for two years, and one of his sled parties managed to wrest the farthest-north record away from E. A. Inglefield, an English officer who had reached a previous high in the same region of Greenland in 1852.

Kane was not really very interested in searching for Franklin, who had been missing for eight years and could be assumed dead. He advocated the existence of an open polar sea, a theoretical fancy that had many supporters but did not actually exist. Geographic theorists sometimes depended more on faith than reason. As Kane so stoutly put it: "There needs must exist a polar sea."[1]

Kane quarreled with the experienced Dane-Greenlander, Hans Petersen, who had been retained as a hunter. Petersen thought the open polar sea concept was nonsense and said so. Petersen had served with the veteran British whaler William Penny on a previous search expedition and compared the two leaders in terms very unfavorable to the American. Petersen considered Kane a mere record breaker who felt that "the stripes and stars ought to wave where no Union Jack had ever fluttered in the polar gale." Petersen was right about Kane's ambition, but he overlooked the serious scientific work the Americans did during their two-year stint. Kane kept daily meteorological logs and made extensive notes on other natural phenomena. Petersen became a bit touchy when Kane disregarded his advice, and he raged at Kane's "blundering braggartism."[2] At times Petersen had cause, as when a party suffered horribly because Kane sent them out too early in the season with an overloaded sled against Petersen's advice.

Kane's inept leadership and his insistence on continuing the search for an open sea after the first winter led to a split in the party. Twelve of his eighteen men, headed by surgeon Isaac Hayes, rebelled and started south for themselves. The escape party found the going too rigorous and were forced to return. Kane accepted them without forgiving them, and it was not a happy camp. Hayes, who later had his own exploration expedition, sulked and refused to carry out his duties. In his narrative of the expedition, Hayes did not mind mentioning that he drugged some friendly Eskimos living near the camp so that the escape party could steal their furs.

The escapees were not technically deserters or mutineers, because Kane gave them approval to go—most grudgingly, and only because he feared an open mutiny. In his journal he grumbled that he hoped to live to thrash the malcontents. If he had been big and powerful, he might have held the party together by physical intimidation; unfortunately, he was a short, slight man.

There were grim moments. Two men tried to escape and join the Etah Eskimos. Kane knocked one of them down after putting a hunk of lead in his mitten for the purpose. The man got away, got some meat from Eskimos, and returned to camp with it. The ungrateful Kane shot at him and the unfortunate man ran for his life. Kane discussed this in his published narrative but did not mention, except in his secret diary, that he had done his best to kill the other deserter with a belaying pin—without success.

After a second winter, and an accidental burning of the *Advance,* Kane resolved to take his party south. By this time he was the strongest man in the party because he understood the diet deficiencies that caused scurvy. He had taken remedies. He even ate rats—much to the disgust of his companions. Later Kane wrote an engaging anecdote about his efforts to persuade reluctant men to eat raw potatoes: "At dinner as at breakfast the raw potatoes come in, our hygienic luxury. Like doctor-stuff generally it is not as appetizing as desirable." He cut out the bad spots, grated the potatoes, and added oil. "It is as much as I can do to persuade the men to shut their eyes and bolt it, like Mrs. Squeer's molasses and brimstone at Dotheby's Hall. Two absolutely refuse to eat it."[3]

Kane showed his greatness during the last months of the expedition. He rescued the sled party that made the farthest-north journey and nursed them back to health. William Morton of the sled party also insisted he had seen the open sea, but, actually, he was deceived by a mirage. Kane pulled the entire scurvy-ridden party together and led them in three open boats south to the safety of a Greenland village. There a whaler picked them up and took them home.

Kane's exploits in the Arctic made him America's chief hero in the mid-nineteenth century, and some sixty books detailing his adventures were spawned. None of them hinted at the truth concerning Kane's leadership abilities or his wretched preparation for the Second Grinnell Expedition. Years later Adolphus Greely reviewed Kane's venture: "Well intended, his expedition was fallacious in plan, unsuitably equipped, inadequately supplied, and manned by inexperienced volunteers." These factors should have added up to total failure, "yet because of Kane the results exceeded those of any other expedition of the generation." Greely, like most of his countrymen, admired Kane too much to condemn the rashness of his preparations. Readers of Kane's narrative had to succumb to the "literary charm, beauty of expression unexcelled by any other polar explorer." Kane was able to unveil the true qualities of Arctic nature and people. "His mind was imbued with the spirit of philosophy."[4] His poetic vision saw the beautiful in all things, yet he was not lacking in strength and will.

The Norwegian Fridtjof Nansen also commented on Kane. Needless to say, polar explorers were inclined to comment on the preparation their predecessors and contemporaries made. They knew that the successful execution of the mission depended upon good fortune and skill in the course of the effort, but that even with this, nothing could be done if the initial planning had been bungled. Elisha Kent Kane's narrative of his voyage constituted Nansen's reading matter during the winter when his ship, the *Fram,* was held in the Siberian Arctic ice, and Nansen was astounded at the American's ill preparation. "Unfortunate man, preparations were miserably inadequate; it seems to me to have been a reckless, unjustifiable proceeding to set out with such equipment. Almost all the dogs died of bad food; all the men had scurvy for the same reason, with snow-blindness, frost bites, and all kinds of miseries. He learned a wholesome awe of the Arctic night, and one can hardly wonder at it."[5]

Kane did not survive his return home very long. The public reaction to him was very revealing. If there was ever a time in the history of a divided nation when an apolitical hero was needed it was in the America of the mid-1850s, and in Kane the people had found a universally cherished hero. His funeral was held on a wintry day in Philadelphia in 1857. For once, political and clerical orators all over the country left off the bitter feuding over the issues that were dividing the Union and roused their auditors with paeans of praise for the universally admired young man. On the question of Kane's virtues and the value of the experience exemplified by his adventures, there could be no dissent. Clearly his life had been sacrificed in the cause of science and humanity.

A long procession of mourners followed the coffin through the streets of Philadelphia, streets lined with multitudes of silent, sorrowing men and women. Drums rolled, minute guns boomed, and bells tolled as a nation paid tribute to a hero. In Philadelphia, as in every town in the country, the Stars and Stripes flew at half-mast. The eulogies had been pouring forth ever since news of Kane's fatal heart attack was received from Cuba. He had voyaged to Havana in quest of rest and health after completing an account of his northern expedition.

This book, *Arctic Explorations,* was an instant success and enjoyed an enormous sale. The light and easy style did not mask the grim sufferings and disasters the explorer and his men encountered, although he did not reveal all of the dissensions. Indeed, Lady Jane Franklin feared that the book's realism could hurt the cause of polar research.

A ship carried Kane's body to New Orleans. There a military guard of honor and the city's leading dignitaries escorted it to City Hall, where it was to lie in state while citizens paid their respects. Another procession attended the transfer of the coffin to a river steamer for the long voyage up the Mississippi and Ohio rivers. Along the river route thousands observed the steamer and recalled Kane's adventures among towering icebergs and treacherous floes. The mystery and exotic appeal of the Arctic gripped Americans as it never had before. Somehow Kane's exploits and ultimate "sacrifice" had triggered an overwhelming emotional response. How did this little man, standing 5 feet, 6 inches, and weighing, when at top form, 135 pounds, captivate the imagination of his countrymen?

As the steamer proceeded upriver, halting at Louisville to permit another public ceremony and finally ending its voyage at Cincinnati, where Kane's coffin was once more displayed to the people, eulogists expounded on the explorer's merits. It was not, one orator declaimed, because Kane had conquered rich provinces or had been successful in the objects of his journeys that he was so famed, but because he devoted himself to knowledge and humanity. Every Christian virtue seemed to have been illustrated by the young man's career. Grieving legislators from Pennsylvania, New York, Massachusetts, Ohio, and New Jersey were among those adopting resolutions of affection and respect, offering to their electorate Dr. Kane's humanity and courage as a model to follow.

Honors continued to shower on Kane as his coffin was conveyed by rail from Cincinnati to Philadelphia. At every town along the line people turned out to see the train containing the revered remains. Only two other funeral journeys in the history of the United States can be compared to it—Abraham Lincoln's and Robert Kennedy's. In Philadelphia eulogists outdid themselves. Civic pride in one of the city's own sons was unbounded. Special music was composed for the funeral services. Pamphlets preserving the eulogies were published. Mourners of Kane were assured that the history of his brief life presented a bright example to young countrymen.

The tributes to the explorer were not limited to one side of the Atlantic. Sir Roderick Murchison, speaking for England's Royal Geographical Society—of which Kane was a gold medalist—noted that few men have ever lived who have earned a better title to the admiration of their race. The British press echoed Murchison's opinions. Kane's participation in two Franklin search efforts, however unsuccessful in shedding any light on the mystery, assured his popularity in England.

Kane's first biographer provided a mere sampling of the funeral orations, which ran to 100 pages of text, but it was more than enough to give the flavor of the whole.[6] Americans added Kane to the thinly populated pantheon housing wholly untarnished national heroes. Cynics of the day— if any existed in Kane's case—might have questioned the explorer's enshrinement on several grounds. From any viewpoint from which Kane's 1853–55 expedition may be scrutinized—its goals, preparations, or execution—the ignorance, uncertainty, and poor leadership of its commander were manifestly evident. Many questions about the venture might have been raised, but criticisms were muted amid the acclamation of Kane's return and his subsequent death. Yet Kane certainly displayed some splendid characteristics, and if his actual attainments were slight, his right to a hero's honor cannot be denied. While it may be questioned whether there was much point to his "sacrifice for science and humanity," he did become a "bright example to his countrymen," and that, in part, was the role of the nineteenth-century polar explorers. When Elisha Kent Kane's coffin was lowered into the earth, his unblemished reputation served as an inspiration to others. His early demise was a tragic loss, yet he was spared the anguish that was so often the aftermath of exploratory expeditions. There were no defaming revelations by his colleagues, no angry denunciations in the press, and no official inquiries. He was lucky.

The case of Charles Francis Hall deserves particular consideration in a survey of some of the aberrations of polar exploration history. Hall was a newspaper publisher and printer in Cincinnati when he became intrigued with the Arctic—possibly stimulated by the death of Kane. Whatever the cause, he came to believe that it was his destiny to clarify the mystery of the lost Franklin party. He was driven by a mystical zeal that inspired him with purpose and confidence. In 1859, at thirty-eight years of age, Hall shocked his wife and friends by selling his business to raise money for a polar expedition. Henry Grinnell and other American businessmen also contributed, and Hall was given passage on a whaler bound for Greenland in 1860.

Hall was overwhelmed with awe and expectation on reaching the region he had read and thought about so long. Off Greenland he saw his first iceberg and exulted: "It appeared a mountain of alabaster resting calmly upon the bosom of the dark blue sea." It was clearly God's work: "Its fashioning was that of the Great Architect! He who hath builded *such* moments, and casteth them forth upon the waters of the sea, *is God,* and there can be none other!" He saw other northern marvels: "I love the snows, the ices—Icebergs—the Fauna and the Flora of the North! I love the circling sun, the long day, *the Arctic Night, when the Soul can communicate with God in silent and reverential awe!* I am on a mission of love." He declaimed his intent to "do or die" for the cause he had espoused.[7]

Hall realized the need for Eskimo assistance in order to search King William Island for signs of Franklin and his men. He was a pioneer in learning to adapt to Eskimo ways and the first explorer to study their language seriously. On this first venture, Hall made a significant discovery—not of Franklin relics but of the first landfall ever made by Englishmen in the Canadian Arctic. He found the ruins of a house built by Sir Martin Frobisher in 1578 on Baffin Island.

Hall's second expedition, from 1864 to 1869, was richer in frustrations than accomplishments. His efforts to travel with Eskimos to King William Island were dashed several times, but he did meet Eskimos who sold him a barometer and silverware that had belonged to Franklin's men.

Hall made the mistake of hiring whaling seamen to assist him, and they were not enthusiastic about his cause. In fact, they considered the explorer to be a little crazed—and it could be that they were right. But one sailor, Pat Coleman, made the fatal mistake of cursing at Hall and challenging him to a fight after Hall had remonstrated with him over some matter. Hall was a burly man, but he decided not to trust his fists. "I hastened to my tent . . . seized my Baylic revolver, and went back and found the leader of the mutinous crowd." Would Coleman now back down? "His reply being still more threatening, I pulled the trigger, and he staggered and fell."[8]

Coleman lingered on in agony for two weeks before giving up the ghost. Hall and the other men nursed the sailor anxiously but it was no use. When Hall returned to New York he admitted his actions in a press interview. "My men mutinied, and if I had not shot and killed the leader, my fate might have been as sad as the fate of Sir Henry Hudson."[9] The whaling men who had been involved protested. They denied any mutiny; it had been a cold-blooded murder done in a cowardly manner and they demanded an investigation. Nothing was done, however; the incident had occurred too far north to interest government prosecutors. The American officials pretended that nothing had happened; the Canadians interviewed the witnesses and let it go at that. Canada had jurisdiction but was not pressing vigorously at the time for a recognition of her sovereignty over the Arctic islands, particularly over such an unsavory affair.

Years later a member of Hall's party, Peter Bayne, described his fear of the explorer after the death of Coleman. Bayne was one of the whaling men, and was tempted to desert but knew that this would give Hall an excuse to gun him down. "I entertained for him nothing but horror and disgust." Hall had called Bayne to his tent, had accused him of provoking Coleman to rebel, and had ordered him out of the camp. When Bayne got back to New York he complained to Henry Grinnell and the police about Hall's "cold-blooded murder," but to no effect.[10]

Hall's final expedition of 1871 achieved the farthest north ever reached by ship at that time. But the party was racked with dissension, particularly due to the wrangling between Hall and the scientist-physician, Dr. Emil Bessels. In October 1871, Hall returned to his northern Greenland base after a sled journey on which he surveyed parts of the northern coast. He drank a cup of coffee and suffered a stroke—or, at least, what Dr. Bessels diagnosed as a stroke. Hall believed that he had been poisoned and lingered on for days in agony, ranting and raving against the doctor during periods of consciousness.

It cannot be known with certainty whether Hall had been poisoned deliberately. Hall's recent biographer exhumed his body 100 years after his burial and found evidence of a heavy dosage of arsenic. Earlier expedition members had noted that whenever Hall had refused to take medicine from Dr. Bessels, his health improved. Bessels had the knowledge and the opportunity as well as the motivation to murder Hall. The doctor was probably brooding about the necessity of spending still another winter aboard a cramped ship, being ordered about by a half-educated boor.

Morale was terrible. One seaman had already been driven to suicide, the others were paranoid. The ship captain was worried about the safety of the icebound vessel and he drank continually. It seems likely that Bessels decided to do away with his nemesis.

On the return of the expedition, a United States Naval inquiry was conducted, and its report indicated that Hall died of natural causes. The investigation was not very rigorous because the government did not care to provoke sensationalism. Rear Admiral C. H. Davis was commissioned to write the narrative of the expedition, and he took care to distort diaries and other source materials. As Hall's biographer Chauncey Loomis put it: "Davis gave the impression that the expedition had been a Boy Scout Jamboree—a bit rough, of course, but enlivened by good cheer and boyish high jinks."[11] In actuality, the exploration party had been divided and embittered from the time the *Polaris* weighed anchor at the commencement of the northern voyage.

The government was not always successful in hushing up polar exploration scandals. When the press was aggrieved or when vengeful relatives of missing men called for an investigation there was a considerable clamor. This was the result of the other two major American exploration efforts of the nineteenth century: the *Jeannette* expedition and the Greely expedition.

THE JEANNETTE
DISASTER

*"All ye icebergs make salaam,
You belong to Uncle Sam!"*
　　　—Bret Harte

A s newspaper reports of polar adventures attracted sensational interest, it soon became inevitable that publishers would promote expeditions of their own. James Gordon Bennett, the flamboyant owner of *The New York Herald,* pioneered journalistically motivated exploration when he sent Henry Stanley off to find David Livingstone in 1871. Stanley's lively reports made the *Herald* the most popular paper in New York and gave Bennett immense satisfaction. Bennett had inherited the *Herald,* and although he fully earned his reputation as an international playboy, he took journalism seriously and possessed a natural talent for it. His flair and genius in finding gifted writers were his outstanding assets.

Thus when United States Navy officer George Washington De Long approached Bennett with a scheme for reaching the North Pole in 1879, the publisher fell in with it enthusiastically. De Long, whose portraits made him appear more a scholar than an explorer, conceived a play that betrayed ignorance and limited experience. He believed that a dash for the Pole could be made from Wrangel Island. This theory rested on the erroneous assumption that Wrangel Island, or other land masses that extended far to the north, could be polar stepping stones.

With this naive hope and Bennett's backing, De Long prepared to take the polar prize. He purchased a ship, the *Pandora,* a veteran of Arctic waters, and renamed it the *Jeannette.* Superstitious seamen always cautioned that ill fortune would follow a ship's renaming, but De Long ignored such warnings, gathered a 32-man crew, and made preparations to steam north in the summer of 1879.

The *Jeannette* was outfitted at the navy yard in San Francisco at Bennett's expense. Engineers at the yard doubted that the ship could make a long polar voyage safely, and so informed De Long. But De Long and the other naval officers who had been given leave to join the expedition ignored such cautions. De Long probably feared annoying his patron, and the others wished to be loyal to De Long. De Long allowed his ambition to overrule his sound judgment as a naval officer.

Bickering among some of the men broke out while the *Jeannette* was still in the navy yard. Jerome Collins, a journalist for *The Herald* who was doubling as a meteorologist, felt that De Haven and Melville looked down on him. Lieutenant John W. Danenhower, the *Jeannette* navigator, openly joked about Collins's lack of scientific training. Clearly the Navy men resented a civilian who presumed to have an equal or superior footing because he represented Bennett. Danenhower's admission of mental illness earlier also caused some anxiety to De Haven. James Ambler, the expedition doctor, urged De Long to dismiss Danenhower. Danenhower's family protested to the Navy that Ambler was persecuting the lieutenant. De Long kept Danenhower as navigator, partly because he had no time to find a replacement.

In July, after being feted by the San Francisco Chamber of Commerce at a banquet, De Long took the *Jeannette* to sea. Enroute to the Arctic he called at Saint Michael, an Alaskan town near the mouth of the Yukon, and hired two Eskimo hunters. Then he steamed into the Chukchi Sea by way of the Bering Strait, hoping to reach Wrangel Island. The ice pack proved to be impenetrable, and soon after entering the pack the *Jeannette* was caught. De Long's optimism betrayed him when he decided to try to force his way through the ice. The *Jeannette* had not been designed to withstand the pressure of ice, and De Long should have anticipated that the chances of survival in such a situation would be minimal. It appears that De Long's ambitions drove him to risk everything to make a successful assault on the Pole. He craved glory and was headstrong. Obviously he rejected the possibility of returning without a report of great discoveries that would bring him fame (and help Bennett sell newspapers).

The trapped ship drifted slowly to the west all through the winter.

Summer brought no release, and the *Jeannette* was held for another winter. In this perilous condition the crew's morale was low. There was little to do but bicker and complain. As George Melville, the hardy engineer of the ship, put it: "Our supplies of jokes and stories were completely exhausted, and their points had long since been dulled by much handling."[1] De Long insisted that all the men exercise regularly. Collins, the *Herald* reporter, refused, and De Long suspended him from his duties.

Neither were the crew in good physical health. Some suffered from lead poisoning caused by defectively made food cans.

The end came for the *Jeannette* in June 1881. Its weary timbers gave way before the pressure of the ice. The crew abandoned ship and marched south toward the New Siberian Islands.

Their journey was an agony. They were not equipped with adequate footwear and consequently suffered from frostbite. The three boats they hauled to cross leads leaked and were cumbersome, but at least they had sled dogs to help with the work. Worst yet, the drift of the ice dictated the pace of their bid for land. Over one stretch of two weeks they walked 30 miles, yet fell back 24 miles from their destination. After a month of strenuous plodding, and with a favorable change of the ice pack's direction, the men reached an island. They were ragged and weary, but delighted to set foot on land for the first time in two years. Since the island was unmarked on De Long's charts, he followed exploration tradition and took possession of it "in the name of God and the United States, naming it Bennett Island."[2]

After a brief inspection of the island, the Americans launched their three boats and navigated toward the Siberian coast. Initially all three boats were lashed together, but in a raging storm they were separated. Melville's boat reached the coast first and he guided it skillfully up the Lena River delta. A few days later the survivors met some Siberian natives, who provided food and agreed to lead Melville to a government official so that a search could be made for De Long and the other men.

Melville directed the search vigorously but did not find De Long's party in time. De Long had reached the mainland successfully, but he and most of his men succumbed to starvation and scurvy. The third boat had apparently been lost at sea. In all only 13 men of the original 32 survived the ineptly planned and capriciously directed *Jeannette* expedition.

Generally, explorers did not have to deal with the press until they returned home. Melville, however, was besieged by British and American newsmen in Siberia and became most unhappy with them. The press reported that one of De Long's men killed himself; a reporter had observed that the dead man had held a pistol in his hand. Melville insisted that the pistol was fully loaded. The news story was "utterly false." The man had been "cheerful and fearless of death, and I know he faced it calmly and manfully as he had done before on the field of battle."[3]

Another incident pained Melville even more. William Gilder, a journalist who had been attached to a naval ship involved in a search for the *Jeannette,* traveled from the Bering Strait to the Lena River delta to investigate the rescue work. After talking to Melville he started back for Europe, and along the way he intercepted Melville's dispatches, which a Cossack was carrying. "The Cossack . . . told Gilder of the contents of the sealed packet, which the spirited journalist straightway induced the derelict carrier to surrender into his hands, and cooly broke open."[4] Gilder scooped Melville by sending *The New York Herald* Melville's report on the death of De Long and his party.

Melville complained to a Russian official about Gilder's "questionable liberties." The official supposed "the breaking of a seal was a matter of little or no consequence in a free country like the United States" but assured Melville that it was a serious matter in Russia and that the Cossack would be punished.[5] Melville would have been happier if he could have had Gilder punished.

Another reporter, John P. Jackson of *The New York Herald,* annoyed Melville by showing up in Siberia "with all the paraphernalia of Oriental travelers . . . , clothed in purple and fine linen, so to speak." Jackson represented James Gordon Bennett, who had a proprietary interest in the *Jeannette,* and he assumed Melville would lead him to the site of De Long's death. Melville would not do so and also refused to turn over diaries of expedition members to Jackson. "The egregious egotism of this kind of person is amusing in the extreme," Melville wrote later on, but at the time he was anything but amused. Jackson wished to take charge of the rescue. "In short, he was prepared to take me in charge and complete in a proper manner the work I had almost finished."[6]

Jackson found other guides to the scene of disaster and infuriated Melville further by violating the graves there. Melville protested this "ghoul-like" work. "I never dreamed," he complained, "that a person born in a Christian land would so far forget the respect due to our honored dead as to violate their sacred resting-place for the purpose of concocting a sensational story, and making sketches, or out of idle curiosity."[7]

Melville's bitterness toward the press permeates his voyage narrative, *In the Lena Delta*. His travails with newsmen continued after the end of his expedition, so he had ample reason for despising men who dared to besmirch heroes. Explorers went forth bravely to face dangers while "their cruel critics away off in comfortable pot-houses are penning their uncharitable and infamous obloquies." Melville denounced the "wolves, and ghouls, and would-be critics of Arctic toil and sufferings" and asked them to stop and consider that the men they traduced, "whose memories you would blast forever, perhaps for a penny a line, are made of finer clay than you." How dare the critics slander men ready "to sacrifice everything on earth save honor for the sake of science and the benefit of mankind." Melville warmed to his theme: "It is a nation's shame that it permits its heroes, living and dead, to be dragged through the slime of public courts and press for the gratification of the prurient multitude of scandal mongers, misguided readers who gloated over the silly effusions of the Arctic critic who never ventures his dear life nearer to the Arctic Circle than can be seen from the window of some tall printing house."[8]

Once Melville and the other survivors returned to the States, a naval board of inquiry convened to deliberate the loss of the ship and men. The board heard that the *Jeannette* had been abandoned in a "cool and orderly manner."[9] No panic had ensued, reflected the board of inquiry with some pride, and good discipline and leadership had further been proven by the health of the shipwrecked men. None of those who formed the three boat parties in a dash for land had shown a trace of scurvy. No blame here. Any ship could have been crushed in the ice in similar circumstances. The naval officers closed the inquiry with satisfaction, and Bennett was able to write the good news to Mrs. De Long: "I am very glad . . . that the Court of Inquiry has vindicated the *Jeannette* and sustained Captain De Long and his brave officers and men."[10]

No questions were raised about De Long's judgment, nor did the survivors admit to any discord aboard the *Jeannette*. All believed that such matters should be suppressed. The expedition had been a tragic fiasco but, if everyone cooperated, it appeared likely to be enshrined as one more example of significant heroism. American boys could well model themselves on De Long and his fellows. The case would have been closed but for the frustrations of a relative. A hustling attorney who had acted as the court stenographer smelled a rat and offered his services to the brother of Jerome J. Collins, the newsman who had been correspondent and meteorologist of the expedition. Dr. Daniel F. Collins was grieved by the death of his brother and was not placated by the assurances of the survivors that all had been well aboard the *Jeannette*.

Dr. Collins petitioned the House Committee on Naval Affairs to consider whether the naval inquiry had suppressed evidence of the indignities De Long had inflicted on his brother and of the mishandling of the rescue efforts. Meanwhile, the bodies of De Long and his nine men reached New York, where proper obsequies were offered. A detachment from Company C of the Ninth Infantry Regiment of New Jersey guarded the remains. The dead were heroes. A huge floral wreath was just one expression of the feelings of the mourning public. It bore the epitaph from the memorial to Sir John Franklin in Westminister Abbey: THEIR COURSE IS SET TOWARD NO EARTHLY POLE.

Bennett of *The New York Herald* had kept silent during the naval inquiry and had suffered without rebuke the thunderings of the rival *New York Tribune* when some testimony indicated that the *Jeannette* was not structurally up to her task. The *Tribune* had charged that "the *man* who bought what a competent critic had pronounced unfit for this work because it was cheap, and the men who suppressed knowledge of its unfitness because they didn't want to hurt his feelings, must divide the responsibility for the horrible tragedy that followed between them." But now Bennett could call the nation to higher thoughts and, by his eloquence, transform an unfortunate venture into a shining example. He proclaimed:

> Amid the thunder of cannon and the tolling of bells and with solemn funeral pageantry America will today press to her bosom the dead heroes she sent forth five years ago to conquer the secrets of the frozen North. None of the dead, wherever they lie, will be forgotten today by the nation in whose service they died.[11]

Dr. Collins's lawyer argued persuasively before the House Committee on Naval Affairs. He did not want to ruin De Long's good name, he asserted, yet De Long had treated Jerome Collins, a civilian, like a criminal for two years and had accused him of insubordination. The Collins family had a right to have this slur removed, to have the record set straight. De Long "was in its highest type a naval martinet." In Frederick the Great's time he would have been a drill sergeant. "His mind was not broad or comprehensive, and I believe thoroughly that his understanding was disordered by his calamities." The attorney related a whole catalogue of blunders concerning the expedition. The *Jeannette* was unseaworthy. The survivors could not hunt birds effectively along the Siberian coast because their equipment included rifles rather than shotguns, and thus they starved. The officers were negligently ignorant of the geography of Siberia and of the true nature of Wrangel Island. When De Long steered into the lead that imprisoned his ship, he went against the sound advice of his ice pilot. "De Long was a very stubborn man; he would listen to no advice."[12]

The uproar created over the alleged bad treatment of Collins resulted in front-page newspaper stories in *The New York Times* and other papers. Letters exchanged between De Long and Collins aboard the *Jeannette,* while the doomed ship drifted helplessly, show the ruffled feelings of the men. Although their dispute seems trifling, it and other similar rows reveal much about explorers' personalities and concerns, although they add nothing to an assessment of the endeavor.

Collins became convinced that De Long and Melville failed to show him proper respect as a scientist and as a *Herald* reporter. He imagined a conspiracy by the naval officers to deny credit to his scientific work because he was a civilian. De Long's remonstrances with him over his late hour of rising and neglect of exercise on the ice seemed motivated by spite.

Such petty grievances became important only because their documentation afforded opportunity to Collins's brother to attack De Long's conduct on all fronts. Dr. Collins told the press that jealousy among the officers predetermined the expedition's failure; that entering the ice pack was an inexcusable blunder; that inferior boats and equipment were used on the retreat. And, worse yet, since this accusation indicted the living rather than the dead, Dr. Collins insisted that the rescue had been unnecessarily delayed, resulting in the death of De Long's party.

Naturally Dr. Collins's accusations lacked substantial support, yet the press played them up eagerly. The charges kept the story alive and could perhaps embarrass the *Herald.* Presumably Dr. Collins got some satisfaction for his brother's loss in launching his accusations, as ill-founded as some of them were. De Long's widow and Melville suffered the most. Like other women placed in the same situation, Mrs. De Long was determined to see that De Long receive full honors for his heroism. Any slur to his reputation must be countered. It was unfortunate that the grief of one relative had to express itself publicly in a way that further aggrieved a sorrowing widow, but this was not atypical in exploration deaths. Surviving relatives also played a role in the adventure, and, as in this case, their personal responses could raise havoc.

But no vindication of Collins came from the naval committee. The Navy published the hearing record of 1,046 pages, as was customary, and that was the end of it. It was never as easy for critics to dethrone dead heroes as living ones. If De Long had returned to face an inquiry into the loss of his ship and some crewmen, he would have been baited severely by members of the board. The press would have been quick to speculate on the significance of questions and answers. Even if the Navy officers decided to close ranks and clear De Long's record, the reverberations of his questionable performance would haunt his career. Dead heroes, however, were to be pressed to America's bosom, and raising questions was in very poor taste. In this case there was no blatant whitewash and little reason for scandal.

But, for all the public's love of sensation, an edifying example of heroism was appreciated, too. Society leaders, in particular, preferred that dissension and failure of expeditions be swept under the carpet. Heroes were needed to set a good example. And that elusive quality—the value of an exploration endeavor—needed to be defined. Orators enjoyed grappling with the value question. It provided a fine opportunity to trot out all the familiar cliches, to summon up the best-loved virtues, to honor explorers for displaying qualities that the speaker most admired.

The survivors of the *Jeannette* expedition were honored with a civic banquet at Delmonico's restaurant in New York City. The venture had been a crashing disaster, but auditors of the Reverend Henry Ward Beecher's after-dinner speech knew what to expect. The Reverend Mr. Beecher could hardly speak of a glorious "sacrifice to science," since the expedition had yielded no significant contribution to knowledge, nor had it been expected to. But at least the debacle gained some luster from the heroic persistence of the engineer George Melville's rescue operation in search of his shipmates.

That evening at Delmonico's, no one wanted to hear anything that would reflect adversely on the expedition. The banquet, Beecher realized, was a tribute to heroism and to survival, and his task was to articulate this. Beecher reviewed the events of the expedition, pointing out specific instances of daring and skill; he eulogized De Long at some length and stressed the bravery and intelligence of Melville. He concluded with the disputable declaration that "there was no invention of art of so much value as that which raises the standard of simple manhood."[13] Raising the standard of simple manhood was the point here. Who could question the value of polar exploration, even when tragic consequences had ensued?

Was exploration worth the sacrifice? Indeed, indeed, acclaimed the speakers who followed Rev. Beecher to the rostrum. "There is no man with capacity to growth who is not made better by contemplation of the characteristic bravery and will of these gentlemen and their dead comrades," intoned New York's Mayor Grace. "It is these things which spring directly out of human nature which touch a symbolic chord in every man's heart, while a Newton or a Kepler are cold abstractions." (In the heat of his emotion, His Honor could be forgiven such anti-intellectualism.) In conclusion, he explained that "it is because these gentlemen have shown themselves the very types of courage and unselfish devotion, that this city and this country welcome them with a joy which is tempered only with grief for the loss of the brave men who would come home no more."[14]

Beecher and Grace were typical of many who made similar assessments of the value of polar exploration. The Reverend W. L. Gage, writing the preface to a narrative of one *Jeannette* survivor, seemed thankful that the world held an Arctic region: "The Arctic Ocean has been for years the nursery of heroic deeds . . . ; what has been shown there of that which is noblest and most admirable in man would have been worth all it cost."[15]

George Melville's neighbors in Sharon Hill, Pennsylvania, expressed views similar to those of the preachers and politicians. "But if you have not brought us tales of new lands and new seas which hide behind the glaciers of the Arctics," they wrote, "there has come to us over that polar messenger, the telegraph, other tidings of frightful suffering, manfully borne—of partial rescues—and finally of a self-devotion and heroism in the search for your lost companions, that throws a melancholy sweetness over the monotonous agony and final deep tragedy of the voyage of the *Jeannette*."[16]

From the pulpit other speakers extolled the values of the expedition. One preacher paid lip service to scientific gains before passing on more fervently to the value that Arctic exploration demonstrated "on higher grounds." He reminded listeners of the heroism of chivalrous knights and crusaders:

"Without the spectacle of disinterested self sacrifice, the world would sink down into a cold, hard selfishness." Explorers awaken "a higher and better life." De Long was a "disinterested martyr."[17]

Still another preacher praised Bennett and vilified detractors of exploration—those who cried, "What a waste of money and men! What useless bereavement!" If anyone asks why "any more human bones thrown to the dogs of the Esquimaux? I answer, that . . . no good is ever gained without great sacrifice." Thousands of men are sacrificed to money-making, and no one cries out at their waste. If men continue to pound "against the barred gateway of those icy palaces, I should not wonder if some great practical good would yet come of it." We must appreciate the explorers, even if "a few wiseacres stand around, hands in their pockets, whistling in a sort of derisive triumph, and say, 'I told you so. It can't be done.'" Ignore such men "maddened at the great undertakings of others," that "most mangy and scabby breed of curs . . . the pest of the church and the world."[18]

The eagerness of the press to capitalize on explorers' notoriety was well illustrated by a front-page story published soon after Melville returned home. A *New York Times* headline blazed the news: "MELVILLE DESERTS HIS WIFE—THE STRANGE CONDUCT OF ONE OF THE JEANNETTE SURVIVORS."

Newspapers in Philadelphia and New York had picked up the news first. They found it singular that the returning hero "did not at once rush to the arms of his family the moment he reached his native country." Why should he wait "to be feasted in New York," then tarry a day and night in Philadelphia, "although his wife and children were waiting in their home, only 6 miles distant." Some neighbors criticized Mrs. Melville for not meeting her husband at the dock in New York, "but this did not appear strange to some who are familiar with her slight eccentricity of character." This forgivable trait of Mrs. Melville's had been manifested while the *Jeannette* was still at sea: She had demanded that the Navy allot her a higher allowance from her husband's pay. The press had reported this with sympathy and had anguished for days over the "long and cruel separation" of the couple. Now the press had the duty of reporting that Melville had deserted his spouse. "My husband has left me," claimed Mrs. Melville. "Gone—I know not where—never to return. Gone without a word of explanation." The *Times* added that Mrs. Melville was said to be without food or money and in the care of a doctor.[19]

This terrible smear of Melville was righted—at least to some extent—in the next day's newspapers. Editors did not apologize but were forced to check on the initial story. It turned out that the unfortunate woman was insane. She had been so certified by her doctor and committed to an asylum. Melville's friends told newsmen that Mrs. Melville had been a source of deep anxiety to him for a long time. Her extravagant spending habits were distressing. She had even squandered the money he had left with her to pay off the mortgage on their home and then had fought with the Navy paymaster in an attempt to raise her $90 monthly allotment.

From the beginning, the *Jeannette* expedition exemplified the gross irresponsibility of the press. Bennett funded an ill-conceived, badly prepared venture in hopes of getting for the *Herald* the kind of sensational news stories that Henry Stanley had provided earlier from Africa. Newsmen interfered with Melville's work in Siberia, uncovered graves, and tampered with his dispatches. This irresponsibility even extended to slanderous reports on Melville's domestic woes—all because the *Jeannette* story commanded so much attention. Rival newspapers strove to keep the tragic event before their readers in one way or another. Bennett feared that he might be blamed for the disaster yet stood ready to take credit for the *Herald*'s sponsorship. *The New York Tribune*'s position was ambiguous as well. Its editors hoped to expose Bennett's folly yet dared not risk unpopularity by denying the heroism of the survivors. In one exasperated editorial the *Tribune* called for an all-out effort to reach the Pole: "There is only one way in which to bring the struggle to reach the pole to an end. Somebody must succeed in doing it. So long as it remains undone, the phantom quest will be taken up again and again."[20]

Public appetite for exploration disasters, scandals, and honors was not satiated by the *Jeannette* affair. Shortly after the uproar subsided, another polar tragedy commanded headlines. Newsmen reporting on the Greely expedition had even more gruesome incidents with which to titillate readers, and the catalogue of blunders logged by rescuers was startling enough to rouse the most phlegmatic of exploration fans.

GREELY'S TRAVAIL

*"Polar exploration is at once the
cleanest and most isolated way of having
a hard time which has been devised."*
    —Apsley Cherry-Garrard

U nited States Army explorers contributed substantially to geographic discovery as the American frontier was pushed westward.
Army men made the first overland crossing of the continent south
of Canada, surveyed for the first transcontinental railroads, and chartered
the courses of the major rivers of the West. But in the North, military
explorers performed rather poorly. The government paid little attention to
Alaskan geography until the gold rush boom of the late nineteenth century,
when the army was ordered to survey an "all-American" route to the
goldfields. Soldiers accomplished some mapping, but their efforts were
disconnected and poorly conducted, and they actually followed in the wake
of prospectors rather than leading the way.

The only army expedition sent to another part of the North proved to be
a disaster. To examine any aspect of the Greely expedition of 1881–1884 is
enough to make one cry at the amazing incompetence that it revealed. This
venture holds a high place among polar expeditions for bungling, suffering,
and squandering of human life. Greely's expedition grew out of an international agreement to undertake a systematic collection of meteorological
and magnetic data. The year 1882–83 was declared by the participating
nations to be the first International Polar Year. Stations were to be
established in Greenland, Ellesmere Island, Baffin Island, and Spitsbergen;

on the Kara Sea; and at the mouth of the Yenisey River. Lieutenant Adolphus W. Greely of the United States Army was charged with leadership of the American station on Ellesmere Island, which had been named Grinnell Land by explorer Isaac Hayes. Greely had ambitions that went beyond information compilation: He had been ordered to launch an assault on the Pole and, failing that, at least to wrest the farthest-north record away from Britain, although neither he nor any of the other soldiers had any Arctic travel background. If this aspiration was "out of tune" with the conception of the International Polar Year, as a contemporary British historian has asserted, it was not the cause of all the woes that beset the military party.[1] Most of the disasters Greely's men suffered were the consequence of the tragic buffoonery engaged in by others responsible for the supply and rescue efforts. But before looking at the fatal fiasco of the relief attempts, it is instructive to examine the conduct of the army men in the field, for it gives a rather apt prelude to the bunglings of the relief expeditions.

Lieutenant Frederick F. Kislingbury became disgruntled with Greely's regulations soon after the party was landed from the ship that carried it north. In proper military form, he asked to be relieved of his duties so that he might return to the States on the *Proteus*. Greely, aware of the threat of discontented officers to the well-being of his command, promptly dismissed Kislingbury from his duties. It took some time for the lieutenant to pack up his kit, and he had not thought first to advise the *Proteus* to expect him. His dallying was fatal. By the time he reached the harborage, the *Proteus* was at sea. Crestfallen, Kislingbury was forced to return to the camp. He was a proud and stubborn man. Presumably he would have been returned to his duties had he asked that of Greely, but he preferred to sulk. Greely understated the case in his narrative of the expedition: "These unfortunate episodes emphasize the necessity of selecting for Arctic service only men and officers of thorough military qualities, among which subordination is by no means of secondary importance."[2] Life at the camp, which Greely named Fort Conger, did not get off to a happy start.

Yet overall, morale was good. Sergeant David L. Brainard was a tower of strength and the founder of the Anti-Swearing Society. A camp newspaper was issued. The first winter was dull but comfortable enough. The men took some sled expeditions in the spring. The second winter did not go so well. The enlisted men were irked by orders restricting them to an area within 500 yards of the camp. Worse yet, the disgruntled Kislingbury had a partner in gloom and bitterness, Dr. Octave Pavy. Pavy felt somewhat superior to his young commander in education and merit. His tardiness in submitting monthly medical reports and his carelessness with equipment bothered Greely. Eventually, rancor boiled to the point where Pavy refused orders and was placed under nominal arrest by Greely.

The highlight of the expedition was a record sled drive to reach a new farthest north. Greely's salutation to the two men who achieved it expresses the spirit of that era of exploration, a bombastic mixture of pride and nationalism: "You placed your name high on the immortal scroll of fame by winning for our great Nation the honors of the Highest North, which England's distinguished explorers had held unbroken for three centuries."[3]

After two years, the soldiers exhausted their food supplies, and game was hard to find. In heroic exertions, they tried to reach caches of supplies that were supposed to have been left by the planned relief parties and by earlier exploring expeditions. On the last effort, Julius Rice and Robert Frederick set out in a temperature of –40° F. A blizzard hampered their journey. Rice died in his tracks of exhaustion and Frederick staggered back alone and without provisions.

Greely eventually ordered a retreat south. It did not appear that a relief party could reach them, and they could not survive another winter. Their boat journey to Cape Sabine took several weeks. There they found to their horror that a relief ship had left rations for only twenty days. Yet Greely did not dare another boat voyage to Littleton Island, where another food cache had been arranged. He decided to remain at Cape Sabine to await rescue or death. For most of the men it meant death. The most macabre incident of the expedition took place in proper military form. Private C. B. Henry had repeatedly stolen food. Only a few starving men remained in Greely's command, but discipline must be maintained. Thus Greely scribbled out an order of execution:

> Notwithstanding promises given by Private C. B. Henry yesterday, he has since, as acknowledged to me, tampered with seal thongs if not other food at the old camp. This pertinacity and audacity is the destruction of this party if not at once ended. Private Henry will be shot today, all care being taken to prevent his injuring anyone, as his physical strength is greater than that of any two men. Decide the manner of death by two ball and one blank cartridge. This order is *imperative* and *absolutely necessary for any chance of life.*[4]

And it was done. Two shots brought down the thieving soldier, who had built up a private food cache. It was a most unusual execution, but when

Greely, on his return to civilization, insisted upon a court martial, he was duly exonerated. "Henry was shot by my order. A liar, a shirker, an incorrigible thief, his continued misdemeanors made capital punishment necessary."[5] Discipline had to be maintained, even among starving soldiers. Henry had been caught stealing food several times. Once he had taken advantage of the confusion created when a smoky fire in a hut nearly asphyxiated several men. He had grabbed and bolted down a ½-pound chunk of bacon, but his stomach rebelled at such unaccustomed dainties and expelled it before the eyes of his hungry companions. On two occasions he stole the small extra rations that had been reserved for the expedition's hunter and shrimp fisherman. Enough was enough. "He was also detected eating seal skin lashing and seal skin boots stolen from the public stock," reported Sergeant Brainard, one of Henry's designated executioners. "The stealing of old seal skin boots, etc., may seem to some a very insignificant affair, but to us such articles mean life."[6] After Greely's order was carried out, it was read aloud to the men. There was no protest against his decision. Men were dying every day of starvation and scurvy, and those still clinging to life had reason to be bitter toward one who seemed determined to survive at the expense of his fellows.

From first to last, Greely was a martinet. During the retreat of August-September 1883, Sergeant Maurice Connell began to side with Dr. Pavy in questioning the commander's judgment. As usual, Greely reacted firmly when he overheard Connell and Kislingbury discussing their situation. He forbade such demoralizing talk and later reduced Connell to the rank of private. "I don't care a God damn about it," retorted the soldier.[7] When the survivors finally reached Cape Sabine and found that the relief ship had cached only twenty days' rations for them, they were further discouraged. Rationing was necessary, and the weakest could not regain their strength. On July 1, 1884, Connell wrote to his former commander and blamed Greely for all that the men suffered.

This is the last you will ever hear from me. I am laying helpless in a starving condition at this point without any hopes of recovery. Twelve of our number has died of starvation since January 17. Lieutenant Kislingbury died at 3 P.M. today and I feel it my turn next; the other thirteen of us are helpless.

It is the blunders of the heads of this expedition . . . who are to blame for our misfortunes and it ought to be a warning to the United States to keep fools and incompetent people at home.

If there is to be fools it is better they should meddle in little things than in great.

I hold Lieutenant Greely personally responsible for the lives of this party. All this has been pointed out to him by Dr. Pavy but it was of no avail, he rushed into where he was not able to lead and it is well that he should not be made a martyr of and if ever he returns to the U.S. he ought to be tried and hung for murder. For my part I have nothing [to] regret in this matter, I die like a brave soldier. I only ask of my Dear Captain to help and see that all that is due from the U.S. government would be duly turned over to my parents if alive or if not to my Brothers and Sister. My Brothers address is Michal Connell portmagee [Port Magee] Co. Kerry Island.

I also request the Chief Signal Officer to turn my journal over to you when he is through with it. So farewell Dear Captain. My love to Freddy and Harry. I hope they can manage Bug now.

My kindest regards to Mrs. Johnson. Believe me I never forgot her or you. Don't [let] our fate frighten Arctic Explorers. It is as safe as any other enterprise providing the right men are at the head of it. Three ships passed this point loaded with provisions and only left 20 days rations, a *shame* to the United States. I recomment to you Dr. Octave Pavy who will explain all to you if he lives to get out of this.

I am just able to crawl but the wind is blowing so hard today and I am chilled through. The Doctor ordered for me 5 drops of spirit. . . . Greely forbids it, says . . . that . . . I am so badly hurt that he cannot afford . . . medicines. This is hard . . . for a dying man. . . .

And on June 4 Connell wrote:

I can still write this date. The wind blew very hard all through the night and went right through me and weakened me very much. We had about 2 ozs. of . . . shrimps and a pint of weak tea. Tincture of iron was issued this morning but I refuse to take any more medicines. He thinks the Doctor is going to die soon so that he will [have] all for himself. . . . This Brute will surely get . . . his reward. Saler passed away.[8]

Greely was perhaps too rigid to have been the kind of leader that a party placed in such dire straits needed, but he did have elements of greatness. He was lacking in command experience, knew nothing of polar regions, and knew nothing of navigation or boating, yet he did manage the retreat from Fort Conger to Cape Sabine by boat. And he survived, while many an expedition commander who carried the pressure of responsibility on top of all other burdens and hardships did not. Greely survived because he maintained his pride in his achievement. He had succeeded. No disaster could smear the honor he had gained for himself, the army, and the nation. Others, most notably, Robert Peary, might later marvel at how clumsy Greely's performance was, but Greely never doubted the excellence of the way he carried on against the terrors of the North. He had won. He had the record. Thus he was able to amaze the navy men who finally reached him in July 1884 by his affirmation, even in his desperate condition.

Arctic relief expeditions were easier to plan than to execute. Ice conditions offered one impediment, but interservice jealousy and ineptitude also played roles in Greely's situation. Greely was supposed to remain at his base at Fort Conger, on Lady Franklin Bay, for two years to make observations. A whaling ship landed his party without difficulty because—for the mysterious reasons that determine Arctic ice conditions—the passage was free of ice all the way. It was understood that during the following summer a ship would be sent north with stores, and if it could not reach Fort Conger because of the ice, it would leave stores at one of the three other designated points.

Ice conditions were quite different in Kane Basin in 1882 when the chartered sealer *Neptune* attempted to reach Fort Conger: The pack was impenetrable. The would-be rescuers cached provisions at Cape Sabine, but when Greely eventually reached there he found a mere 250 rations. After the relief effort of 1882 failed, the army should have seen that in 1883 relief had to be carefully planned. There could be no bungling; determination and resolution were essential to success. Yet unfortunately, both were lacking.

As in 1882, the army refused to turn the rescue effort over to the navy. Pride of service dictated that army men win glory for saving their fellow soldiers. There must have been officers with grit and leadership ability, but the command was given to Lieutenant Ernest Garlington, a man of vacillating purpose. As one naval officer noted, it was a cruel situation in which the young cavalry officer had been placed. His six years of service on the Dakota frontier were scant preparation for the endeavor. The army chartered the *Proteus* once more, and with this sturdy vessel Garlington would try to reach Fort Conger. Failing that, a sledge party would be left on Littleton Island for the winter, and from there a search mission would be carried out. At a late stage in the planning, a naval ship, the *Yantic,* was chosen to support Garlington. The *Yantic* was not fitted for ice work and was a slow sailer that could not keep up with the *Proteus.* Its commander outranked Garlington but did not show any more initiative or imagination.

Garlington failed to stop at Cape Sabine on his way north. Had he done as he was instructed and left stores there for Greely, many lives would have been saved. Instead he pushed into the ice pack and wrecked the *Proteus.* The crew got ashore and did not worry overmuch about saving stores that could be cached for Greely. Garlington led the three-boat party of sailors to Littleton Island, where a rendezvous with the *Yantic* had been scheduled. Then, for some reason—panic, probably—he decided to head south without waiting for the *Yantic,* which arrived some days later. Amazingly, Garlington left a message for Greely but not for the *Yantic* commander, whose relief work was under his direction. Thus the naval officer was justified in following his vague orders calling for cooperation with Garlington by doing nothing—even failing to leave a cache—and sailing south.

A military court of inquiry examined this sorry relief venture in 1884 and slapped the wrists of the officers involved. General William Hazen, chief of the Signal Corps, was censured for not seeing that a winter station had been established on Littleton Island. "This strange blindness to this palpable and most urgent necessity of this case . . . is lamentable and incomprehensible."[9] Garlington was criticized for not waiting for the *Yantic* to reach Littleton Island and for not leaving caches for Greely. Although the court conceded that the officers had done everything wrong, neither man was court-martialed.

In 1884 Commander Winfield Scott Schley of the United States Navy pushed his ship through the ice to reach the Greely camp. When he entered the tent, the army men were lying in their own filth, some dead, others dying. One soldier, a frostbite victim, had neither hands nor feet. A spoon was tied to the stump of his right arm. "Directly opposite, on his hands and knees, was a dark man with a long matted head, and brilliant, staring eyes." Schley asked this creature if he were Greely and drew this firm response: "Yes—seven of us left—here we are—dying like men." Greely paused briefly for breath, then cried out in the passion of his pride: "Did what I came to do—beat the best record."[10] If we consider the circumstances—the sudden flame flashing from a man more dead than alive, the triumphant claim of a near ghost—we get much closer to understanding the spirit of men like Greely. Great God, what zeal!

When the expedition survivors returned to the States, the army was quick to exonerate Greely of any blame for the execution of Private Henry. Officials hoped to draw public attention away from an unsavory event and insisted that the execution had been necessary. But because of the sensation-seeking press, another aspect of the expedition could not be covered up. *The New York Times,* which was zealous in the cause of getting General William Hazen sacked, broke the horrible news: "HORRORS OF CAPE SABINE—Terrible Story of Greely's Dreary Camp—Brave Men, Crazed by Starvation and Bitter Cold, Feeding on the Dead Bodies of Their Comrades—HOW PRIVATE HENRY DIED—The Awful Results of an Official Blunder."[11]

The *Times* charged the army with attempting to cover up the scandals of cannibalism and the execution of Henry and got much mileage out of its news stories "of inhumanity and cannibalism." Other newspapers picked up the *Times* articles and embellished them as their imaginative editors saw fit. Readers learned that the remains of the 17 men said to have died of starvation were only clean-picked bones. And there was an even more gruesome note. One of the survivors was hysterical when the rescuers reached the Greely camp, and as the sailors carried him to the ship he begged not to be shot and eaten, "as they did poor Henry." The *Times* editorial page reflected somberly on such black deeds: "The facts hitherto concealed will make the record of the Greely colony . . . the most dreadful and repulsive in the long annals of Arctic exploration."[12]

Greely insisted that he knew of no cannibalism at Cape Sabine, and the public celebration of his return went on. Greely was a strong man and he faced the scandal with fortitude. If there was cannibalism, it was done secretly. Furthermore, all of the survivors had come to him and sworn that they were innocent of the deed or any knowledge of it. Of course, the corpses of Kislingbury and others did suggest some cannibalism, but the extent of it did not approach what the *Times* made of it, and there was not a shred of evidence that anyone had been killed to provide food.

Vilhjalmur Stefansson once reflected on the Greely scandal and on the taboo against eating human flesh, "to which we attach an irrational horror." He and others "talked of it in whispers, and fell silent if he [Greely] or another of the six [survivors], came within possible hearing."[13] Later Stefansson became convinced that none of the survivors had been culpable. He rested his argument on dietary considerations. The survivors had been the strongest men, and they would have been less strong had they feasted on lean flesh. On his first journey down the Mackenzie River, Stefansson had learned about "rabbit starvation," or protein poisoning. Indians sometimes died when they ate the fatless meat of skinny rabbits or caribou.

The public's fascination with the horrors of cannibalism was stimulated by the publication of pamphlets that dwelt on such "awful tales." With the approval of his family, Lieutenant Kislingbury's body, which had been buried with military honors at Rochester, N.Y., was exhumed in the presence of press representatives well schooled in ghoulish wonder. "Slowly and reverentially the blanket was removed and then there was a suppressed cry of horror upon the lips of those present. The half-body, half-skeleton remains lay outstretched in all their ghastly terror." On the dead man's breast were discovered wounds "caused by the knives of those who stripped the body of its flesh and skin to still the terrible cravings of long-aggravated hunger."[14]

Kislingbury's brother, speculating on what knowledge he possessed of the bad feeling between Greely and Kislingbury, decided that the expedition had been divided into two factions and that "one perished because the other had gained possession, by force, of the supply of food." Dr. Pavy and Kislingbury were the ostracized party, and those "not in favor with the commander were compelled to die that the others might live."[15] Other family members protested that they could understand the cannibalism but not the reason for keeping the matter from the public, and they demanded a thorough investigation.

The same pamphlet quoted the imaginative *New York Times* on the condition of the Greely camp when the rescuers reached it. Much was made of the decline in the standards of body butchering after Dr. Pavy's death. His surgeon's skill had disguised the fact that the survivors had been subsisting on human flesh. "After his death the survivors were forced to dismember the bodies and denude them of flesh in a way that left nothing but bones." In the last days before rescue, the survivors were ruled by "the doctrine of the survival of the strongest." The *Times,* uninhibited by lack of evidence, painted the savage scene. "All sense of honor and of feeling had been lost." The survivors were unable to stand upright and were reduced to crawling. Sergeant Brainard's knees were calloused to a thickness of over half an inch. How did the men keep their reason? asked the *Times,* while implying that they did not. "About the camp were scattered bones of the dead, and dissected and mutilated bodies were half exposed in the little burial plot back of the tent. It was a scene at which the rescuers shuddered as they looked and the truth stood revealed."[16]

Among some "startling scraps of documentary evidence" was a diary allegedly kept by one of Greely's men. Some hack had a good time concocting this romantic piece, which described the writer's demented belief that he had discovered a fortune in jewels. "The secret is mine, and mine shall it remain if I live, but should I find myself no longer able to hold out, my diary will be placed where future brave navigators of the Arctic may find it."[17]

But the truer passion "recorded" in this "diary" is that of fear. "Things are desperate. From the glaring eyes of some of my companions in this dreadful prison of glaring, glistening ice, I fear that the awful thought of cannibalism is gradually working upon their already overwrought brains." The author described his own loss of control as he crawled toward an unidentified piece of food with a knife clenched between his teeth. "My God! Is it any wonder? Men under such awful circumstances lose all control over their better natures, and may become even cannibals."[18]

It is probable that Greely and his surviving companions protected themselves from such rot as the *Times* and other papers featured by avoiding it. Had they been exposed to it, they might have been soured by such sordid exploitations of their sufferings. But such stories spurred circulation of the *Times,* which was then in deep financial distress. Other papers used dubious material, too—but not all of them. *The New York Daily Tribune* censured "the vultures who have been gloating over these exaggerated and revolting stories" and quoted Clements Markham of England's Royal Geographical Society: "The accusation of murder and cannibalism made against the Greely party is a disgrace to American journalism."[19]

Greely's capture of the farthest-north record heated the rivalry for the Pole. Fans of exploration sensed that the ultimate triumph loomed near. Who would take the prize? Some prodigious men entered the field in the 1880s and 1890s. In 1888 Fridtjof Nansen crossed the Greenland ice shield, and three years later the tough, moody Robert E. Peary explored North Greenland for the first time. Both men served long apprenticeships and eventually achieved worldwide fame for their brilliant work.

Other lesser lights competed with Nansen and Peary. Evelyn Briggs Baldwin caught the polar fever in the late 1890s. On hearing about Salomon Andrée's preparation for a polar balloon flight, he hurried to Spitsbergen in hope of joining the Swedes. Andrée's *Eagle* had soared aloft before Baldwin reached the balloon base. Baldwin's frustration eased when the *Eagle*'s loss was reported, but his ambition burned on.

Baldwin had some experience in polar work with Peary and some meteorological training, although he did not profess to be a scientist. But he possessed the indispensable talent of attracting patronage. In 1900 Baldwin found in the American multimillionaire William Ziegler a bountiful source of support. There was something refreshing in the unbridled zeal and aggressiveness of Ziegler and Baldwin. Neither man indulged in scientific pretensions. They lusted to win the polar game; nothing else would do. Ziegler told the press with candor: "I intend to plant the stars and stripes on the North Pole if it costs me a million dollars to do it."[20]

Baldwin declared the same dedication. "I desire here to emphasize the fact that the Baldwin-Ziegler Expedition was organized *to reach the Pole.* Neither scientific research, nor even a record of 'Farthest North,' will suffice; only the attainment of that much sought for spot can satisfy our purpose."[21]

The British press commented disdainfully on such blatant record seeking as this. For Americans like Baldwin and Peary to refuse to mask their ambitions as scientific investigations seemed improper and "still another example of Yankee pushfulness."[22]

Ziegler spent $250,000 to outfit Baldwin's attempt. He had determined purely and simply to buy the Pole with the most lavishly equipped expedition ever sent to the Arctic. Equipment included three ships, an electric heating plant, a telephone system, prefabricated houses, signal balloons, 400 sled dogs, and 15 Siberian ponies. Baldwin headed a group of 42 men, including Russian hostlers who attended the Siberian ponies. The main party steamed off in the yacht *America* for Franz Josef Land, where their base was to be located. Another ship, a whaler, carried provisions and one of the prefabricated houses to Shannon Island, in East Greenland, to establish a retreat station in anticipation of Baldwin's return from the Pole. The *America* and an auxiliary transport called at Archangel to take on dogs, ponies, hostlers, dried fish for the dogs, and hay for the ponies, and left the Russian port dangerously overloaded.

In Franz Josef Land, Baldwin took over the base used a few years earlier by the English explorer Frederick Jackson. Baldwin showed less ambition in the field than one would expect from an expedition leader. Rather than make preparations for the next year's sled journey he took the *America* to sea, leaving the base manned. He either longed for civilization or felt it essential to supervise personally further provisioning. But the ice prevented his escape to the south and forced him to return to his base.

The Americans had poor luck with their dogs. Thirty died on the passage from Archangel to the Arctic for lack of water and 200 died over the winter.

Little attention was given to proper handling of the dogs. Baldwin and most of his men spent the winter aboard the *America,* which was connected by telephone to the shore base, where the ponies roamed at will and the dogs killed each other in endless battles.

Perhaps Baldwin was too preoccupied with personal squabbles to bother about the dogs. He quarreled with the *America*'s skipper, Captain Johannsen, and tried to fire him before leaving on the spring sled drive to the north. The crew refused to take orders from the chief engineer, whom Baldwin had elevated to command, claiming that obeying the engineer would be mutinous. Baldwin raged that he was commander and shipowner and threatened to punish any disobedience of his orders.

Dissension was widespread. Baldwin quarreled with Ernest de Koven Leffingwell, surveyor and astronomer of the expedition. As a consequence Leffingwell refused to carry out his duties. Other men complained of Baldwin's treatment of them, but the work went forward in the spring nonetheless. Eighteen relay bases were set up to the north.

In June, when Baldwin should have been set to dash for the Pole, he became anxious because an expected supply ship had not arrived. He frantically released 15 balloons carrying 300 messages strung on floats triggered to be released at intervals. The messages called urgently for a shipment of coal. Why the commander expected a ship as early as June is unfathomable, but, as he had done the year before, he steamed south instead of north. Baldwin reached Norway on August 1 and learned that the supply ship had sailed for his base two weeks earlier.

Ziegler, who was in Norway waiting for news of a polar triumph, marveled that Baldwin was there as well. Baldwin bragged to Zeigler and to the press of his fine scientific attainments and played down the dissension. Scientific work seemed more meaningful to him now than earlier. But after hearing from other expedition members about the discord and limited accomplishments, Ziegler fired Baldwin, replacing him with Anthony Fiala.

In the 1903–04 season, Fiala's work produced disappointing results. He progressed a mere 10 miles over the ice before giving up. Meanwhile, Ziegler died, his polar ambitions having been thwarted.

Fiala wrote a narrative of his 1903–04 attempt in which he disparaged the notion that money alone could assure a polar victory. Explorers needed luck, endurance, and courage, and all expedition members needed patience, "the highest qualities of Christian character."[23]

Fiala explained that a polar explorer "operates in a decidedly hostile and uncultivated territory, where there are no cornfields or henroosts along the line of march, but instead an active enemy in every wind that blows from the north, and opposition to his advance in every pressure ridge and water lane that crosses his path."[24]

Dissension plagued Fiala's venture, as it had Baldwin's. In 1904 two attempts over the ice were diverted by foul weather and ice leads. Fiala wanted to winter over and try again in 1905 but allowed his men to retreat south for an agreed-upon rendezvous with a rescue ship if they preferred. Fiala lost more men than he had anticipated. "The politicians in the retreating party used their influence and persuasiveness to enlarge their own party—until those to whom 'Northward!' had become a shibboleth, became, like Gideon's band, fewer and fewer."[25] As it turned out, the relief ship missed the rendezvous and the unhappy men returned to base.

Fiala wrote nothing of what was seemingly an assassination attempt upon him. Russians who visited Fiala's base on Rudolph Island in 1969 found an electrically wired explosive device planted in Fiala's quarters. Also found was a note signed by three defectors: "We, the opposition, are leaving the camp on Saturday, July 2, 1904, having 18 dogs, two ponies, and an Indian boat."[26]

More would be known of the Ziegler expeditions if participants had cared to write about their experiences. But only Fiala contributed a narration of the Fiala-Ziegler Expedition, and his account was a guarded one. No one chose to narrate the Baldwin-Ziegler Expedition. The entire Ziegler-sponsored endeavor left a bad taste with everyone concerned.

After his dismissal Baldwin sought funding for another polar venture. Patrons shied away from him. Malicious wags remarked that his fame rested on his discovery of Mr. Ziegler rather than of the Pole. Baldwin faded from public view. For fifteen years he held a minor position as a government clerk. When he lost his job because of cutbacks in employment, a better-known explorer, General Adolphus Greely, appealed to the President on Baldwin's behalf. The President ignored this plea in behalf of a man whose patriotic devotion to planting the Stars and Stripes on the Pole had once been a dominating urge.

This summary of American involvement in polar exploration from Kane to Baldwin demonstrates that controversy over exploration was common prior to the Cook-Peary affair.

III

BLOWUP

THE SCANDAL
ON THE MOUNT

*"The dangers of an expedition really
begin on its return."*
—*Frederick Jackson*

Before Cook's North Pole expedition became a sensation, very little attention had been paid to his 1906 mountaineering feat. *To the Top of the Continent,* Cook's book on his 1903 and 1906 Mount McKinley climbs, appeared in 1908 without provoking any particular comment. There were few readers. Insiders like Professor Herschel Parker and Belmore Browne scrutinized it carefully and found their suspicions of 1906 sustained. If anything, the narrative exposed Cook's audacity further in their eyes. The colorful language describing the ascent obscured the feat. Mountaineers expected full details on the route, yet Cook's account omitted details and dates. But Cook was in the Arctic, and a reopening of the question in his absence would be ungentlemanly. For all anyone knew, Cook might even be dead.

When headlines heralded Cook's polar claim, Professor Herschel Parker wasted no time in renewing his attack. Within three days of newspaper accounts of Cook's reception in Copenhagen, he reopened the Mount McKinley case in *The New York Times.* Three years earlier his charges in similar interviews had not caused much excitement, but in September 1909 Cook was a celebrated man, and Parker's accusations attracted more attention. Parker did not have any new evidence, but another news story indicated that other expedition members shared his doubts.

Doubts of Cook's Mount McKinley claim were expressed two weeks later by R. S. Tarr, a noted glaciologist and Cornell professor. Tarr wrote his views to Herbert L. Bridgman, secretary of the Explorers Club. With Cook in the news and Peary's men, including Bridgman, in an uproar, the Club was not inclined to brush off Parker again. An investigation was undertaken by a carefully chosen committee that did not include anyone conspicuous for supporting Peary. Members insisted that Peary, the Club's president that year, did not order the investigation; the Club's Board of Governors assumed the responsibility.

As early as October 1, newspapers reported that Edward Barrill, who had been Cook's packer, had denied Cook's ascent. A week later Barrill's visit to New York was reported.

Barrill's denial did not cause an immediate sensation, yet clearly Mount McKinley was now a more important factor in the evaluation of Cook's career than formerly. The exploration elite, at least those of them favoring Peary, were keen to hear all about Mount McKinley. Peary partisans gained a "smoking gun" to impeach the word of the adventurer who had robbed his better of polar honors.

The New York Globe and Commercial Advertiser bannered the news on October 14: "HOW DR. COOK CLIMBED MOUNT MCKINLEY: TESTIMONY OF BARRILL. ONLY MAN WITH HIM. Guide who Went on Alaskan Expedition Swears Alleged Discoverer of the North Pole Was Never Nearer than Fourteen Miles of the Summit of the North American Continent's Tallest Peak—Highest Elevation Reached Not in Excess of Ten Thousand Feet."[1]

Details followed, but the revelation was simplicity itself. Barrill had released an affidavit to the press asserting that the alleged climb was wholly fraudulent and that the photographic evidence to support it had been contrived. Photographs and maps included in the initial article and follow-up stories illustrated the deception practiced by Cook.

Barrill said that the climbers started up the glacier on September 9. Cook told him that the climb was only a reconnaissance in preparation for another Parker-Cook expedition the following year. All Barrill's diary entries from September 9 through 18 were made under Cook's direction. Dates and elevations were misstated. On September 12 Cook told his companion to stop making diary notes. "At this time we had been to the top of the point claimed by the doctor as the top of the mountain, and the doctor had taken a photograph of the point with me standing on the top thereof, with the American flag in my hand."

Cook had offered the photograph taken at this point as a record of the summit victory. It appeared opposite page 227 of his book. Barrill insisted that he had not stood on the summit: "The truth being that the summit of Mt. McKinley was over twenty miles distant in an air line from the point where my picture was so taken." When Barrill told Cook that higher peaks above the photographed point would appear in the picture, Cook said that "he had taken the picture at such an angle that those peaks would not show."

Corroboration followed in the *Globe* on October 15. Fred Prinz, Cook's chief packer, swore that Barrill had told him of the fake within a month of their return to Montana from Seattle in early November. Walter Miller, another member of the expedition, swore that Barrill told him of the fake in May 1908.

Newspaper readers had a choice: They could believe Barrill or Cook. It would have been easier to believe Cook and to assume Barrill lied if other circumstances supported Cook's claim. Unfortunately for Cook, Samuel Beecher, an expedition cook, recognized some of the peaks in photos Cook used, particularly "the view from 16,000 feet," which "could not have been taken at an elevation of more than 7,000 feet."

Other affidavits indicated that Barrill had also told Beecher in 1907 that Cook faked the ascent. This statement corroborated Prinz's story that Barrill had not kept the truth from his acquaintances. Barrill's early revelations were significant because they undermined Cook's argument that Peary partisans had fabricated the Mount McKinley exposure to avenge Cook's polar claim.

Cook's ineffective response to Barrill's disclosure decisively undermined his credibility with the public. He called Barrill a liar and a receiver of bribes, but something more was needed to hold people's confidence.

When the sensation erupted, Cook was lecturing in Buffalo. Reporters flocked to him for an explanation and he handled the matter with commendable poise, saying that he had sent for both Barrill and Prinz. "I want to have them where everybody can question them and end this talk about my ascent of Mount McKinley. By having them in New York, where everyone can get at them, the facts can be known."

Cook also announced that he would send out a party to Mount McKinley to confirm his record.

One reporter asked whether it was true that Cook owed money to several expedition members at the termination of the Alaskan journey. Cook recalled that such had been the case, disclaiming any responsibility for tardy settlement. "I was not responsible for the bills, but the society that had charge of the expedition must have overlooked these payments. When my attention was called to the bills I promptly paid them. As in everything else, I invite the closest inquiry in this matter."

Two little lies. He had not been sponsored by a society. He did not pay the bills promptly.

Cook's charge that Barrill had been bribed was answered in the *Globe* on October 16. Thomas Hubbard of the Peary Arctic Club did not hide his hand. He had asked James M. Ashton, a well-known Tacoma attorney and a friend of his, to interview all the expedition men who lived in the Northwest. Barrill freely admitted his part in the hoax. Hubbard denied Cook's charge of a $5,000 payment to Barrill.

On the same day, October 16, Cook replied confidently to eager reporters: "Within the last forty-eight hours affidavits made by prominent citizens of Hamilton, Montana, would be handed over to the Associated Press, and would be to the effect that during the last three years Barrill has continually rehearsed the Mount McKinley story and has at all times insisted that we succeeded."

Cook told reporters at his customary 6:00 P.M. conference that he knew nothing of Barrill's diary; he had never seen the packer make entries. "Why do you think Miller corroborates Barrill's story?" a newsman asked. "Miller was always hostile to me," Cook replied. "He was not on the mountain, at any rate." As for his own diary, "I will produce it, though, of course, it is in storage with my other property. Still, a fully worked out record [his book] would contain more detail than a diary would."

Cook's promise to give evidence that Barrill's Hamilton neighbors had heard him confirm the climb was not fulfilled. The Associated Press received no affidavits. Instead, the news out of Montana only damaged Cook's shaky defense further. *The New York Times* wired the Hamilton Chamber of Commerce asking for verification of Cook's statements. Its president, M. A. White, responded by wire: "Have been informed by reputable citizens of Hamilton that Barrill has repeatedly said for years that members of Dr. Cook's party failed to reach the summit of Mt. McKinley. Opinion here Barrill's statements are true."

After this, Cook's response to queries about Mount McKinley was "no comment." Cook rested his defense on the bribery charge and a fresh lie that could be exposed. He insisted that his photographs of McKinley had not been faked. As a great statesman once remarked, this was worse than a crime, it was a blunder. Faked photographs are subject to close scrutiny, and the deception could only be temporary.

From October 14 Cook's standing with the public eroded. It could hardly be otherwise when the only other man who allegedly stood on Mount McKinley's peak with him totally denied the whole story. People weighed the possibility that Barrill lied, and a majority rejected it on the balance of probability. Barrill had little to gain by lying. He exposed himself to slander from Cook, to a lawsuit, and to the disapproval of those who wondered why he had not come forward earlier. Cook, on the other hand, would lose everything he had gained if he, rather than Barrill, were stamped as a liar. If Barrill lied, he must be ranked as one of the most perfidious and successful rogues in history; yet there is nothing in his pre–Mount McKinley background or in his subsequent life that corroborates such incredible venality.

Poor Cook was in deep trouble. He dared to confront Barrill at a public meeting in the latter's hometown. This showed he had nothing to fear on a lecture platform from an inarticulate blacksmith, but that is all it showed. Even if Cook could have taken Barrill with him on tour around the nation and confronted him nightly before large assemblies to demonstrate his larger forensic skills, the result would probably not be different. Through the efforts of Peary partisans (legitimate efforts, it should be noted), Barrill did Cook in, but only because Cook did not dare to present his "evidence" before an impartial scientific or geographical group.

In the press the celebrated Mr. Dooley (Finley Peter Dunne) commented: "Moreover he could not have reached the pole because he did not climb Mt. McKinley and he did not climb Mt. McKinley because he is a liar."[2] Both of Dooley's propositions were acceptable: Mount McKinley had nothing to do with the North Pole. Cook's claim to the Pole remained intact; it was as good as it ever was, assuming evidence actually existed. Even the slowest mind had to recognize that Cook's word had been tarnished. Unfairly perhaps, but tarnished just the same. He must offer more.

Sensibly, Cook hired a lawyer, H. Wellington Wack. Wack and Cook appeared before a committee of the Explorers Club, where Wack complained of possible bias. Peary, the Club president who succeeded Cook, had convened the committee, Wack complained, and it looked as if an organized attack against Cook was under way. Club officials denied that

Peary had anything to do with the committee. Wack then agreed to present Cook's original records if the publisher of his narrative released them. Since the records remained the property of Cook and were in his possession, this did not seem to be much of a problem.

Later Cook vilified the Explorers Club, as well as any other individual or organization that questioned him. Club members were divided and unhappy about the polar controversy regardless of which man, Cook or Peary, if either, they believed. The continuing scandal in the press embarrassed Club members. An endeavor they considered fine and noble had been smeared, and two Club presidents were involved. The Club made no offer to arbitrate the polar claims, but Mount McKinley was another matter. Only Cook was involved, and a settlement would not tear the Club apart; a judgment on the Pole was much touchier. Members would accept a favorable committee decision on Cook's Mount McKinley proofs, and, equally, they would accept an adverse decision.

Grounds for consideration of the dispute existed. Cook had reported to the Club in 1906, thus recognizing the Club's interest. Furthermore, Herschel Parker had asked the Club to investigate the issue in 1906.

Some club members objected. General Adolphus Greely, a polar hero who initially much preferred Cook's claims over Peary's (probably for personal reasons), threatened to resign. Another member, Caspar Whitney, begged Greely to reconsider in a letter written October 5 (before the Barrill affidavit). The investigation would be a "proper and friendly thing," Whitney argued, and "Cook agrees it is the only way to settle discussion."[3]

Greely replied on October 15, just after the Barrill news broke. He had been shocked at the news. "If true, Cook must fall into eternal disgrace."[4] Greely made no further objection to the examining committee.

Cook got some help when Alfred H. Brooks, the head of the United States Geological Survey in Alaska, told the press that Cook's published account was not inconsistent but only vague and lacking in detail. All Cook had to do was clarify his story. Later Brooks realized that Cook could not clarify his climb.

Brooks's support cheered Cook. Just as soon as he got his North Pole data off to Copenhagen, he told newsmen, he would lead a party of scientists to Mount McKinley.

The Explorers Club's rejection of the Mount McKinley claim, published on Christmas Day, confirmed a conviction many people had already reached. The Club's committee did not mention Barrill's affidavit in reaching its conclusions. With the testimony of Herschel Parker, Belmore Browne, and the sportsman-author Charles Sheldon bearing on key technical matters that seemed to rule out a genuine climb, and with Cook's failure to answer their objections, Barrill's statement could be ignored. In the committee's view, the evidence showed that Cook lacked the intent, equipment, time, and opportunity of access route. His photographic evidence had been questioned, and he would not provide the original pictures. His breach of the agreement with Parker and his failure to meet financial obligations to party members suggested that his statements could not be trusted. Thus the committee concluded that his claim must "be rejected by the Explorers Club as unworthy of credence."[5] The unanimous decision of the committee was accepted by the general membership because of its reasonableness, and because the presence of acknowledged friends of Cook on the committee created confidence in its impartiality.

12

DUNKLE AND LOOSE

"A doubtful throne is ice on summer seas."
—Alfred Tennyson

To regain his standing Cook desperately needed the affirmation of the University of Copenhagen. While the interested public waited for the Danes to report, it was treated to the Dunkle and Loose revelations on December 9. Dunkle and Loose were two down-at-heel, cunning opportunists who saw the chance to make a few easy dollars. Like other New Yorkers, they followed the Cook drama in the newspapers and they discerned that the explorer might need help. It was not charity that moved them to approach Cook, but the guile of rogues who were a little desperate themselves and capable of smelling out the desperation of a fellow rogue.

Captain August Wedel Loose was a navigator of some experience, and George H. Dunkle was an insurance salesman. Together they formed a good combination of technical expert and front man; there was no reason why their pooled talents could not yield them a small bonanza. They had more time to speculate than more prosperous citizens, and so it was, as Dunkle told it later, that they began discussing the matter. Whether it was in a saloon over refreshing drinks, or elsewhere, we are not told, and it does not matter; their proceeding was sober enough.

Loose figured that Cook's narrative in *The New York Herald* claimed too much and that his observations "had the earmarks of having been faked." This was not a singular deduction; other more honest readers had reached similar conclusions. Loose bragged to Dunkle: "I could frame up better observations than those." Dunkle demurred: "But they say it is hard to manufacture observations. Can it really be done?" Nothing to it, said the hearty mariner; "It's easy when you know how." Dunkle, a cautious landlubber, sensed an opportunity: "Do you mean to say you can sit down and fabricate observations that would bolster up a claim that you had been to the North Pole?"[1] To this Loose laughed with the ease of an expert; he was rather pleased to show his more worldly and somewhat more prosperous friend that his life at sea had not been entirely misspent. Loose assured Dunkle that with his eyes shut he could manufacture records that would pass the scrutiny of a group of scientists.

One thing that bothered Loose about Cook's observations was his explicitness in putting down the seconds for his sextant recordings. Such fine detail could not be recorded on the instrument on such a long journey and neither could the exact position at the Pole. And things were growing hot for Cook. He had to answer Barrill's Mount McKinley affidavit and delayed sending his records to Copenhagen. Loose told Dunkle that Dr Cook probably lacked complete observations and needed more convincing truth. "Maybe I could help him out," said Loose smugly.

Dunkle, the front man, got right to work. He contacted John R. Bradley Cook's sponsor, and boasted of his willingness earlier in volunteering to join the relief expedition that had been planned when it was feared that Cook was lost. Now Dunkle was eager to meet the great explorer. Bradley complied and took Dunkle to Cook at the Waldorf-Astoria on October 17

Since Dunkle understood the ways of the world and appreciated the sensitivity of men whose reputation was under attack, he approached his interest warily, speaking of records and the need to safeguard them—no with more data, but with insurance. Cook seemed to understand this implausible opening and laughed with Dunkle over the little joke that an insurance man never missed a chance to talk business. He agreed that insuring his records when under way to Copenhagen might be a good idea

Cook's agreeableness suggested that he took the hint. Only a very obtuse or distracted man could miss it. Cook was not obtuse but had plenty of reason to be distracted. Before leaving, Dunkle had to be more explicit: " told the doctor that perhaps he might need the help of someone in getting his records off at the time he wanted, and that if he did I might be able to offer a suggestion." Dunkle had a knowledgeable friend who could help. Cook admitted his observations were not yet in shape and showed interest; he did not take offense, as Dunkle feared he might.

Should Cook (assuming his conscience and motivations were pure) have shown Dunkle the door with calm disdain or irritated indignation? Dunkle offered either something fraudulent or help that could be construed as such. Perhaps Cook could have believed, as he stated later, that he was merely interested in an independent check of his figures. Anyway, as he was preparing to travel west, he only took Dunkle's card and indicated he would get in touch if Loose's services were needed.

Cook's wife smelled a rat. She took an intuitive dislike to Dunkle and warned her husband. Of course, she was not privy to all of his needs.

Returning from the trip on which he confronted Barrill in Hamilton, Montana, Cook was eager to see Dunkle and Loose. The three men made arrangements that showed the circumspection of all parties in interesting detail. Dunkle did not report that Cook ever betrayed himself by asking for help or that he ever acknowledged an intent to deceive. Cook thought Loose might help with a few points. "It's nothing vital, you know, but some details that I want." A tentative agreement was reached on November 3 and on November 4 Dunkle brought Loose to meet Cook. By then Cook had been assured—probably by Captain Lewis Nixon, an acquaintance—that Loose knew his navigation.

Loose learned at their first meeting that Cook had not taken altitude observations ("that is, the altitude of heavenly bodies above the horizon") and told the explorer that scientists would not accept his evidence without such data. Happily, Loose could provide such data by working out observations backward from the Pole. Cook seemed very pleasantly surprised that this could be done. "Then," he told Loose, "you can be of some service to me."

Now if this bargain was actually struck, as Dunkle and Loose insisted, Cook was unquestionably willing to manufacture fraudulent evidence. So either Cook lied in professing his shock when Loose later gave him the faked figures, or Dunkle and Loose lied in saying that a bargain had been reached. The team insisted that they knowingly agreed to participate in a fraud in return for cash payment. It is possible, if not probable, that Cook did not understand the deviousness of the scoundrels he hired and that he was amazed when they gave him what they believed he asked for.

Who lied? Perhaps the reaction of Cook's attorney, H. Wellington Wack, whose every action for his client showed skill and honesty, is the key. Apparently Cook never asked Wack to do anything illegal, and the lawyer did the best he could with what information his client gave him. When Wack heard the news from the University of Copenhagen, he commented that Cook's behavior revealed some mental instability, and he may have thought that Cook's dealings with Dunkle and Loose were clear evidence of derangement. Wack did not say whether he knew more of the affair than Dunkle and Loose told *The New York Times*. He may well have heard about it from Cook and advised him to drop the pair and eschew any use of such questionable data in his Copenhagen report. Either on Wack's advice, or on that of someone else, or independently, Cook did not send the manufactured data to Copenhagen.

Cook knew where to go for reputable verification of his data if that was really all he wished to have done. Among his acquaintances at the Explorers Club and Arctic Club, there were several men whom he might have contacted, including Captain Lewis Nixon. He could have asked the help of respectable academic or government scientists skilled in navigation; instead, he allowed the approach of two dishonest men.

In *My Attainment of the Pole,* Cook tells how Dunkle and Loose worked their way into his confidence and how he came to rely upon them. "When I think of the incidents leading up to the acquaintance of Dunkle and Loose, it does seem that I had lost all sense of balance, and that my brain was befogged." On the basis of Loose's claim of having some influence with Scandinavian newspapers, Cook agreed to let Loose write some friendly articles. The articles "seemed weak and irrelevant," but it seemed worthwhile to send them off.[2]

Cook said he agreed to Loose's checking of his figures because "all observations were subject to extreme accuracy." Loose knew navigation, while "I was not a navigator, and, moreover, had had no chance of checking my figures." So Cook told Loose to work on the data published in *The New York Herald* articles. He approved of Loose's moving into his hotel, paid him $250, "which was to compensate him in full for the articles and his running expenses," and worried about how much time Loose was taking to do the job. Dunkle and Loose claimed the $250 was only a down payment on the $4,000 promised for the job, plus the $500 bonus due Loose if the University of Copenhagen accepted his figures.

Then Cook described the climax. He went to Loose's room late one night. Dunkle was there, too, and papers were strewn all over the place. "'Well,' said Loose, 'I think we have this thing all fixed up.'" And Dunkle, "smooth-tongued and friendly as ever, said, 'Now, Doctor, I want to advise you to put your own observations aside. *Send these to Copenhagen!*'" Loose admitted that he advised just that. He had been appalled at the paucity of Cook's data and even more at Cook's apparent ignorance of basic navigation. He knew the University of Copenhagen would reject what paltry evidence Cook could offer without his help. But Cook professed to be devastated by Dunkle's recommendation that Loose's figures be used.

Cook, revolted by their "nefarious" suggestion, stunned a trifle (as always in moments of tension), finally thundered at them: "Gentlemen, pack up every scrap of this paper in that dress suit case. Take all your belongings and leave this hotel at once."

Cook glowered at them while they packed up. "Not a word was spoken. Sheepish and silent, they shuffled from the room, ashamed and taken aback." For all their smooth-tongued confidence and audacity, it is amazing that they showed so little spirit. Not that Cook thought it odd, as he described the end of a collaboration fraught with uneasiness and alarming risks. From the outset he suspected that hiring Dunkle and Loose to calculate his North Pole navigations could lead to scandal. Sure enough, they mentioned the unthinkable, and he felt "sick at heart at the thought that these men should have considered me unscrupulous enough to buy and use their faked figures."

Dunkle and Loose made no response to Cook's righteous wrath then, but their abrupt dismissal and a certain default in payment hurt their feelings. Later, looking around for a shoulder to cry upon, they reached *The New York Times.*

Cook was hiding in South America when the *Times* story, a very full one supported by affidavits from Dunkle and Loose, was published. He thought the *Times* would have rejected the story had not Dunkle and Loose lied to the editor, claiming that the fabricated data had been sent to Copenhagen. That it was not sent protected Cook against charges of fraud, or so he felt. Neither of the men indicated in their stories that the faked data was enroute to Copenhagen; they could not have known it, but they and the *Times* might well have believed that the data would be used for the purpose for which it was concocted. Subsequently, the *Times* erred in reporting that the data had been sent and later retracted its report. This report was careless, but its publication was the only occasion on which the *Times* acted rashly. Contrary to Cook's belief, the *Times* would have welcomed the Dunkle-Loose story, even without assurances that the data was going to Copenhagen. It was a great sensation, a story that, if true, showed Cook in a very bad light. Two men had sworn to it. Beyond trying to reach Cook, who had fled the country by then, the *Times* could not check further.

13

A PLACE TO HIDE

"He abhores to take the lie but not to tell it."
                    —*Bishop George Berkeley*

Robert Peary's attention to Cook's travails from October through December was dedicated. His initial blasts launched from Greenland had been followed by repeated declamations against his rival's fakery after he returned to the States. When public reaction was adverse, he was counseled by Hubbard and Bridgman to keep his peace. Consequently, Peary refused to discuss Cook with the press and complained bitterly, although privately, that the press was mistreating him. *The New York Times* argued that Peary had every right to refute Cook, but other papers took unkindly to his pugnaciousness. Peary's towering ego was matched only by his fiery rage whenever anyone thwarted or criticized him. He reacted as savagely as a wounded bear. By contrast Cook seemed so gracious and manly, even under nasty assaults on his character.

When the Mount McKinley sensation broke on October 14, 1909, Peary rallied his friends to an all-out battle against Cook. "I am not vindictive. I cannot afford to be," he wrote Hubbard, president of the Peary Arctic Club. "But Cook has been unmasked and should be handled without gloves." As unpleasant as the matter was, they had to look it squarely in the face. Cook's treachery created "a National Disgrace which has lowered our prestige, made us a laughing stock abroad, and incurred the resentment of a friendly nation [Denmark], which has been simply insulted."[1]

In a sense the polar controversy was indeed a national disgrace, a mar on exploration tradition. Some British newspapers sniffed at the incident contemptuously, reflecting on the squalid consequences of Yankee pushiness. No one who loved exploration could be happy over the demeaning clamor, although Peary's concern for the nation's honor or for Denmark's friendship could not compare with his outrage at the personal blow he suffered.

Peary's indictment of Cook and those who abetted him was thorough: "An unprincipled adventurer disgracing the name American, has deliberately insulted the Royal family of a friendly nation and placed an ineradicable slight and slur upon their entire people." On other occasions Peary referred less kindly to the Danes, lashing them as dupes and fools. He went on: "Then, backed and aided and abetted by a gambler, and a yellow paper, [Cook] has caused this country to make a hysterical fool of itself; and finally has deliberately and intentionally stolen thousands of dollars, by as fraudulent a trick as was ever practiced by green goods man or confidence sharp."[2]

In England or Germany the people would retaliate sternly, Peary argued, and Americans must purge themselves from national disgrace "by drastic and immediate action." What Peary then proposed was not as drastic as his indictment: Send copies of the Eskimo and Barrill statements to every organization to which Cook belonged, and "Any society that does not then expel him from membership will discredit itself."[3] Also, the United States government should be alerted to Cook's injury to the Danes.

If Peary really believed that the United States government might apologize to Denmark on Cook's behalf or somehow rap Cook's knuckles, he hoped for too much. His tactic regarding the societies Cook belonged to was sensible enough, although such professional groups did not require any urging from Peary's friends. The Explorers Club had already begun its investigation, and others would act in time, including even the Arctic Club, which had honored Cook so unreservedly. Peary recognized Cook's place in the exploration Establishment and knew the importance of the societies' rejection of one of their own. In no sense was Cook an outsider or outlaw at that time, but Peary hoped that the Mount McKinley exposure would result in Cook's professional disgrace. Peary's hopes were realized eventually, although not as swiftly as he wished. It took the decision of the University of Copenhagen in December, coupled with the Mount McKinley fraud, to bury Cook.

Peary was vindictive for reasons easy to understand. But he was also impotent in speeding Cook's downfall. Parker, Browne, Hubbard, and others delivered the fatal blow by exposing the Mount McKinley fraud, as they had every right and reason to do, and the rest was up to Cook.

Peary's contributions to the destruction of his nemesis are more interesting for showing his state of mind—and his pettiness. Peary insisted to Bridgman and Hubbard that no individual or organization tainted by having supported Cook be represented at any ceremony honoring his own achievements.[4] Toward the Arctic Club he showed particular vehemence. Otherwise his efforts consisted of little more than nagging at his friends to pressure Cook's critics to express publicly what reservations they held privately. It annoyed him when authorities failed to come forward. "What good does it do for Professor Davis to tell you and me things that we already know?" he asked Bridgman. "Why don't [sic] he put the thing in definite shape and put it out over his own name?" Peary explained the situation: "If I make the statement it will be simply a continuance of the jealous blackguard abusing a perfect gentleman."[5]

Even Herschel Parker, who did more than any individual to expose Cook's mountain caper, even when it was unpopular to do so, was abused by Peary. "We have the spectacle of the man who accompanied Cook and who claimed to have had just as much financial and other interest in the expeditions as Cook, saying in private and behind Cook's back that Cook never got to the top of Mt. McKinley, and yet sitting at the same public dinner table with Cook and listening to him recounting his ascent of Mt. McKinley (as I saw him do on two occasions) and never raise his voice in protest."[6]

As Bridgman, Peary's correspondent, knew, and as Peary should have known if he read the newspapers or tuned in to Explorers Club gossip, Parker tried hard to expose Cook publicly. At the time Peary cared nothing about mountaineering controversies, even though he was informed by Stefansson and others of a possible fraud. Only public-spirited men or interested parties were inclined to jump into travel controversies, and in 1906 Peary was neither. Only one cause, his own polar saga, ever compelled Peary's serious attention. His ambition lifted him above the squabbles of others; in short, he did not give a damn until his ox was gored.

Peary was pleased when authorities held correct views on the controversy. In discussing a Russian geographer with Bridgman, Peary suggested: "He too is on the track and should be cultivated."[7] Peary was also keen to raise protests against Cook's delay in presenting his polar evidence to a scientific body, although during the same period, critics like General Greely censured Peary for delaying his own presentation.

Peary indirectly, and others directly, urged the University of Copenhagen to insist that Cook send his data promptly. The Peary clique also pressured the university to allow American representatives of the National Geographic Society to participate in its Cook deliberation. The Danes rejected all such appeals and queries. The university officials may have regretted ever having involved themselves in the polar affair, yet understood that a submission to pro-Peary pressure could only add to their embarrassment.

As the University of Copenhagen investigation neared, Peary tried to anticipate Cook's strategy, little realizing that Cook was drifting as helplessly as a fire-gutted ship at sea. An announcement that *New York Herald* publisher James Gordon Bennett was traveling to Europe alerted Peary's suspicions. Was Bennett going to Copenhagen to direct Cook's campaign? he queried Bridgman anxiously. Any *Herald* reader—and certainly Peary was one—could observe that the newspaper had lost interest in Cook. Bennett had smelled a losing cause before the Barrill exposure and, even in September, had not backed Cook with anything like the vociferous enthusiasm the *Times* threw behind Peary. Still, Peary stewed on. He was a worrier, and the obvious shift in public opinion did not placate him.

Peary's correspondence does not reveal him to be an endearing personality. He fought for his cause against Cook with every weapon at hand and was as interested in hurting Cook by finding a blemish in his medical school record as by more germane exposures. He was not scrupulous, nor was he particularly astute. As alert as Peary was, his personal participation did not bring about Cook's downfall. It is true that Cook might not have been exposed but for the timing of Peary's claim, but that fact did not make Peary the author of Cook's woes.

In November the momentum of the controversy quickened again. Peary presented his data to a committee of the National Geographic Society and received its highest award, a gold medal, as did Captain Bob Bartlett, the hearty Canadian mariner who had helped his commander reach a point 135 miles south of the Pole. Matt Henson, Peary's only other companion aside from Eskimos after Bartlett was sent back, did not share National Geographic Society honors with the two white men. No one complained of the slight to a colored man in 1909.

A few days after Peary's award, and following other attacks on Cook's polar journey, Dr. Cook told the press that his records would go to Denmark on November 25. He also offered to give his original records to the National Geographic Society if Peary would submit his to the University of Copenhagen. Peary did not respond. Peary and his friends wished to monitor the Danes' look at Cook's records, but were satisfied with the National Geographic Society's judgment on Peary's. They reasoned that foreign authorities would go along with the National Geographic Society's award, and they were right.

About the same time, Cook dropped from sight—or tried to—by moving to the Hotel Gramatan in Bronxville, N.Y. The only news concerning his current activities related his plans to send his records to Copenhagen. He feared their interception by his foes, his friends told the press, but the *Times* scoffed at this. Meanwhile, as Cook presumably labored to prepare his data, Peary made a number of public appearances and received other honors. His star waxed as Cook's waned.

On November 27 Cook's attorney, H. Wellington Wack, told the press that Cook needed rest and would travel to southern Europe. When he left the country is not clear, and nothing more was heard from him in November or December, except for unconfirmed reports that he was seen in sanitariums in White Plains, N.Y., in Maine, and elsewhere. Wherever he was, Cook had clearly gone to ground after dispatching his records to Copenhagen.

Cook's disappearance did not end the speculation and recriminations reported by the press. Indeed, the frenzied debate ran on more intensely despite his silence. Excitement mounted as a worldwide public waited for the University of Copenhagen to complete its investigation.

While the public waited, Cook crashed. The scandal he created engulfed him; the pressure was too much. The frenzy had started in Copenhagen on his return from the Arctic. Offers for lectures and publications poured in on him, and he had no time to respond. Once aboard the steamer *Oscar II,* bound for New York, he and his newly hired secretary, Walter Lonsdale, had time to sort out the business. Cook calculated on an income of $1,500,000 from his book, articles, and lectures. The North Pole victory could yield a bonanza of fantastic proportions.

Rumblings of doubt did not initially dim his glowing expectations. At sea he received a wire asking for a lecture at the Saint Louis Fair shortly after his arrival in New York. According to one report he was offered

$25,000 for a single appearance, but Cook said he received less than half of that amount. In various cities he lectured about twenty times in all, receiving from $1,000 to $10,000 per lecture.

Clearly the strain of traveling and lecturing in the weeks after his return was extremely wearing. "Everywhere I went crowds pressed about me. I shook hands until the flesh of one finger was actually worn through to the bone. Hundreds of people daily came to see me."[8]

Some people wondered why Cook launched himself on such a demanding schedule instead of resting or preparing his data for the University of Copenhagen. Cook could not understand criticism relating to the preparation of the data. "Every explorer for fifty years has done the same thing, all had delivered lectures and written articles about their work after a first preliminary report. Supplementary and detailed data were usually given long afterwards, not as proof but as a part of the plan of recording ultimate results." Cook could not see why people insisted upon proof. He could not admit that the pressure created by competing claims altered the old leisurely, trusting tradition. "My feeling at the time was that I was under no obligation to patrons, to the Government, to any society, or anyone, and that I had a right to deliver lectures at a time when public interest was keyed up, and to prepare my detailed reports at a time when I should have more leisure."

Cook needed money; he was broke; the public was fickle. Who could blame him for striking while the iron was hot?

In his flurry of activity, Cook had trouble responding to various blows. Harry Whitney returned from Greenland without the instruments and mysterious data Cook had left there in his care. Peary had refused to allow Whitney to carry any of Cook's possessions aboard the *Roosevelt,* so Whitney buried them. Cook had not considered this material of great importance when he left it with Whitney. Now the material seemed important because of the suspicion aroused against him. "At the time I felt crippled; my feeling of disgust with the problem, with myself, and with the situation began." His report would be deficient without the data left in Greenland. He could not check his instruments. He could not send a ship to Etah to pick up the material until the following year.

Meanwhile the Mount McKinley scandal broke over Cook's head. His friends confused him as much as his enemies by giving him conflicting advice. Some friends urged him to attack Peary. "Such a course was distasteful to me, and, furthermore, the selfish, envious origin of all of Mr. Peary's charges seemed evident."

Under such pressure, Cook made mistakes. To accompany his *Herald* articles, he submitted a number of photos. Some of these were taken on earlier expeditions to the Arctic. Although he recalled telling a *Herald* editor that some photos did not relate to his polar trip, there was such a rush that one of them was used. "Whereupon, Mr. Herbert Bridgman, secretary of the Peary Arctic Club, shouted aloud, Fraud! and others took up the cry."

Other criticism seemed unfair. From Cook's first report of his victory, critics cried that his speed on the dash exceeded the possible. Yet when Peary reported a faster daily record, nothing was said. "I asked myself the reason of [sic] this sudden hush."

Cook claimed that he did not read the newspapers during this period. Friends and reporters told him about the accusations, but it was hard to understand the clamor.

Alone, I was unable to cope with matters, anyway. I underestimated the effect of the cumulating attacks. Oppressed by the undercurrent, feeling that it was all a fuss about very little, a thing of insignificant worth, and disturbed by the growing uncertainty of proving such a claim to the point of hair-breadth accuracy by any figures, despair overcame me.

I was so busy I could not pause to think, and was conscious only of the rush, the labor, the worry. I no longer slept; indigestion naturally seized me as its victim. A mental depression brought desperate premonitions.

I developed a severe case of laryngitis in Washington; it got worse as I went to Baltimore and Pittsburg. At St. Louis, where I talked before an audience said to number twelve thousand persons, I could hardly raise my voice above a whisper. The lecture was given with physical anguish. I was feverish and mentally dazed. Thereafter, day by day, my thoughts became less coherent; I, more like a machine.

There was no pleasure in such circumstances, except on those rare occasions, such as the Waldorf-Astoria banquet, when he felt the close presence of hundreds of warm friends. At the ceremony of the presentation of the Freedom of the City of New York, "I was so confused and half ill that I was not in a condition to appreciate the honor."

After I had been on my lecture tour for a few weeks, I began to feel persecuted. On every side I sensed hostility; the sight of crowds filled me with a growing sort of terror. I did not realize at the time that I was passing from periods of mental depression to dangerous periods of nervous tension. I was pursued by reporters, people with craning necks, good-natured demonstrations of friendliness that irritated me. In the trains I viewed the whirling landscape without, and felt myself part of it—as a delirious man swept and hustled through space.

Cook was heading for a breakdown. He knew it and knew also that he had to get away. He finished his report to the University of Copenhagen and entrusted it to his secretary, Lonsdale. For days he had been paranoid about the security of the report, fearful that his foes would steal it before it reached Copenhagen. Now his work was finished. Lonsdale helped him disguise his appearance. He removed his mustache, cut his hair short, donned a black slouch hat, and departed Pennsylvania Railroad Station for Toronto on November 24. He could no longer face the storm, and who could blame him?

THE VERDICT OF
COPENHAGEN

"If he has been a traveller, he certainly says
true, for he may lie by authority."
                    —*John Dryden*

On December 22, 1909, the world received news of the University of Copenhagen's decision. Arctic exploration had dominated front pages internationally since Cook's claim on September 2. The news from Copenhagen climaxed four months of excitement. In no period of history, before or since, has the world been gripped so intensely by Arctic events.

The university reported that it received two typewritten documents from Walter Lonsdale, Cook's secretary. The expedition report was identical to that printed in *The New York Herald* in September and October, and the typescript of Cook's journal did not contain "any original astronomical observations whatsoever, but only results." Furthermore, "the documents presented are inexcusably lacking in information which would prove that the astronomical observations therein referred to were really made; and also contains no details regarding the practical work of the expedition and the sledge journey which would enable the Committee to determine their reliability." The university's conclusions were not complicated: "The Committee therefore is of the opinion that the material transmitted for examinations contains no proof that Dr. Cook reached the Pole."[1]

In a more perfect world, the Cook affair would have ended at this point. The Danes were embarrassed by their role in the obvious deception, and several members of the committee went beyond the restrained language of the report to make this clear. No one had anything good to say about Cook. "The most flattering opinion expressed of him," according to a *Times* reporter, "is that he was an incredibly stupid bungler." Earlier, some Danes had been willing to believe that he suffered from a hallucination, but the data submitted disabused them.

The cock-and-bull story the embarrassed Walter Lonsdale issued in Copenhagen crowned the farcical nature of Cook's response. Lonsdale said he did not bring the original travel records because Cook feared that foes would steal them. It had been arranged that Cook would sail to Europe on another ship, and his wife on still another. Cook would then contact Lonsdale and arrange for him to meet Mrs. Cook, receive the diaries, and carry them to Copenhagen. All Lonsdale received was a noncommittal letter Cook sent from Marseilles with an enclosed message to the university's Dr. Carl Torp, asking that the final verdict be withheld until Cook gathered his instruments and other records from Etah.

Prof. Elis Stroemgren, the president of the committee, preferred to add nothing to the report, but Commander Gustav Holm, a member, asserted that "the whole of the record concerning the last stages of the alleged polar journey is so childish that nobody in any degree worthy of serious consideration as an explorer could possibly have submitted it." Holm noted a few material differences between the account submitted and the one originally published in the *Herald*; he found one change concerning Cook's position near the Pole "designedly obscure—in fact, scientifically unintelligible."

Knud Rasmussen, the great Danish polar expert who was destined to gain great fame after later expeditions, was not a member of the committee but had been asked to advise on technical details, dog handling, sledging, and the like. He had little to advise on. "The details of the sledging given by Cook fail to satisfy anybody with practical experience, but the report is full of absurdities which on their face are concoctions." Earlier Rasmussen had taken Cook at his word and praised his work publicly, so he now had reason to be chagrined by the data Cook submitted.

The Associated Press dispatch on the university's findings appeared in the *Times* and in other subscribing newspapers. "The report [of the University of Copenhagen] shatters completely, almost contemptuously the American explorer's title to such discovery, and fills the officials and people of Denmark with chagrin at the figure Denmark is made to assume in the eyes of the scientific world." According to the Associated Press, the public was prepared for a verdict of "not proved" but did not expect its recent hero to be "branded as an imposter." Many Danes, the Associated Press went on, believed that Cook acted in good faith but harbored a delusion.

On the surface this dispatch seems confusing. The university's report did not, in so many words, brand Cook as an imposter, but the press accounts implied that it did. This kind of journalistic reporting outraged Cook's partisans. They had reason to grumble at the press's failure to distinguish between the precise language of the report and its fuller implication, which was aptly interpreted by individual committee members and by consultants such as Rasmussen. All of Denmark and all the rest of the world understood the implication; the committee did not need to spell it out. Interpolating the obvious made no difference, then or now. Cook was finished; however, it was not because of a sensational press, but because his long-awaited evidence was farcical and because the surrounding circumstances—his disappearance, the delay in submitting, the claim of records arriving via Mrs. Cook and Lonsdale, and the last-minute call for a deferral of final judgment—compounded the farce. In the eyes of virtually everyone who considered the affair objectively, Cook *had* been branded as an imposter.

Apparently all that the Danes expected of Cook's presentation to the committee was that "he would at least supply some plausible data and supporting material which, while it might not suffice to establish his claim, would at any rate furnish some corroboration of his earlier statement." If only Cook had offered more, the committee could have saved Denmark's face. There would not have been an abrupt dismissal; instead the committee could have let Cook and the public down easily with polite, circumspect language, perhaps lauding him a bit for his tremendous travels and calling for specific evidentiary data, while claiming its inability to reach an ultimate decision. Instead the committee, shocked by Cook's evidence and by other tactics that suggested deception and disdain, shocked the nation and the world with a report so brief and definite as to be insulting in other circumstances. Then some members described their personal feelings to the press, and the press reported them, somewhat carelessly in some instances, but with absolute adherence to what these committee members believed. Cook was a fraud!

Professor Olafson, secretary of the Danish Geographical Society, which had honored Cook earlier, called the committee finding "the saddest event in my life." "As an explorer, there seems to be no doubt that Cook is absolutely unreliable."

An elaboration of Knud Rasmussen's views was carried by the Associated Press. "The University would not call me at first because I was one of Dr. Cook's strongest supporters." Later, he was invited and he realized the scandal. "My confidence in Cook had been based on personal impressions, on reports that I had received, and also on the testimony of the Eskimos when they all said that he had made the trip from Cape Sparbo to Etah, and such a trip during the dark of winter would suffice to make a man famous." What happened to Rasmussen's good regard? "The papers Cook sent . . . are almost impudent. No schoolboy could make such calculations. It is a most childish attempt at cheating. Cook has killed himself by his own foolish acts."

In London the news from Copenhagen was received with appreciation for its news value and with the sense that justice had been done: "'I told you so,' was the expression heard from the man in the street." London papers took sly digs at the original credulity of Danish scientists and noted that everywhere in Europe, excepting Denmark, Cook's claims had been discounted. Such captions as "WE HAVE BEEN HOAXED—DENMARK'S LAMENT OVER COOK'S RECORDS AND SAD AWAKENING" headed newspaper stories.

No anti-American sentiment marked British press reviews; in fact, the positive side of the story—its supposed vindication of Peary—received emphasis. The press reported that New Yorkers accepted the University of Copenhagen's decision and predicted that the result would be the same everywhere: "So ends what would seem to be one of the most audacious attempts upon record to obtain fame by false pretenses, an attempt which was the more disgraceful because its success would have deprived a heroic fellow-countryman of his hard-won laurels."

The London Daily Mail reminded readers of earlier expressions of disbelief in Cook: "We pointed out that never had such amazing distances been covered in so short a time in the whole history of polar exploration, and that many of the statements belonged to the realm of fantasy." Like the other papers, the *Daily Mail* saw the University of Copenhagen's decision as the final act: "So ends one of the greatest hoaxes in the annals of exploration." No one expected a Cook comeback; the world assumed that he would sink into obscurity.

Robert Scott, the Antarctic explorer who was soon to lead his party to their terrible, glorious deaths, indicated the general relief felt by those active in the exploration field. Such unseemly clamor as the Cook-Peary rivalry and the resulting slander discredited the entire enterprise. Scott knew something of rivalry too—a more muted, English kind of rivalry. When he said, "It is very satisfactory for the matter to be cleared up," we understand that he expressed the feeling of a gentleman who shuns the vulgarity of the American affair. Scott admitted that he had found Cook's original account unconvincing. Scott's rival, Sir Ernest Shackleton, was more circumspect: He refused to comment on the issue, as it was his rule to forbear criticism in polar matters.

After the news from Copenhagen, the public heard a few charitable comments. The American astronomer John N. Stockwell must be mentioned, even if he did not make much sense. Stockwell had been the first astronomer to point out the "fatal errors" in Cook's story, errors that revealed his abysmal ignorance. Stockwell believed that Cook's location of Annoatok did not tally with fact; Cook did not even know where his winter quarters were located, according to his recorded data. Thus Stockwell considered Cook to be confused, rather than willfully misleading. Cook traveled somewhere, and not knowing where, he assumed he had reached the Pole. "He is merely a mistaken enthusiast." Stockwell's conjecture overlooked all other signs of fraud, such as sledge distances and the like, and suggested that Cook's stupidity in risking a long journey over sea ice was even greater than his ignorance.

Cook's so-called ignorance amazed many individuals, and confused them, too. To divert criticism Cook needed to explain how he could find his location despite an inability to calculate it.

New York Times reporters wasted no time in soliciting the views of those who originally doubted or supported Cook. George W. Melville, a naval engineer and a veteran of the disastrous *Jeannette* expedition, had been one of the doubters, and his blunt comments were refreshing amidst all the others. He was not elated. Originally he had doubted Cook's capabilities. Now he would not discuss the question of whether Cook was himself deceived into believing he had reached the Pole. "It would be the charitable thing to do to suppose he was deceived." Melville had long since become disgusted with the controversy; people had badgered him on the streets about it, "stopping me to tell me what a fool I was." Some former friends actually fought with him over the issue. "Do you wonder I don't feel like talking about it?"

Roald Amundsen felt sorrow over the Danes' "crushing statement," for he appreciated Cook as a devoted friend and an honest man. "The important question now is whether he is a swindler, or merely ignorant." Amundsen believed that Cook thought he had reached the Pole. "This must have been a fixed idea with him. If he is swindling he must have changed his character in the past ten years." The *Times* did not comment on Amundsen's remarks, which it headlined "AMUNDSEN STANDS BY COOK," but they were not forgotten. Some years later Peary fans in America treated Amundsen shabbily when he repeated his kind words for Cook.

From Brussels, the head of Belgium's Royal Observatory expressed his astonishment and admitted having had confidence in Cook: "I have always found him honest and upright, but of course the observatory accepts the verdict of Copenhagen without question." He knew that Cook "was never very capable in making astronomical observations" and thought Cook either made a mistake or was an imposter. If the latter, it was audacious and unpardonable; at any rate, the observatory regarded the matter as closed and would probably invite Peary to lecture.

New York's aldermen, who had given Cook the Freedom of the City, revealed some aplomb. A resolution withdrawing the honor was rejected; one alderman said that New York had done no more honor than the Danes. Rescinding Cook's honor commanded no enthusiasm, and a Brooklyn alderman quipped that Cook was bigger now than he was before: "He's added two letters to his name. He used to be called Cook, now he's 'Cooked.'"

Harper and Brothers denied that Cook's book was forthcoming on their list. A tentative arrangement had been canceled by mutual consent.

Not a few newspaper writers saw the humor of the situation. "And what a magnificent liar he was!" crowed *The New York World*. "Hailed by half the civilized world, welcomed by a king, greeted with an arch of triumph in his home city, mobbed by cheering thousands, he was indeed one of the most audacious and memorable imposters in the annals of science."

Even *The New York Times* set a light tone in some comments. "Who could forget the picture of Dr. Cook sitting at a royal banquet between Queen Louise and Princess Ingeborg, regaling them with stories of the dash to the Pole and afterwards telling the royal children diverting stories of hairbreadth 'scapes?" Rich memories indeed. "Who could forget the bestowal of the gold medal of the Royal Danish Geographical Society or the ostentatious gift of the Freedom of the City of New York?"

On the whole, however, whatever guffawing rang through city news-rooms, editors adhered to a line of dismay, and even sympathy in some instances. *The New York World* suggested that Cook may be "one more in the long list of men who have fallen prey to hallucinations of their own greatness." *The New York Sun* commented similarly: "Cook was too hastily acclaimed as the discoverer of the North Pole. Let us not be too hasty in acclaiming him the prince of imposters. . . . Insane delusions are caricatures of the time and place where they are developed."

Cook's most persistent champion, *The Springfield Republican,* admitted that his box of proofs for the University of Copenhagen "might about as well have been filled with sawdust," yet it maintained that Peary's friends should not insist that the case was closed or brand Cook "as the greatest imposter of all history." Somewhat startlingly, the paper said that word of Cook's suicide would end questions of his imposture, but would leave other questions unresolved. Why did Cook present so meager a case when a better one could be easily trumped up? And how was he able to describe conditions at the Pole so exactly? The *Republican* insisted that the case remain open "until further developments in satisfactory explanation of these strange features have appeared."

Generally, the press did not hesitate to declare Dr. Cook an imposter and a swindler, using such epithets as "intrepid liar," "monumental faker," "master of duplicity," and other denunciatory terms.

Some papers stressed Cook's wrong to his nation, others stressed his wrong to Peary, and still others considered both equally. *The Newark Evening News* recalled that the nation had trusted him and had been shamefully wronged: "The popular decision must be that he is a faker of colossal assurance."

The Washington Times sorrowed at the thought that "the huge fake will inevitably be set down by many people as characteristically an American bluff."

And *The Philadelphia Press* set Cook down as "a conman, long-continued fabricator, fabricating for sheer vanity, and worse, to deprive another man of the honor nobly won and justly his due. . . . It is a blistering fact, not easily put aside, that an American was guilty of this double dishonor of his own falsehood and his attempt to filch by this falsification the honors of another."

"His flight was a confession," said *The New York American.* Cook had "nothing left to live for."

Money was Cook's object, stated several papers, and estimates of his gain over a few weeks of acclaim reached a figure of $100,000.

The New York Times, which was not then among the circulation leaders in New York, became leader of the field in polar stories for the three-month period and made a mighty surge forward in popularity for its reports. It may be that the *Times* gained more from the great dispute than any individual, but its editors wanted Peary to gain too: "Imposture has met its doom, merit should have its full reward." *The Brooklyn Eagle* also stressed the terrible damage done to Peary.

A few American newspapers knocked the Danes, especially in response to a Danish editorial urging Denmark to wash its hands of the matter in these words: "Our country must now leave this sad affair to America and Cook." Not so fast, cried *The Philadelphia Ledger.* "Until they have made amends to Peary for the wrong they helped inflict on him the Danes have by no means fulfilled their whole duty in this matter." Sternly *The New York Evening Post* pointed out that "the fact that determined the whole subsequent history of the case" was the University of Copenhagen's conferring of honors on Cook after a mere two-hour examination.

The New York Herald argued that the University of Copenhagen's decision meant only what it said: It was a verdict of "not proven" rather than "guilty." Of course the *Herald* had invested in Cook's story and had good reason to reject the clear implications of the university's report. In part the *Herald* had built fame and circulation on exploration enterprises; this time Bennett had backed a loser. So the *Herald* scoffed at newspapers that labeled Cook fraudulent on the basis of the university of Copenhagen's report, but that paper did not campaign further for Cook.

Thus was the verdict of Copenhagen greeted in the press. Apparently Cook was finished as a plausible public figure.

PEARY'S CAMPAIGN

*"Be thou as chaste as ice, as pure as snow,
thou shalt not escape calumny."*
— *William Shakespeare*

After the University of Copenhagen's decision, Cook moved off center stage. In 1910 Americans could turn to other matters: Charlie Chaplin was amusing New Yorkers with his vaudeville act; the Senate passed enabling bills allowing Arizona and New Mexico to form state governments; Teddy Roosevelt proclaimed his Square Deal; in April, intense cold destroyed crops in the Midwest; and in May, Halley's comet passed without the dire results that had been predicted.

Peary emerged from the shadows of the controversy and delivered lectures to appreciative audiences. At a gala "national testimonial" ceremony in the Metropolitan Opera House, his wealthy fans presented him with a $10,000 purse. London's Royal Geographical Society, the Chicago Geographical Society, the National Geographical Society, and other prestigious European and American groups awarded Peary gold medals and other honors.

Reports of Cook's whereabouts surfaced occasionally, but he remained silent. Peary could not forbear mention of Cook in his *Hampton*'s articles and in his lectures, describing how he guarded Cook's supplies for him and protesting that Cook plagiarized from Peary's earlier book. The magazine *Fourth Estate* praised *The New York Times* for exposing Cook. A simmering interest in the polar controversy remained, but other events surpassed it

135

in the public's attention. For most people the matter had been settled: Cook was a fraud and better forgotten; Peary had won the Pole.

While Peary and his partisans later complained that criticisms of him continued even after Cook's thorough exposure as a fraud and Peary's vindication by the National Geographic Society, his own ambitions kept the issue in public prominence. Whether driven by the need for official honors or by a Navy man's natural drive for promotion, Peary opened a new campaign in 1910. He wanted a promotion to rear admiral on the retired list and rallied his friends to the cause. His drive to secure this advancement gave his foes a prime opportunity to savage him, and the assaults hurt him deeply. It is too bad that his good friends did not advise him against the promotion struggle; but they were jealous for his honors as he was himself, and perhaps they could not foresee the consequences.

In February 1910, Senator Frederick Hale (R) of Maine, Peary's home state, introduced a promotion bill that passed unanimously in the United States Senate. The House of Representatives did not choose to act so hurriedly, and a similar bill was referred to a subcommittee of the House Naval Affairs Committee. At once, Peary faced trouble. Congress is a forum for public debate, and Peary had thrust his record before that disputatious body. Peary knew that Cook's partisans would continue to attack him, and must have anticipated some opposition by the Navy. Naval opposition was the more formidable obstacle, and it had nothing to do with the North Pole. Traditionally, high rank in the United States Navy went to line officers, those who commanded ships and fleet units. Peary's rating as a civil engineer left him well outside the prestigious circle of deck officers who competed for the top brass ratings. The shift from windpower to steam power had opened up the higher ranks to some extent, and Peary was promoted from commander to captain in 1910 on the basis of seniority in the Civil Engineer Corps. But admirals were few, even admirals on the retired list, and Peary was demanding a good deal from the naval Establishment. After all, he had served the Navy far less than his personal aims. Precedent existed, however, in the earlier promotion of another polar explorer, George W. Melville, to rear admiral. However, Melville had served actively as a naval ship's engineer and had gained his laurels on the *Jeannette* expedition while serving in that capacity.

Peary enlisted Bridgman, Hubbard, and other influential friends in his campaign. He even retained a lobbyist in Congress to look after his interests. In October 1910, he told Bridgman of his promotion to captain, explaining that it occurred automatically because of the retirement of another engineer and that it had nothing to do with his Arctic work. "Note this," he urged Bridgman, "because papers, some ignorantly and some intentionally, are likely to say this is a reward and promotion for my Arctic work, and thus put many people in the way of believing that my friends need ask for nothing more for me."

Peary's correspondence over 1910–11 indicates how hard he lobbied for promotion. He left nothing to chance and provided his most powerful supporters with all the essential information, including the current list of rear admirals and a listing of members of the House Naval Affairs Committee. He identified the congressmen supporting him, opposing him, and those "whose sympathies should be enlisted." Peary warned about the hostility of Congressman Ernest Roberts, (R) Mass., in particular: "It is the line element that is in back of Roberts."[2]

But instead of pursuing his promotion quest, Peary might have devoted more attention to the preparation of his polar narratives. A carefully produced narrative was essential to his cause in the long run, since any inconsistency or any weakness in recording his voyage in permanent book form could be the basis of an attack by opponents. Although Peary recognized this, he was disinclined to pass up his leisure and other affairs, including lecture opportunities and appearances before the geographical societies of Europe and America. And his schedule was made heavier by commercial concerns, including the design and patenting of a fur coat that would be marketed under his name. Something had to give way, and it turned out to be his *Hampton's* narrative, which was largely ghostwritten, and his book. His publisher suggested a ghostwriter, A. E. Thomas, for the book, and Peary agreed. Thomas was a professional writer and a good one, but he had to work for the most part with the *Hampton's* articles that writer Elsa Pedersen had composed.

The utilization of a ghostwriter was neither unusual nor unethical, but it involved the risks of loss of clarity and consistency. Peary's devoted biographer William Hobbs found *The North Pole* a literary classic and quoted Peary's half-truth that the book occupied him for a year: "In longitude the manuscripts and proof covered the distance between St. Louis and Budapest, Hungary; in latitude . . . just between Maine and Rome. . . . It has been planned and written in hotels, on trains and street cars and taxi-cabs even, on steamers and everywhere and anywhere I might find a few spare hours or minutes during the last year. Of necessity I had to make constant use of dictation."[3] Actually Peary did little work on the magazine articles beyond turning over some records to Miss Pedersen. However, he did correct proofs on the articles and the book.

Hobbs insisted that discrepancies did not mar the text, although journal dates were omitted, and claimed that "there is . . . no difficulty in supplying the lacunae when the serial narrative is used."[4] Others have found difficulties, even when they supplemented the text with the published magazine articles that were Peary's initial narrative.

Peary's letters to his book publisher reveal that he anticipated some perils in using a ghostwriter. "Thomas' work must be entirely confidential," he wrote to Frederick Stokes. Let him start working on the first three *Hampton's* articles "according to your ideas," then "forward each chapter as blocked out to me." Five months later he exorted Stokes to "have someone not concerned with typos, etc. go through the text looking for apparent discrepancies, lack of correlation in sequence of narrative, lack of clearness, etc." Peary knew what was necessary: "Someone who could put himself in the place of a critic, anxious to prove Peary a liar out of his own mouth."[5]

Well, critics anxious to prove him a liar out of his own mouth existed, and Peary asked the impossible in expecting a ghostwriter to relate his story in a manner defying close scrutiny. Aside from reading the galley proofs, meeting with Thomas a few times, and providing him with the articles and perhaps the diaries, Peary contributed little toward the book. For its failure as an historical document, he alone could be blamed.

Meanwhile Peary tried to map a cohesive campaign for his promotion struggle. He warned his supporters that congressional apathy—a reflection of legislators' selfish concern for their own political welfare—would be the chief obstacle. Ranking next in significance was the opposition of the line officers and their friends, opposition he saw as vicious, thorough, and forewarned. Next in importance was Cook-generated feeling, and, finally, fiscal conservatism.

When the House subcommittee refused to pass a promotion bill, the unsavory wrangling began in earnest. The affront stung and embittered Peary and his backers. Even General Adolphus Greely, no friend of Peary's, expressed his chagrin at the House's ingratitude. *The New York Times* editorialized in Peary's favor repeatedly in February and March, but the House adjourned without passing the Peary bill. Peary voyaged to Europe and the honors awaiting him there, reflecting bitterly on the opposition at home. He had not given up on the promotion and returned in plenty of time to campaign during the next session of Congress. In March, 1911 the House passed the Peary bill by a large majority.

Meanwhile there were other events. A fresh Cook scandal was revealed in May when Charles H. Townsend, director of the New York Aquarium, accused Cook of passing off a Yahgan dictionary as his own work. On his 1899 Antarctic expedition Cook had agreed to publish the life's work of Thomas Bridges, a Tierra del Fuego missionary. Bridges died, and years later the Belgian publication of the dictionary showed Cook, a "Doctor of Anthropology," as author, while merely acknowledging the missionary as "instrumental in collecting the words." It was another case of fraud, but not one of interest in 1910. Even the vigilant, pro-Peary *New York Times* gave the story only one day's middle-page coverage.

In the spring of 1910, Mount McKinley was in the news because of three expeditions to the mountain. One of them, the Sourdough Expedition, achieved success. This little-heralded venture came about as some of the boys passed the winter of 1909–10 sitting in Bill McPhee's saloon in Fairbanks, Alaska, speculating on Cook's alleged climb of Mount McKinley four years earlier. The sourdoughs doubted the New York doctor had done it, and figured it would be a good thing if a group of hearty Fairbanks mining men took on the job. The genial McPhee put up $500, and in the spring of 1910 the party headed south for the great mountain.

They lacked proper equipment and clothing, but they were lucky in finding the best approach by way of the Muldrow Glacier, For days they toiled up the glacier, hacking steps, bridging crevasses, until they reached the glacier's head at 11,000 feet. Tom Lloyd quit. Three men remained in the party at this time: Pete Anderson, Billy Taylor, and Charley McGonagall. On April 10, when the weather broke favorably, they pushed on. McGonagall quit. The remaining two men went on, reached the summit, planting a spruce pole from which an American flag fluttered bravely in the wind. Dragging the 14-foot spruce pole with them was a measure of their strength and doggedness. It was their hope that the flag might be spotted by telescope from Fairbanks, where their friends waited expectantly. Perhaps it was with Fairbanks viewers in mind that they chose the north summit rather than the south summit, which is 50 feet higher. So, as heroic as their feat was, they did not gain credit for the first triumph over Mount McKinley. Not that they minded; they accomplished what they set out for and professed no interest in writing or lecturing about their adventure. In fact, some Alaskans doubted their story until Archdeacon Hudson Stuck and Walter Harper ascended the south summit in 1913 and saw the sourdoughs' flagpole opposite them.

Although the sourdoughs proved Mount McKinley could be climbed, the Mazama Club's 1910 expedition indicated that Cook's account and route were unreliable, while the Explorers Club's attempt of the same season did not accomplish anything conclusive. Unlike the Explorers Club expedition of Parker and Browne, the expedition of the Mazama Mountaineering Club of Oregon hoped to confirm Cook's claim. Mazama Club members were helped by financing from *The New York Herald, The Portland Oregonia,* and *The Pacific Monthly,* and led by C. E. Rusk, who determined to follow Cook's route and show that the summit could have been reached.

Following the route Cook described, Rusk reached a place on the Ruth Glacier where the Cook map made no sense. Where Cook's map showed the Ruth Glacier flowing in from the east and northwest, the glacier actually made a sharp turn flowing in from the west, close under Mount McKinley's sheer south wall. Instead of a climbable glacier, Rusk saw a hopelessly tangled knot of high mountains. As the Mount McKinley historian Terris Moore put it, "Cook's 1907 map abruptly departs from reasonable accuracy into complete fantasy."[7]

Rusk could see no possible alternate way to climb Mount McKinley from a point 9 miles from the summit, which was still 14,000 feet above them. At this the Mazama Club party were forced to give up. They had taken photographs along the way, not of the "summit" Parker and Browne subsequently discovered, but of other mountains whose heights and locations were falsely placed by Cook. Among the Mazama Club party the disenchantment with Cook was thorough.

Rusk published his narrative in *The Pacific Monthly* in January 1911 and regretted that he had not been able to vindicate Cook's claim. He praised Cook's reputation for courage and as an all-around good mountaineering fellow and did not doubt that had Cook persevered he eventually might have been able to climb Mount McKinley. Cook had pioneered the Susitna and Chulitna river routes as entries to the mountain and had braved the Ruth Glacier with one companion. As Rusk gazed upon the forbidding crags of the great mountain from far up the Ruth Glacier at the point of farthest advance of his party—and, presumably, of Cook's—he realized that it would require perhaps weeks or months more to explore a route to the summit. "We realized how utterly impossible and absurd was the story of this man who, carrying a single pack, claims to have started from the Tokositna on the eighth of September, and to have stood on the highest point of McKinley on the sixteenth of the same month." Such a feat was inconceivable. It was not a situation in which two men of remarkable powers might accomplish what lesser individuals could not achieve. "The man does not live who can perform such a feat," wrote Rusk in 1911, and his statement has not been disproved by achievements since that time.[8]

Thus, sadly, Rusk had to join the Cook doubters. This informal group was composed of men who had tried hard to sustain Cook and, accordingly, suffered personal disappointments exceeding those of ordinary newspaper readers. Men like Rusk did not laugh about the matter; the immensity of Cook's fraud hurt them. Rusk called for understanding: "Let us draw the mantle of charity around him and believe, if we can, that there is a thread of insanity running through the woof of his brilliant mind. . . . If he is mentally unbalanced, he is entitled to the pity of mankind. If he is not, there is no corner of the earth where he can hide from the past."[9]

When Cook later discussed Mount McKinley in his book *My Attainment of the Pole,* he made no mention of the Mazama Club's climb.

On December 22, thirteen months after his disappearance, Frederick Cook reappeared in New York. Rested, healthy, and determined, he was far from the shaken wreck he had become before disappearing. He planned to emerge with suitable fanfare and profit—something over $4,000—for a series of articles.

The publisher of *Hampton's* was eager for Cook's story. Circulation was down and the magazine was fading. Paying $50,000 for Peary's polar articles had not given the hoped-for impetus, but the publisher figured that Cook's story might create a sensation.

The editor of *Hampton's* knew what he wanted. According to Cook, the editor told him that he must confess his fraudulent claims and explain how he was driven into hiding. Cook saw no merit in this proposal; he wanted to reiterate his claims and defend his reputation. After negotiations in London, Quebec, and Troy, N.Y., carried on after Cook voyaged from Europe incognito in October to avoid the press, it should have been obvious to *Hampton's* that Cook was unrelenting. The editor hinted that a plea of temporary insanity would do the trick, but Cook was adamant. All Cook was willing to confess was the possibility of missing the precise spot of the Pole by a little distance, due to imprecise navigation instruments.

Obviously Cook's story was useless unless the editor could tease it up in some manner, and he decided that he could do so without destroying Cook's basic claim to veracity. Accordingly, the publisher asked for the story and scheduled its publication date, and Cook returned openly to New York.

Hampton's released portions of the story to the newspapers to stir interest. Cook's arrival in New York did make some news. And the *Hampton's* story, which began in January 1911, drew attention, too, but did not create the profitable sensation the editor hoped for. Although the cover billed the articles as a "confession," they were no such thing. Some weasel words added to Cook's text by the editor implied that he might have been confused about what he had really accomplished, but this was intended to tease readers without retreating from Cook's position. As publication proved, *Hampton's* did not have much of a story. Not even a direct confession would have caused a sensation. Neither a recantation nor an affirmation was news of far-reaching interest.

Cook may have been disappointed that the articles did not produce great sympathy, but he did not give up. Perhaps by less dramatic and patient means he could reverse public opinion. He began lecturing again, and prepared what he considered his ultimate defense, the narrative of his journey, *My Attainment of the Pole,* which appeared in December 1911.

Dr. Frederick Cook in 1909

PROF. PARKER LAYS BARE MT. M'KINLEY FAKE OF DR. COOK

Makes a Duplicate Photograph of His Famous "Top of the Continent" at an Elevation of Only 5,000 Feet and Twenty Miles Away From the Base of the Giant Alaskan Peak.

EXPOSURE BY EDWARD BARRILL IS COMPLETELY CORROBORATED

With Map Made by Former Guide and Dr. Cook's Own Photograph Noted Explorer and Mountain Climber Has No Trouble in Locating the Spot.

Indisputable evidence of the falsity of Dr. Frederick A. Cook's claim to having ascended to the top of Mt. McKinley, the highest peak in North America, is furnished by Prof. Herschel C. Parker of Columbia University, who has just returned to New York City from his latest trip to Alaska. Prof. Parker undertook the journey during the past summer to settle once and for all time the question of Dr. Cook's veracity as to the Mt. McKinley episode, and the proofs he has brought back with him show beyond a shadow of a doubt that the man who failed miserably in his attempt to rob Captain Robert E. Peary of the credit of having discovered the North Pole was twenty miles away in an air line from the "Top of the Continent" at the time he claims to have stood on the utmost height of the snow-capped peak.

The most important piece of evidence obtained by Prof. Parker, and which not even the most ardent supporter of Dr. Cook can question, if there be any left who still believe in him, is a duplicate photograph of Dr. Cook's "Top of the Continent," or, as he was pleased also to term it, the Ultima Thule of his ambition. The Globe presents in another column a reproduction of this photograph taken by Prof. Parker, together with the one Dr. Cook, as he says in his book, "To the Top of the Continent," took "of Barrill, with the flag lashed to his axe, as the Arctic air froze the impression into a relief which no words can tell." The most cursory examination of the two pictures will show that they are photographs of the same rock, while a tracing of the outlines of each leaves no doubt of it.

New York Evening Telegram
account alleging Mt.
McKinley fraud.
September 8, 1909

Cook's summit photogra

Belmore Browne's photograph of
the "fake peak" taken in 1910

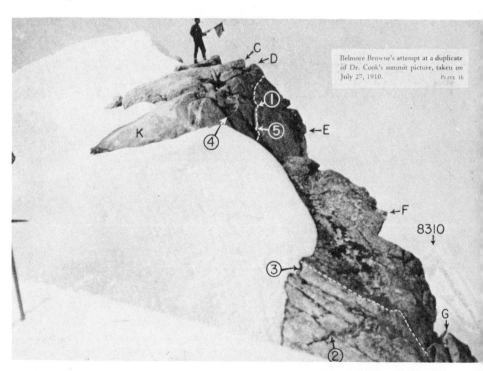

Bradford Washburn's picture of the upper part of the "Fake Peak," taken in August 1956—enlarged from a part of a photograph taken at a considerable distance. PLATE 1c

Bradford Washburn's photograph of the "fake peak" taken in 1956

ams Carter's photograph of the same peak taken in 1957

Adams Carter's picture of the top of the "Fake Peak" taken in August 1957 from the top of a pole, closely approximating the positions occupied by Cook and Browne when they took their photographs a half century ago. PLATE 1d

Title page of a Peary Arctic Club brochure

PEARY
ARCTIC CLUB

ROBERT E. PEARY, C.E., U.S.N.

THE WHITE HOUSE,
Washington, May 26, 1905.

I wish I could be present to bid good-bye and god-speed to Commander Peary and to express in behalf of the American people not only my appreciation of what he is doing, but my appreciation of the action of those men who, headed by Mr. Morris K. Jesup, have enabled him to undertake this work. We have a right as Americans to be proud of the courage, energy, and hardihood Commander Peary has shown, no less than of the wise generosity of those who have stood behind him.

With all good wishes believe me,

Faithfully yours,

THEODORE ROOSEVELT.

Peary's ship, the *Roosevelt*, from the same brochure

Peary to Tell Contemporary Club of His Dashes to the North Pole

Arctic Explorer Says He Will Succeed, Despite Brooklyn Rival.

HE DENOUNCES A "TRICK"

Declares Dr. Cook Has Engaged Quietly Supply of Dogs and Esquimaux.

Arctic Explorer Peary, the man who fears not cold, hardship or hunger in his determination to reach the North Pole, and who will be a guest of the Contemporary Club Wednesday night at Hotel Jefferson, is undaunted at the report that his rival for frigid honors, Dr. Frederick A. Cook of Brooklyn, has stolen a march and cornered the available supply of dogs and Esquimaux in the polar regions.

"Nothing Dr. Cook has done or can do will delay my trip in an endeavor to push farther northward than I have already been," said Commander Peary, in a recent interview in Washington. "I expect to reach the Pole this time.

"Dr. Cook's plan to reach the Pole is fantastic," said Peary. "No geographer need be told that the route which Cook proposes in his letters is impracticable and I do not think the expedition should be taken too seriously.

"I do not think most men would approve of the way he left on his trip—going off subrosa for the admitted purpose of stealing a march on me and utilizing the dogs and Esquimaux of the region. However, Cook's plans will in no way interfere with me. My dogs and Esquimaux I have hired for years from the same tribe in the whale lands, and they will be ready for me whenever I am ready for them. I expect to start in July and shall equip the ship 'Roosevelt' for a three years' trip, although I do not expect to be gone more than 16 months.

"I expect to reach the Central Polar

LIEUT. PEARY.

Sea, 500 miles from the pole, in September. In February the trip on sledges will begin. I shall take soundings on the way and collect specimens of birds, animals and fish."

Peary will have practically the same officers and crew on this trip as on the previous one, which ended 174 miles from the pole. The Peary Arctic Club of New York is backing Peary. Morris K. Jessup is president of the club. Peary is remarkably robust. He says he must remain young and strong until he has achieved the great object of his life.

"Then," he remarked, with a laugh, "I shall remain young because of the success I have achieved."

His lecture will be delivered following the banquet of the Contemporary Club. The talk will be illustrated with 60 lantern slides made by Peary, on his trips.

Peary announces his plans in January 1908. From the *New York World*.

First report of Cook's progress to the Pole

DR. COOK HEADED FOR NORTH POLE AND MAY REACH IT

Alone but for a Few Esquimaux, Explorer Starts on a 560-Mile Journey Over the Ice for the Long Sought Northern Apex of the Globe.

FIALA THINKS CHANCES OF SUCCESS ARE GOOD.

Noted Fellow Explorer Says We May Hear Next Summer that Cook Has Reached the Goal —Is Splendidly Equipped, and Friends Have No Fear for His Safety.

Dr. Frederick E. Cook, the Arctic explorer, is believed by Anthony Fiala to be close to the North Pole, if he has not already reached the target of many former expeditions.

No word has been heard from Dr. Cook since March 17 last. He was then on the Polar ice north of Cape Thomas Hubbard, about 560 miles from the Pole. He was the only white man, with several Esquimaux and a big equipment of dogs, sleds and supplies. When he wrote then he was on the eve of making a das...

FIALA THINKS DR. COOK MAY REACH THE POLE.

By Anthony Fiala, Arctic Explorer.

It is very good news the letter brings from Dr. Cook. It gives us a thrill of interest to know that he was on March 17, on the Polar ice north of Cape Hubbard and on his way to the Pole.

If Cape Hubbard is where I suppose it to be, about 560 miles from the Pole, and a good part of the journey is over level ice, he may cover the distance, and more, if he has a spell of good weather. We may receive word of his successful reaching of his goal, and his return, by next summer.

Dr. Cook took plenty of supplies and is a splendid equipment. He and his Esquimaux companions should be able to make very good time...

Anthony Fiala

WOULD PUT POLICE IN

Cook's Eskimo companions

Copy of ards in Tube
Apr. 21, 1908 at the North Pole
Accompanied by the Eskimos boys
Ahwelah and Etukishook I reached of
noon to-day 90°, a spot on the pole
Star 520 miles N. of Svartevoeg.
we were 35 days enroute. hope to
return to-morrow on a line slightly
west of the arch around through
Nero land was discerned along
the 102-m. between 84 & 85°. The
ice proved fairly good with few
open leads, hard snow and little
pressing trouble.
We are in good health and have
food for 40 days This with the meat
of the dogs to be sacrificed will
keep us alive for 50 or 60 days
The water is deposited with
a small am. flag in a metalic
tube on the drifting ice.
It return will be appreciated
to the International Bureau of
Polar Research at the
Royal observatory Uccle Belgium
Frederick A. Cook

Cook's diary at the Pole

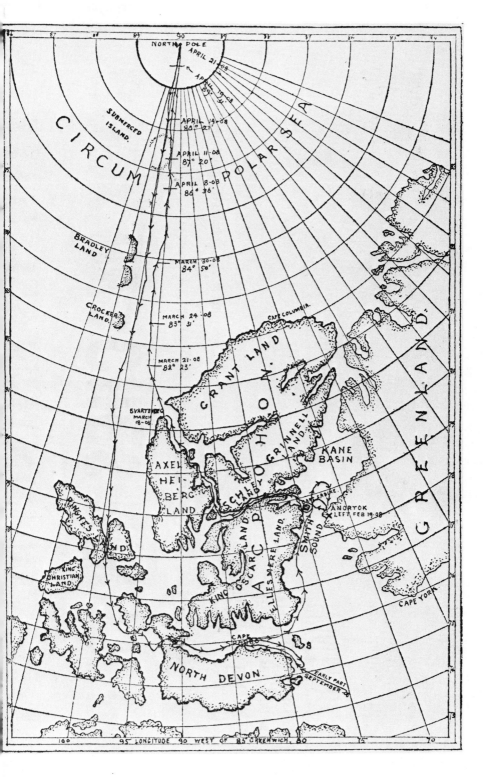

Cook's map of his polar journey

HOME EDITION

VOL. LXXIII. NO. 209.

Fair, cooler.

THE EVENING MAIL

NEW YORK, WEDNESDAY, SEPTEMBER 1, 1909.

HOME EDITION

ONE CENT.

DR. COOK REACHES NORTH POLE

Cook's photograph of his companions at the Pole

News of Cook's success was worth an "Extra."

EXTRA

GOAL LONG COVETED BY WORLD'S EXPLORERS WON FINALLY BY AMERICAN

Dispatch Received at the Danish Colonial Office from Lervik, Norway, Says Cook Accomplished His Great Feat, More Than a Year Ago, on April 21, 1908.

Copenhagen, Sept. 1.—Dr. Cook, the American explorer, reached the north pole April 21, 1908, according to a telegram just received at the Colonial office here.

Peary's announcement

VOL. L. NO. 17,540.

The World

"Circulation Books Open to All."   "Circulation Books Open to All."

NEW YORK, TUESDAY, SEPTEMBER 7, 1909.   PRICE: ONE CENT

NURSE'S HURRIED TO HARRIMAN, WHO SUFFERS RELAPSE.

His Physician, Who Admits that His Patient Has Had a "Sharp Attack of Indigestion," Replies to Inquirers at the Home on Tower Hill that "We Hope for the Best."

TWO NEW YORK SURGEONS SAID TO BE WITH HARRIMAN.

Dr. Lyle Refuses Either to Confirm or Deny the Report, and Talk of an Operation Is Renewed—Examined Recently by Cancer Specialists—The Daughters Give Up Outing.

HOW PEARY TRAVELLED TO THE POLE BY DIFFERENT ROUTE FROM COOK.

PEARY HAS FOUND THE POLE.
HE ANNOUNCES IN TRIUMPH.
'HAVE MADE GOOD AT LAST.'

In a Message to His Wife, Who Frequently Shared His Arctic Perils In the Past, American Explorer Announces: " I Have the Pole."—Another Despatch Tells the Safety of His Ship and Me

"STARS AND STRIPES NAILED" TO IT, HE EXULTINGLY WIR

Date of Discovery Is Fixed by Another Telegra as April 6 of This Year—Dr. Cook S He Is Glad of Rival's Success Addir "There Is No One Living Whom I Wo Prefer to the Brave Peary to Follow N Footsteps."—Peary's Message Alm Universally Credited.

Commander Robert E. Peary, U. S. N., reached the North Pol
April 6, 1909.

After repeated attempts, after most careful preparations for
largest, his successful expedition, this fine American attains the goal m
has compass scientific adventures of every nature to graves in the e
ipeding for.

Having arrived at the top of the earth and the summit of its a
ition, Peary's thoughts turned not to the glory, the acclaim, that il w
him, but to home, to his wife, who has shared some of the danger
has passed.

First Message to His Wife.
Peary cabled to his wife, who is at Eagle Island, near South H
well, Me., yesterday

Indian Harbor, via Cape Ray, Sept. 6, 1902.

PEARY FOUND NO TRACE OF DR. COOK'S FOOTSTEPS.

Capt. Bartlett of the Roosevelt Brings News of Explorer's Failure to Discover Signs of Having Been Preceded by a Rival in the Arctic.

ROBERT E. PEARY, AFTER 23
ADDS "THE BIG NAIL" TO
DR. COOK TO SUBMIT

ROBERT E. PEARY AND MRS PEARY ON BOARD THE HERALD
DESPATCH BOAT OWLET JUST BEFORE HIS DEPARTURE FOR
THE NORTH.

E. H. HARRIMAN SUFFERS RELAPSE

Dr. Lyle, Admitting Change, Says There Is No Cause for Alarm.

NURSE HASTILY CALLED

SAVES GIRL FROM CHINATOWN LURE

Louise Elbert Walks Into Trap When Comfortable Home Is Promised to Her.

IS TAKEN INTO A DEN

Met at Ferry by Woman Whose Letter to Florence Crittenden Herne in Newark Brings Her Here.

ROBERT
FROM "NEAREST THE

Peary claims the Pole.

SIEGE, REACHES NORTH POLE;
EW YORK YACHT CLUB'S TROPHIES
RDS TO UNIVERSITY OF DENMARK

THE ROOSEVELT LEAVING NEW YORK HARBOR.

MISS MARIE A. PEARY, DAUGHTER OF ROBERT E. PEARY.

ROBERT E. PEARY, JR., WITH THE ROOSEVELT'S MASCOT

CAPTAIN "BOB" BARTLETT OF THE ROOSEVELT

Attains Highest Point on April 6, 1909, Year After Dr. Cook's Discovery

Sends First News of His Achievement from Indian Harbor via Cape Ray, on Newfoundland Coast.

FILES MESSAGES OF SUCCESS, THEN

PEARY'S CHARGE
FIND POLE WIL

SCORES SEE MAN
IN LEAP FROM
BROOKLYN SPAN

Jumps Off Swiftly Moving Car and Plunges from Bridge Rail to River.

PICKED UP UNCONSCIOUS BY PASSING TUG

Is Hurried to Shore in Craft and Taken to Brooklyn Hospital.

DIVER   MADE   A   PRISONER

Unidentified by Authorities, Who Are Puzzled to Find Solution for Act.

Jumping from a swiftly moving street car and mounting the high guard rail of the Brooklyn Bridge, an unidentified man this afternoon dove into the East River while scores of passengers on several cars looked on and shouted.

The man was picked up by a passing tug and taken to the Brooklyn shore. He was unconscious and an ambulance hurried him to the Brooklyn Hospital, where he is a prisoner.

The man got on an open Flatbush avenue car near the Borough Hall, in Brooklyn. He occupied a seat in the middle of the car, and all during the trip busied himself

OFFERS LIFE
FOR BABY IN
THIEF FIGHT

Mrs. Vogel Dying from Fractured Skull After Battle in Bedroom with Armed Intruder.

CHILD'S CRIES BRING HELP, BUT TOO LATE

Baker's Wife Victim of Desperado Who Was After Supposititious Savings of Couple.

MAN USED BLACKJACK.

Fells Woman and Attempts to Strangle Baby as It Cries "Mamma."

Alone with her two-and-one-half-year-old son, Samuel, in her apartment on the third floor of No. 325 East 100th

Says W
of C

Mrs. R. T. Davidson, Her Frie Says Explorer's Wife Has th Necessary Records.

Nerved by her quick understanding the issues in the momentous controv raging about her husband, as the dis erer of the North Pole, Mrs. Frede A. Cook, wife of the explorer, decl without any reservation whatever to that she had received detailed acco from Dr. Cook which would set at all doubts as to his dash to the Pole they were made public.

"There is not the slightest doubt Dr. Cook will be able to produce a lute proof of his discovery of the N Pole when he gets back to the Un States," declared Mrs. Cook.

This statement was given out by Cook through her close friend, Mrs. R Davidson, of No. 833 Bushwick ave Brooklyn. Although Mrs. Cook is kn to be in this city, having arrived from Portland, Me., late last night her two children, she succeeded in kee her whereabouts from the public, and utmost efforts of newspaper men did succeed in locating her.

According to Mrs. Davidson, who of all of Mrs. Cook's friends knows w the explorer's wife is stopping, she is shopping, and wishes to be free for immediate present from the news set by newspaper men upon all the cipals in the great drama growing ou the discovery of the Pole.

It was expected, however, that Cook would be located during the and it was said that she might decid answer fully all questions put to her a her husband's exploit.

"Don't Worry About Dr. Cook," S Peary in Message to Wife.

SOUTH HARPSWELL, Maine, Wednesda Mrs. R. E. Peary received a second sage early to-day from Commander P stating that he had been delayed at dian Harbor and that she "need not w about Dr. Cook." Mrs. Peary did not out the exact wording of the message.

Mrs. Peary spent part of the da making preparations to start for Syc N. S., immediately upon receipt of fu direct advices from her husband.

Miss Marie Peary was kept busy be all day answering the minutes of pas steamers, yachts and tug boats. E craft possessing a whistle saluted a

Mrs. Cook denies Peary's charges.

g Telegram **FINAL NEWS**

..BER 8, 1909.—SIXTEEN PAGES.   PRICE ONE CENT.

T RIVAL DID NOT
LL, SAYS MRS. COOK

as Proof
Discovery

Wife of Brooklyn Explorer Declare: Recent Message Tells of Proof Absolutely to Substantiate Claim.

PEARY QUOTES ESKIMOS AS SAYING COOK WAS NOT OUT OF SIGHT OF LAND

Asserts Companions of Dr. Cook on Tri: Affirm He Went No Distance North.

REPORTS MEETING THE JEANIE RELIEF

Scientist Who Reached Copenhagen with Dr. Cool Takes Up Cudgels in Behalf of Latter.

MRS. MARION F. H. COOK

ESKIMOS' TESTIMONY FIRST GUN IN NORTH POLE CONTROVERSY

What Mr. Peary Says.

"I have nailed the stars and stripes to the North Pole. This is authoritative and correct.

"Cook's story should not be taken too seriously. The two Eskimos who accompanied him say he went no distance north and not out of sight of land.

"Other members of the tribe corroborate their story."

What Mrs. Rasmussen Says.

"My husband, who is in Greenland, was the first to congratulate Dr. Cook, and he listened to the testimony of the Eskimos, which is by no means negligible. They do not understand the use of instruments, but they know how to make observations of solar light."

"My husband does not doubt in any way Dr. Cook's veracity.

h were unfurled yesterday upon the tars and Stripes

rs except a few passing the sum——

thing except his of furs, and his pparel to Sydney the snow baby." "I don't like it." he distinction of d born north of w sixteen years tern High School,

s being longer dly called atten-d may be home th birthday next

child, had his sixth birthday a week ago Sunday.

Mr. Bridgman Sees Mrs. Peary on His Way to Meet Explorer.

PORTLAND, Me., Wednesday.—Mr. Herbert L. Bridgman, secretary of the Peary Arctic Club, who left New York last night for Sidney to meet Mr. Robert E. Peary upon his arrival there the latter part of this week, passed this forenoon in this city while waiting for the departure of the St. John express. He will reach Sidney tomorrow night. Owing to the receipt of news that the telegraph station at Chateau Bay had been discontinued and that Mr. Peary would be unable to wire this wife from there when to start for Sidney, Mrs. Peary was invited to join Mr. Bridgman.

Dr. Frederick A. Cook's claim to be the first to discover the North Pole is directly challenged by Mr. Robert E. Peary in despatches received from the latter here and in London to-day. Mrs. Peary, at Harpswell, Me. also received a message to-day from her husband telling her she need b-

Peary's Eskimo mistress and their child. A photograph Cook displayed in his lectures and his book, *My Attainment of the Pole*.

Hampton's Magazine with Cook's "confession" story. Cook did not confess.

HAMPTON'S
MAGAZIN[E]

Dr Cook's Confession.

"Did I get to the North Pole? * I confess that I do not know absolutely. * fully, freely and frankly I shall tell you everything."

Dr COOK'S OWN STORY IN THIS ISSUE

Roald Amundsen, the great Norwegian explorer, who discovered the South Pole in 1911. As late as 1926 he told the newspapers that he believed Cook's claims as plausible as Peary's.

IV

COMEBACK

OUT ON THE HUSTINGS

"Winning isn't everything, it's the only thing."
                        —Vince Lombardi

Cook stood quietly a moment looking out at his audience, then began to tell his familiar story. Lecturing provided his income and his opportunity for a comeback in public esteem from 1911 through 1916. He traveled all over the country during the lecture season, appearing in city auditoriums, chautauqua tents, and sometimes in three-a-day stints on vaudeville programs.

He began performances with a description of his Arctic travels, supported by lantern slides. After recounting the adventures he had experienced enroute to his triumph over the North Pole, he discussed the detractors who had conspired to deny him honors. Peary and the National Geographic Society received most of his scorn, although anyone who doubted him was fair game. At times, when the political mood seemed propitious, he knocked former President Teddy Roosevelt for publicly supporting Peary.

Usually he made four charges against his rival:

1. Peary stole Cook's food supplies at Annoatok with the deliberate intent of causing Cook's death by starvation;

2. Peary was guilty of immoral conduct with Eskimo women in the Arctic and left neglected children there whom he refused to acknowledge or support;

3. Peary and his backers bribed Barrill, Cook's Mount McKinley companion, to state that the ascent had not been made;

4. Peary's claim to the North Pole rested entirely upon the dictum of three National Geographic Society members who were shamefully anxious to accept Peary's inadequate records.

Cook performed during the peak era of America's infatuation with lectures as a medium for entertainment and self-improvement. His popularity benefited from the aggressive management of Fred High, the manager of one of the many chautauqua bureaus in the country. High realized the value of attacking Peary to stimulate interest, and placed articles in his magazine, *The Platform,* to titillate theater operators. High and his press agents also effectively disseminated Cook's sensational charges to local newspapers. It was some feat for Cook to maintain public interest, but he did have an exotic topic in polar exploration. Throughout the nation there were hundreds of communities where the polar controversy had not been overexposed, and they were willing to hear Cook's story.

As a lecturer Cook benefited from a personable manner, modest bearing, and a soft pleasing voice with the touch of a lisp. He did not rant and rave in strident, declamatory style to hold his auditors; rather he amused them with witty assaults on Peary's defenders. The National Geographic Society, which affirmed Peary's records, was "a scrub association," and the congressional subcommittee that approved Peary's promotion in 1911 was a group of "three scrub politicians in Washington, not one of whom had ever seen a piece of Arctic ice themselves."[1]

Cook mocked Peary for twenty-five years of "passing the hat" for expedition expenses, while accepting a government salary for duties he did not perform. And now that Peary had retired, he promoted a fur company, which, Cook said, gained Peary and his friends $1 million.

Here is a segment of Cook's lecture that gives a fair idea of his style.

For a year I have tried to treat Mr. Peary as a gentleman—since I was able to reach the Pole in 1908, I have been ready to credit Peary with the same success in 1909, but the unfair after-battle has now thoroughly convinced me that Peary has stooped to depths so low that he is forever deprived of a claim to manly manhood. I have therefore resolved to uncover the dark side of the polar campaign, and to open the eyes of my countrymen to a conspiracy which for injustice is not matched by anything in the history of the world. The problem is a very complex one, and can only be handled in sections.

What I will say tonight is a call and a challenge to Mr. Roosevelt and Mr. Peary, who, as a team have pulled together on a wagon freighted with pro-Peary lies and the loot of other men's credit.

Perhaps Roosevelt did not know the moral rotten-ness of the load which he helped to pull down the hill of degradation or up the slope of polar dishonor, but he should know, for he has been in the harness with Peary. A man is known by his companions. A horse is rated by its mates.

There is no charge of uncleanliness on Mr. Roosevelt. When alone he stands as a spotless white horse with traces taut in an effort to uplift mankind, but here he is cross-matched with a black animal, covered with leprous spots of immorality and I charge him to free himself from this dishonor.

Two months after the Pole was reached, Peary started for the Pole. His hat had gone the rounds of easy money for twenty years, the profits of a lucrative fur trade had gone into his pockets for a decade. All this was threatened by my polar efforts, and accordingly Cook must be discredited at all costs. Publicly I was accused of trying to steal Peary's route, his Pole, and his people. Mr. Roosevelt endorsed Peary, and therefore endorsed this accusation.

The map shows that I did not take the Peary route, and I did not take the Pole. I simply left my foot-prints there—now as to the people, here there is room for an argument.

The most Northern Eskimos belong to no one; they are under no flag; they are as free as the birds of the air, but Peary has there a legitimate claim upon two people. They are children and they are illegitimate. I did not take these hybrid children; they are today in the cheerless North, fatherless with unwiped tears on their cheeks, crying for bread and milk and the comforts required to protect white blood.

For twenty years, Peary has gone North at public expense, not so much to explore new lands, as to enjoy beyond the reach of the law, the privilege of a plurality of wives. The same privilege which is denied the Mormons of Utah. Peary gets that privilege, with the endorsement of Mr. Roosevelt, the consent of the Government, and the backing of the Navy.

Peary has taken money from the hands of our innocent school children. We have a right to ask the question "How much of our children's money has been expended to make Mr. Peary's arctic concubines comfortable." Let Mr. Roosevelt, the champion of domestic morals, explain.

The ship *Roosevelt,* flying the American flag, loaded with luxuries paid out of the public purse, entered Etah Harbor in August of 1908. My companion, Rudolph Franke, was then there. He was sick, starved and expected to die. He had tasted no civilized food for months. He had had no news from the world for a year. Of course the coming of a ship gave him cheer. He pulled himself together, boarded that ship, asked for a cup of coffee. In reply, he was put off the ship. A few days later, Peary learns that after all Franke, though ragged and sick, was not a beggar. He had furs and ivory worth ten thousand dollars. He was in charge of my house and supplies some distance North, which was worth twenty-five thousand dollars. With the eye of a thief and the heart of a hypocrite, Peary now invites Franke aboard, and by methods that would put a Buccaneer to shame, seized all of my belongings, and those of Franke. A man who would do that in a mining camp would be justly hung to the nearest tree. Let Mr. Roosevelt investigate this. His attention has been called to it before, but he has turned a deaf ear.

We next follow a campaign of bribery and conspiracy, ending in Washington, where Rear-Admiral Chester, Professor Gannett, and Professor Tittman barter their souls to Peary interests. I asked Mr. Roosevelt to investigate. The honor of the Government and that of the Navy is at stake. This is not an idle back-fire. I am ready to back up my charges with legal documents, with my money, and my fist if necessary.

Peary has proven himself a Buccaneer in the arctic, an assassin in the field of geographic honor. His murderous assault has left the stain of the blood of envy on the flag of Freedom. History will deal with Peary, the Explorer; but I call upon Mr. Roosevelt and manly men to quarantine Peary, the man, to the island of immoral contagion. His bearing on the polar problem is a leprous blot on the fabric of clean human endeavor.

I do not for one moment accuse Mr. Roosevelt of being responsible for the shame of Peary's infamy, but he is associated unconsciously with a band of bribers, conspirators and thieves of other men's victory. Roosevelt and his magazine have upheld this black hand movement.

Let Roosevelt and *The Outlook* and the Government and the Navy each and all free themselves of this entanglement.[2]

Aside from attacking Peary, Cook defended his own record. He related all the familiar testimonials, even those from explorers and others who had since rejected him, pointing to the purity of his motivation and the quality of his evidence. Little of what he told was new. As he said, it was all in *My Attainment of the Pole.* Touting the book in his lectures was a good argument and good business as well.

To attract interest, Cook called for a congressional investigation of the polar controversy and invited audiences to sign a petition.

People did respond to Cook. He held many auditors with the story of Peary's cruelty, relating how he faced starvation because Peary stole his supplies in Greenland. "As we came back to Greenland," he told his listeners, "we were half starved, almost unable to walk, really at death's door; and we looked around for something to eat. We had left there a camp in which we had packed away food enough for several years. That was our life-saving station; our very existence depended on that camp; but during our absence, during the time that our backs were turned, Mr. Peary came along and took that camp, took all of our food supplies and left us hopelessly stranded to starve. There Mr. Peary attempted a deliberate murder, for in taking our supplies he knew that he was trying to starve us out, and he was told so by his own men."[3]

In his book *My Attainment of the Pole,* Cook described his arrival in different terms: "So weak that we had to climb on hands and knees, we reached the top of an iceberg, and from there saw Annoatok. Natives, who had thought us long dead, rushed out to greet us. . . . The world now seemed brighter. The most potent factor in this change was food—and more food—a bath and another bath—and clean clothes. Mr. Whitney offered me unreservedly the hospitality of my own camp. He instructed Pritchard to prepare meal after meal of every possible dish that our empty stomachs had craved for a year. The Eskimo boys were invited to share it. Between meals, or perhaps we had better call meals courses (for it was a continuous all-night performance—interrupted by baths and breathing spells to prevent spasms of the jaws)—between courses, then, there were washes."[4]

Cook's indictment of Peary extended to strong hints that his rival ordered the murder of Ross Marvin. Marvin, a member of one of Peary's support parties on the polar dash, was lost on his return trip to the *Roosevelt.* His Eskimo companions reported that he fell through thin ice. Years later one of the Eskimos confessed to killing Marvin in a fit of anger. It was Cook's innuendo that Marvin's diary would show Peary had falsified his trek records, although Cook could not have known at his writing that Marvin's death was other than accidental.

On at least one occasion lecture guests protested, but like any experienced speaker Cook knew how to use the audience to overwhelm heckers. In July 1914 at Hamilton, Ohio, a listener stood to confront Cook's charge that Peary robbed his camp. Why did you not say this in your *Hampton's* article? he asked. Cook brushed off the questioner to the approbation of the audience, and a policeman conducted the offender out of the tent.

This proved too much for Allen Andrews, a local attorney, who rose to complain that Cook had solicited questions, then refused to answer. Pandemonium broke loose until the manager finally settled the crowd. Cook then castigated the local newspaper. Cook did not specify his complaint, but apparently the editor had told Cook's press agent that he would not walk across the street to hear Cook.

Andrews addressed a letter to the newspaper, insisting that his sympathies had been with Cook. He had even signed Cook's petition for a congressional investigation. But the lecture and Cook's handling of the ejected questioner upset him. "I cannot believe that the Congress of the United States, the convocation of scientists at Copenhagen, the National Geographic Society and the many men of science, and the press generally throughout the country, had united in a conspiracy to ruin Dr. Cook's reputation, as he stated from the platform." Nor did Andrews believe that Peary "is a thief and a murderer, as stated by Dr. Cook."[5]

As war threatened Europe in the summer of 1914, newspaper coverage of Cook's lectures indicated that his campaign was not prospering. Some papers joked that the early reports of war, assumed to be false, originated with Cook. "Doc Cook is on the other side and has captured a telegraph office." "Heavy firing was heard to the southwest this morning. It is believed to have been Dr. Cook making a general assault upon Fort Truth." A Saint Louis paper marveled at the easy money on the chautauqua circuit. "Even Dr. Cook can garner a princely salary by repeating his fairy story of the north pole." A Grand Rapids newspaper editor sneered at Cook's efforts to influence Congress. Detroit vaudeville audiences signed petitions, but only because "few people can refuse the temptation to sign something addressed to Congress. . . . Michigan does not support Cook." In Texas an editor deplored the reopening of Cook's case, observing that he "naturally has everything to gain, never recently having had anything but lecture receipts to lose." Nobody will give Cook a gold medal, "but really he ought to have a leather one for audacity. There isn't one man in ten million with such a cast iron nerve."[6]

Some papers accepted Cook and damned Peary, so Cook was not wasting his time lecturing. He was not able to reverse the public's decision against him, but he did keep the pot boiling and he earned a living.

CONSPIRACY!

"No retreat, no retreat,
They must conquer or die,
Who have no retreat."
    —*John Milton*

From innumerable lecterns, Cook proclaimed that a fair reading of his book would convince doubters of his integrity. His book, *My Attainment of the Pole,* appeared in 1911. Cook published and distributed the book himself and promoted it to lecture audiences. A second edition, published in 1913, indicated a total of 60,000 copies in print.

As an exploration narrative—one of the strangest in the literature—the book stands in a class by itself. It is more than a defense and justification of his polar claims; it includes thoroughly savage attacks on Peary, Peary's supporters, the press, and other challengers of Cook's exploration claims. As a rational achievement, the book holds together only if its guiding theory is convincing. The account of Cook's polar journey added nothing to either his newspaper articles or the University of Copenhagen's evidence that would induce anyone to change an earlier evaluation. Its value is not in its evidence, but rather in its exposition of a theory by which his downfall could be understood. His defense, beyond a repetition of his discredited "evidence," rested on a single theory: He was victimized by a conspiracy. The conspiracy explained everything. But for the conspiracy he would be an honored man. Because of it he stood as "the most shamefully abused man in the history of exploration."[1] He asked readers to appreciate that stinging rebukes and derision had always characterized exploration history because of its competitive nature and the reluctant acceptance of novel facts. It had always been part of the explorer's hazard, requiring each victim to reply in whatever manner satisfied most. James Bruce, an eighteenth-century traveler to Abyssinia, threw one detractor down a flight of stairs, while other abused explorers either suffered in silence or mounted defenses or vituperative counterattacks. Choice of conduct was a matter of style.

Cook's style called for the construction of a conspiracy theory. His complaints ran the gamut from expressions of humble, incredulous wonder at his fate to damning indictments of the criminal conspirators. Earlier he might have been a confused, innocent victim, but now he struck back virulently. There is nothing muddled or incoherent about his attack, although elements of it are hard to reconcile with the actual circumstances.

Cook argued persuasively. He explained that he had always believed that Peary reached the Pole. There "was glory enough for two." But Peary had not felt the same generosity and had formed a powerful, affluent organization "with unlimited money" to destroy Cook.

In contrast to Peary's, Cook's position was frail. Powerful foes were out to get him. They spewed out misinformation. And how could he protect himself without an organization behind him, wires to pull, or money for defense? Little wonder he felt overmatched. "I felt what anyone who is not a superhuman would have felt, a sickening sense of helplessness, a disgust at the human duplicity which permitted such things, a sense of the futility of the very thing I had done and its little worth compared to the web of shame my enemies were endeavoring to weave about me."

Then Cook launched into one of the most remarkable arguments of a remarkable book, showing, in essence, that the conspirators used journalistic repetition to "create as a fact in the public mind a thing which is purely imaginary or untrue." The press had been induced to call for "vague and obscure proofs," mere unreduced reckonings; Cook claimed he once had such data but thought so little of it that he had left it in Greenland. Because he neglected the growing demand "for this vague something," and because people did not understand that his published narrative was far better evidence than meaningless figures, they turned on him.

In a chapter entitled "The Key to the Controversy"—and throughout the book, mainly in footnotes—Cook blasted Peary unmercifully. To Cook, Peary was indeed the key to the controversy. Peary could not have prevented Cook from scaling Mount McKinley or reaching the Pole, but he could and did prevent the public from recognizing the truth.

To understand Cook, we must consider his attack on his rival carefully, not for its truth—it contained a mixture of truth, lies, exaggerations, questionable inferences, and venom—but for its elucidation of Cook's psychological state. He was angry, unjustly injured in his own eyes, and he would show the world how the truth had been tarnished by Peary's diabolical conduct. Cook's scourging of Peary was vicious and defies the accuracy of Peter Freuchen's celebrated appraisal: "Cook was a liar and a gentleman, Peary was neither." Freuchen's comment came before *My Attainment of the Pole* appeared, before Cook abandoned his mild approval of the "second man" to reach the Pole.

Cook described Peary's desperation when he first learned that a rival had beaten him to the Pole. Peary and his "coterie of conspirators" burned up the news cables and launched an abusive campaign" that the press, eager for sensation, lapped up. The press and the public were induced to believe that Peary's original, unkind insinuations came from one who was himself above the shadow of suspicion—which was far from the case.

Initially Cook withstood Peary's slanders calmly, reasoning that truth would ultimately prevail, "and that the rebound of the American spirit of fair play would quell the storm." Certainly Cook did respond wisely to Peary's attacks and was well advised to do so. He won much sympathy by not lashing back at Peary. Name-calling would gain him nothing. And what could be more effective in shaping public opinion than praising Peary's attainment and turning one's cheek to ill-tempered blows? Cook did not act as he did out of respect for Peary but because a dignified bearing "would be most effective in a battle of this kind."

Cook knew Peary well; he had served on two of his expeditions without pay, watching his successes and failures, admiring his strong qualities; and he "shivered with the shocks of his wrongdoings." Yes, there were ugly things to report of Peary, but Cook had hesitated to resort to retaliative abuse because he was a charitable man. Besides, the truth would out. Eventually "this warfare of the many against one, under the dictates of envy, must ultimately bring to light its own injustice."

Cook decided that his patient waiting had been a poor strategy: "The old Christian philosophy of cheek turning did not give the direct results." The press jumps on those who are gentle. On Cook's homecoming, the press had "lavished praise and glowing panegyric"; then it swung around and heaped on his head terms of opprobrium and obloquy: "Faked news items were issued to discredit me by Peary's associates; editors devoted space to jibes and sarcasms at my expense; clever writers did their best to make my name a humorous byword with my countrymen." The suddenness of the injustice overwhelmed him: "The plaudits of the multitude were still ringing in my ears when this horror of a world's contumely burst on my head."

In explaining the suddenness of newspaper attacks, Cook did not mention the effect of the Mount McKinley revelations, although in the next chapter of his book he credits them with overturning public opinion. Instead he painted an affecting picture of his mood at the unleashing of the storm, which he withstood with bowed head. "Sick and hurt and dazed in mind, conscious of a vague disgust with all the world and myself, I longed for respite and forgiveness within the bosom of my family." So, quietly, he retired for a year, out of the reach of yellow newspapers, "out of reach of the grind of the pro-Peary mill of infamy, still maintaining silence rather than stoop to the indignity of showing up the dark side of Mr. Peary's character."

Actually, the record does not confirm Cook's memory of events. He gave battle as long as he could—until he broke down under pressure. He battled cooly and superbly for weeks, keeping a masterful rein on tongue and temper, forbearing to slander Peary. Facing down Barrill in Montana used up Cook's last reserves; lecturing or any concentration must have become a terrible ordeal; newsmen besieged him constantly; detectives shadowed him, or so he felt; and Copenhagen kept calling for proofs. At his wits' end, he turned to Dunkle and Loose; then, realizing the hopelessness of his position, he fled.

Now Cook had returned to defend his good name. "I am compelled, with much reluctance and distaste, to reveal the unpleasant and unknown past of the man who tried to ruin me; showing how unscrupulous and brutal he was to others before me." Cook held evidence in hand: "I shall reveal how he wove his web of defamation and how his friends conspired with him in the darkest, meanest and most brazen conspiracy in the history of exploration."

Consider this man Peary, Cook exhorted his readers as he had his lecture audiences. Peary's twenty-year polar effort was undertaken primarily for personal commercial gain. He passed the hat for contributions, accepted a government salary while engaged in private enterprise that gave him hundreds of thousands of dollars, and lobbied for naval promotions. "Such a man could not afford to divide the fruits of polar attainment with another."

From 1891 Peary's brutal, selfish spirit caused him to lash out at every explorer who had the misfortune to cross his trail. Peary belittled Fridtjof Nansen's crossing of Greenland; he denounced Eivind Astrup because, without Peary's approval, Astrup wrote a book of scientific observations taken on Peary's expedition; and he treated another companion, John M. Verhoeff, so shabbily that Verhoeff "left his body in a glacial crevasse in preference to coming home on the same ship with Mr. Peary."

In 1897 Peary stole the Eskimos' only source of metal, a great meteor, and, in the name of science, robbed a poor people of their greatest spiritual and practical resource. Greed, cruel greed, drove Peary to this wretched act.

Peary carried some Greenland Eskimos to a New York museum, where they were locked in a cellar awaiting their exhibition. Unhealthful surroundings and improper food killed six or seven of them, and the surviving child was denied passage home by Peary. Peary also stole presents left for the Greenland Eskimos by the Danish government, and yet he called them "my people."

Then there is the Greely story. For years Peary and his press agents had discredited Greely's expedition, while "his own inhuman doings about Cape Sabine and the old Greely stamping grounds have been suppressed."

In 1901 Peary's ship carried an epidemic to the Eskimos, and Peary allowed them to die, although Dr. Dedrick wished to treat them.

Peary refused common courtesy to Otto Sverdrup because Sverdrup was a rival explorer, denying him Eskimo guides and dogs that did not belong to Peary.

For years Peary treated the Arctic as his private preserve, discredited and thwarted other explorers, exploited the Eskimos, denied credit to his own companions, and made money selling ivory and fur. But for the distraction of trading profits, Peary would have reached the Pole ten years earlier.

Cook had affidavits from members of Peary's expeditions, some from rough seamen who shuddered in speaking of Peary's deeds. These affidavits revealed gross actions that demanded an investigation by the Navy.

Again and again, Cook could not help contrasting his conduct with Peary's. Peary assumed the attitude of one above reproach and tried to rob Cook of his deserved honors. Cook remained silent, although he possessed facts that "the people of this country, who are clean, honest and fair, will not stand." Cook bore terrible insults manfully; Peary lied about him without scruple; and, even now, Cook hesitated to tell the full truth.

The full truth! Cook teased a little before disclosing to his readers Peary's ultimate infamy, an infamy he had already told the thousands who attended his lectures. "In the white, frozen North a tragedy was enacted which would bring tears to the hearts of all who possess human tenderness and kindness." What now? Ah, Cook hated to name it, despite the ruthlessness, the selfishness, the cruelty of the man who tried to ruin him. "I prefer the charity of silence, where, indeed, charity is not at all merited."

Yet one's preference for charity does not always rule. Peary blackened Cook's name, stole food although others might die, and somehow held credit in the public eye. Yet this man, this brute, "has deserted two of his own children—left them to starve and freeze in the cheerless North." The children would cry for food and for a father, "while he enjoys a life of luxury at the expense of the American taxpayers." And Cook appended a photograph of an Eskimo mother and her child labeled "Polar Tragedy—A Deserted Child of the Sultan of the North and Its Mother."

Cook packed a lot of punch in one short chapter, and some of what he wrote was true. Peary had done things that reflected unfavorably upon himself, but Cook's attack widely exceeded reason and decency.

The parts of Cook's narrative that tell of reaching the Pole are primarily descriptions of the hardships and emotional sensations. If one had no reason to doubt Cook's veracity, one's reaction to his narrative might depend upon one's sensitivity to a particular style of language. Some readers have labeled Cook a phony on the basis of his writing manner alone; others have found it sincere and expressive of such a high achievement as he claimed. Cook argued stridently that "the real proof—if proof is possible—is the continuity of the final printed book that gives all the data with the consequent variations." Aware that the data alone did not satisfy the University of Copenhagen, Cook wished his claims to be considered within the "continuity" of the narrative.

In an appendix Cook includes his field notes from March 18, 1908 (his start from Svartevoeg) to June 13, 1908 (his sighting of Heiberg and Ringnes Land on his return trip). The matter is recorded on eight pages of printed text. For each day he lists the mileage covered, and sometimes he describes his physical state or mood. Other data include temperature, barometer readings, weather and ice conditions, and various other information such as measurements of the sun's shadow. He gives compass direction and position infrequently: on March 24, 26, 30; on April 8, 11, 14, 19, 20; and of course, on April 21, the day of triumph.

This scant data is what the University of Copenhagen pondered over before dismissing it as proof.

Additionally, Cook appended an essay entitled "Questions That Enter Calculations for the Position of the North Pole," a six-page section. Cook introduces this material with the explanation that at the Pole it had never occurred to him "that there would be a cry for absolute proof." We can believe this statement with one reservation: He was asked for convincing data, not absolute proof. Since no one before him had ever claimed either Pole, we cannot be sure of the meaning of his complaint that "such a demand had never been presented before. The usual data of a personal narrative had always been received with good faith." Explorers claiming a farthest north or farthest south had never been questioned as Cook was questioned because (1) their data were not open to such obvious questions; (2) their claims were not the most significant of travel records; (3) the surrounding circumstances did not create such dramatic conditions.

The essay itself is not impressive. It mocks Peary and other critics of Cook, and ends with Cook's claim for the "continuity of the final printed book" as the best evidence.

More space is given to the matter in another essay, Evelyn Briggs Baldwin's "Positive Proof of Dr. Cook's Attainment of the Pole." It is nine pages long and is notable because Baldwin later repudiated it and claimed that Cook altered the original draft in part. It is notable, too, for Baldwin's ridiculous arguments.

Evelyn Briggs Baldwin may have been a double agent, but it is more likely that he was just a very foolish man. Baldwin, a portly fellow and a disgraced polar explorer, behaved in a peculiar fashion, not just in turning on Cook, recanting solemnly stated convictions expressed earlier, but in the manner of changing his colors. Many others reneged on Cook after the Mount McKinley scandal and the University of Copenhagen decision, fleeing like rats from a stricken vessel, washing their hands piously, and sending up loud huzzahs for the opposition to cover, Cook felt, their treachery and embarrassment. But Baldwin stood by Cook and helped him prepare *My Attainment of the Pole.* He lashed out at "armchair geographers and renegades." And he called up witnesses whom no Peary zealot could discredit: "The seals and polar bears and little foxes will bear testimony of unimpeachable character to substantiate Cook's discovery of the North Pole." Little foxes do not lie or recant—that was Baldwin's point, and very well put, too. Seals and polar bears would testify to Cook's character if they could—and because they could not, Baldwin would speak for them. This has to be the most singular appeal in the annals of exploration.

In other respects Baldwin analyzed the evidence foolishly. Had he been a bright man, one might be paranoid enough to believe that his defense was a pretense, and that he was working for Peary to make Cook look ridiculous. But we should not confuse mediocrity with cleverness. Baldwin's insistence that Peary's observations confirmed Cook's was used as an argument out of desperation. Baldwin pointed out that Cook reported no animal life at high latitudes, and Peary reported the same absence of life. Since the current theory among geographers urged that the Arctic Ocean near the Pole was lifeless, this argument glowed with truth. Baldwin's second "negative" argument was far more subtle: Cook sighted Bradley Land and Peary discovered Crocker Land at the same location.

Now if these arguments seem silly, since both explorers reported on the existence of land that actually did not exist, it is because we fail to grasp the limited arguments available when the essential data was lacking. While Cook, besieged by vociferous enemies, was harassed enough to miss the opportunities for spoofing in Baldwin's ludicrous appeal to bears, seals, and foxes as "unimpeachable" character witnesses, and to miss the joke of using the "evidence" of Peary, whose own evidence of his polar conquest was unsatisfactory, we can only marvel that Cook thought it sensible to print such stuff.

What Baldwin admired primarily in Cook was his thwarting of Peary. Baldwin hated Peary for publicly calling him a quitter and a coward years earlier, just when Baldwin was trying desperately to raise money for his own exploration. Baldwin got the money anyway and the chance of showing his incompetence, and suffered a public dismissal from the command of a polar expedition. Both Cook and Peary bad-mouthed him to his sponsor, and he disliked both polar claimants, but disliked Peary more than Cook. By helping "confirm" Cook's claim, he struck at Peary. Despite the accusation of bribery, there is no evidence that Baldwin took money from Peary's crowd to renounce Cook later. He just saw the light, as did others. His denunciation of Cook made him appear silly rather than insincere or dishonest. The polar controversy helped Baldwin maintain stature as a polar expert. Both claimants were discredited by his pronouncements, and Baldwin's availability to newsmen did nothing for his long-term reputation.

One of Peary's friends thought Baldwin's exaggerated defense of Cook, followed by a passionate denunciation, supported by depositions of others, indicated some mental instability. Whatever the truth, Baldwin's behavior does not stimulate any great confidence in his mental capacity.

Baldwin's funniest defense of Cook, aside from the unbeatable seal and fox testimony, was his answer to Gilbert Grosvenor, editor of *National Geographic* and a leading Peary fan. Grosvenor wrote that Cook probably filled his head with the books of Otto Sverdrup and other explorers in creating his own narrative. In answering this grave charge, Baldwin was somewhat less than powerful, and his reply must have been tongue in cheek. "Now, since Sverdrup is a real navigator . . . I do not consider Mr. Grosvenor's armchair criticism of the writings of Capt. Sverdrup and of Dr. Cook quite in keeping with the principles of a square deal and fair play." And the defense rests. From the author of an essay entitled "Positive Proof of Dr. Cook's Attainment of the Pole," this retort lacked vigor—not to mention positive proof. Worse, it lacked sense.

Baldwin's lack of discernment and political sense showed up later in 1913 when he asked Fred High, editor of *The Platform,* a lecture-circuit trade magazine, to assist him in getting a lecture contract. Baldwin was foolish on two counts: first, in believing that the newspaper notoriety he gained by initially defending, then renouncing Cook made him a "name"; second, in assuming High might be sympathetic or at least neutral. High's lyceum and chautauqua enterprise had a stake in Cook, and if crowds had been easier to draw, Cook would not have been forced to take less prestigious, less lucrative vaudeville engagements. And High was also a friend of Cook's. Yet poor, naive Baldwin dared to solicit High's help.

High blasted Baldwin in a long, venomous letter. He acknowledged "the first great surprise of the New Year" and marveled that Baldwin thought his "duplicity or treachery" deserved rewards. High said, "When I desert a friend I must have more reason for doing so than you have given me," but he told Baldwin to write a story for *The Platform* "if you have any facts to present." Remember, High cautioned, I am too wise to the game to allow anyone to work me for free chautauqua publicity—"I am no easy mark."

Baldwin's original defense of Cook had appeared in *The Platform* after the explorer solemnly assured High that he could prove Peary a fake and Cook truthful. If Baldwin saw no embarrassment to himself in reversing his view in a new article, High knew the implications for *The Platform* and for Cook's success as a lecturer. High probably believed that someone put Baldwin up to the whole embarrassing scheme. It was hard for him to conceive of Baldwin being as dumb as he appeared. High twisted Baldwin's explanation to show his suspicions: "You say in your letter that you are forced to acknowledge Dr. Cook to be one of the most monumental frauds of all times. Who is forcing you? What is forcing you?" Maybe "the forcing is tinged with the same taint as was the money that Judas took."

What outraged High is plain to see. Here was Baldwin denying his own article and publicly claiming that Cook had altered its last three paragraphs, yet, on its publication, he had thanked High for printing it. Were you lying earlier? High asked. Give me the facts and I will print them, and never mind Mount McKinley and other immaterial matters. "You need not explain why you timed your treachery, and bit the hand that fed you, when it would do him the maximum of harm. . . . Judas at least had manhood enough left to go hang himself, but what's the use?"

High's indignation in this instance can be appreciated. On other occasions his defense of Cook boiled over to extreme, unwarranted nastiness. A woman mountaineer, Annie L. Peck, made the mistake of writing to High to set him straight on Cook's Mount McKinley fraud, while dropping the hint that her lecturing career had not prospered, despite the fact that "some people say that I am the most wonderful woman in the world" and that they find her lectures the best they have ever heard.[3]

High discredited her arguments and mocked her: "Now, Miss Peck, I have only sympathy for a woman of your age and experience, who is so credulous that you are taken in by that irrepressible flatterer who sits in every Lyceum and Chautauqua audience. . . . we have all fallen for this, but for you to write such gush to a Lyceum editor shows that you have either entered into your second childhood or you are too innocent for this world. Heaven is your home." Let us hope that men who tell you such things are sincere, he went on. "But why do you still have Miss as a prefix to your name? . . . Why Aunty, those are terms that lovers use—they are not always true and should not be used in a scientific discussion."[4]

Poor Miss Peck. And poor, disagreeable Fred High, too. They are only two of a legion of individuals who suffered in one way or another over the Cook controversy. What did it all mean, except that it often made people treat others contemptuously? The cause of Cook enriched no one, regardless of what position the commentator took.

LOBBYING CONGRESS

"Do not go gentle into that good night."
　　　　　　—Dylan Thomas

Lucien Alexander earned $500 monthly plus expenses from Peary for keeping a watch on Cook and countering his attacks on Peary. Alexander, a Philadelphia attorney who was instrumental in developing the American Bar Association's code of ethics, only worked for Peary from time to time. In 1911 he had successfully lobbied Congress for Peary's promotion, then became active again from 1914 through 1916.

Why all the concern for the discredited Cook in 1914? Cook's fortunes had dipped rather low as the year began. A projected lecture series at the London Pavilion began and stopped on December 30, 1913, after a sparse audience expressed their disapproval. Various American papers commented humorously and sarcastically on the meaning of such a snub. Yet Cook returned to New York in mid-January and denied that he "met with a frost in London. I had good audiences and I expect to return to Europe again in a few months." Alexander drew up a memo contrasting Cook's statement with contradictory reports from the Associated Press, the Sun Press Association, and various special correspondents.

But Peary, Alexander, Bridgman, and Hubbard remained worried, particularly because of Cook's demands for a congressional investigation. Friends of Peary's who did not share his fears wondered at his anxiety. When Peary sent anti-Cook material to Scott Keltie, secretary of Britain's

Royal Geographical Society, Keltie lamented Peary's effort. Keltie had no time to read such material—and saw no reason for it. "Nobody here is taking any notice of Cook." Keltie had just read Belmore Browne's book on Mount McKinley and thought it showed clearly that Cook's story "was a fake."

A year later Alexander pursued Cook in full cry. *The Congressional Record* had printed Peary's side of the controversy through Congressman S. D. Fess of Ohio, an argument that countered another congressman's defense of Cook and attack on Peary in *The Congressional Record.* Alexander and Peary ordered 101,000 copies of the extract for mailing to doctors, grade-school teachers, theater managers, and others. Alexander urged Peary's approval of a general publicity campaign to "throw a sort of anti-Cook net over the entire country . . . which will tend to confine Cook's efforts."[3]

One thing that stirred Alexander up was the belief that Rudolph Franke, Cook's polar companion, had gone north with Captain Joseph Bernier. Franke might bring to the States the Eskimos who accompanied Cook on his polar trek. It would be easy for Cook to coach them to affirm his own version of the journey, even though they had contradicted it before. On the stage the Eskimos would be extremely effective.

If this worked for Cook, he would probably climb Mount McKinley by the Parker-Browne-Stuck route and "find" the record of his climb. Then he could laugh off the fake photos he published and convince a number of people.

Alexander urged counteraction and wished to go north with Bernier himself to oversee Franke's negotiations with the Eskimos. "If Franke brings back one or both of the Eskimos, Cook *and* his Eskimo would be the biggest vaudeville drawing card Keith [the vaudeville agency] ever put on the circuit."[4]

A year later Peary's indignation soared to new heights after Congressman Henry T. Helgesen of North Dakota introduced a bill to repeal Peary's 1911 promotion. Helgesen decried Peary's "discovery" of two nonexistent places, the "Peary Channel," in northeast Greenland, and Crocker Land. Although Peary kept mute publicly, he jotted down his opinions: "Helgesen is first a deliberate, unmitigated . . . liar. He is second the mouth piece and cat's-paw of a notorious lobby engaged in exploiting Congress for press-agent work in the interest of a vaudeville venture."[5]

Peary and Alexander had nothing to fear from Congress. Among its priorities for deliberation in 1914–1915, the North Pole controversy ranked in popularity with the commemoration of Benedict Arnold or the abolition of the Post Office. But Cook partisans did not appreciate their efforts' futility, and tried twice to pressure Congress.

On the first attempt to engage the attention of lawmakers in the Senate, the matter was dispatched with the usual dignity and efficiency of legislative machinery. Senator Miles Poindexter of Washington introduced into the Senate a resolution that was shunted promptly to the Committee on the Library, a casual group with little occasion to meet and small appetite for controversy. The committee passed up a chance for notoriety by ignoring the issue.

Would the House of Representatives weigh "the American Dreyfus case" more gravely? It was worth a try, and a member introduced a resolution to determine which of the polar discoverers deserved credit for priority. The House leadership passed the buck to the Committee on Education, a group as active and disputatious as the Senate's Committee on the Library—that is to say, one composed of members who had more important duties and committee assignments and who did not strain themselves over the Committee on Education.

However, courtesy cannot be denied to colleagues, so the committee chairman convened an evening session on January 28, 1915, banged his gavel ceremoniously, observed the impossibility of getting a quorum together, and urged Cook loyalists to make their pitch.

Edwin Swift Balch of Philadelphia, author of two pro-Cook books, led off with a short dissertation on the evidence of Cook's polar and Mount McKinley claims. It was a most succinct summary of his two books, and made as much sense as they did.

To committee questions Balch made faltering responses. Congressman John W. Abercrombie (D), Alabama wondered whether Congress ought to be concerned with the polar controversy: "Is it not a question for scientists rather than for lawmakers?"[6]

A good question, and Balch contributed little to encourage his listeners' interest. "I am afraid I am not informed as to that. That is not a geographical question." Recovering the initiative somewhat, Balch went on, "Of course, I think that scientists ought to take it up, but I think they are very much afraid of it."[7]

Balch's friends must have winced at his confused, tepid advocacy. His answers could not have encouraged committee members to believe they were faced with a mission of significance.

Balch's main thrust was simple. Since Peary's articles and book had described the North Pole in language similar to Cook's, Peary had in effect corroborated Cook's narrative. This point was worth mentioning, and certainly Cook did so in *My Attainment of the Pole,* yet it was hardly the substantial kind of argument one might expect of an expert of Balch's stature.

Neither Balch's credentials nor his testimony impressed Congressman Horace M. Towner (R), Iowa. Towner demanded to know who had the facts of the case. Another witness, Clark Brown, answered that Dr. Balch could set the facts in juxtaposition. Towner sharply denied any need for Balch's juxtaposition: "We will juxtapose on facts, and we will have to do it." In some impatience, Towner stressed his point: "Let me say this to you: I do not think that what you have stated tonight is of any particular value to us." Congress had to make its determination—if it decided to do so—on the evidence presented by competent people. "Now, let us have concretely from you a statement as to what we should depend upon outside of what they tell us, so that we can tell whether or not they are telling the truth about these matters."[8]

Clark Brown tried to clarify Towner's doubts. Brown explained the inconsistency of some of Peary's evidence. Brown's summation reminded Towner of the real problem: "Has not most of the time of Dr. Cook's advocates and of Admiral Peary's advocates been spent in criticism and vituperation of the other?" What would be the advantage, Towner wished to know, of listening to the respective advocates discrediting each other? Brown suggested that it might add to the knowledge of the world. Towner blazed back: "It seems to be that there has been so much of it given to the world already that the world is pretty sick of it."[9]

Here was the crux of the Cook dilemma: The world was indeed bored with the controversy—and for good reason. What issue could be at once so stale and yet so fraught with unbending emotional advocacy by the few zealots who remained intrigued by it? Towner wished for no more arguments and vituperation and called for names of experts. At this point Congressman Charles B. Smith of New York, who was apparently responsible for getting the committee to meet, called on Ernest C. Rost.

Rost had a list of names, 32 in all, of men presumed to be Arctic experts who would offer evidence in support of Cook. The experts could be called and would be happy to testify.

Rost confined himself to the accreditation of absent experts who would defend Cook. His own expertise was in photography. Had committee members been particularly hostile to Cook's cause, they might have interrogated Rost more sharply on his role. Towner asked him his calling, and Rost confined his self-identification to admitting only that he was a friend of Dr. Cook's. Committee members did not press the matter of Rost's calling, because they knew him as Congressman Helgesen's aide. Whether they also knew him as a hired lobbyist for Cook is not known.

The pièce de résistance that Cook's friends prepared for Congress consisted of the testimony of Lillian Kiel. She testified to a fraudulent deed committed in her presence six years earlier when she worked for *Hampton's*. Kiel's testimony made these points: (1) Elsa Pedersen wrote Peary's polar narrative for *Hampton's* and had trouble getting data for it, which suggested that Peary lacked proofs; (2) the editors of *Hampton's* changed Cook's 1911 articles because of a contract with Peary forbidding them to print anything detrimental to him.

As to the first point, ample evidence confirms Kiel's story of Pedersen's difficulty in writing the Peary articles, although this does not necessarily show that Peary lacked data.

On the second point, Kiel's testimony is dubious. The editors of *Hampton's* did alter Cook's copy a little so that the text would provide a slight tie-in with their cover banner proclaiming "Dr. Cook's Confession." But there is not a shred of evidence—aside from Kiel's unsupported eavesdropping on a conversation between two editors—that the alterations had anything to do with Peary. And a connection with Peary makes no sense. *Hampton's* had sound reasons for altering Cook's copy. Some sensational revelation was necessary to make the story salable, so the delicate hint that Cook did not always know what he was doing on the polar journey was introduced.

The additions made to Cook's story approached the "confession" heralded by its title. One suggestive insertion stated that he "may have unconsciously lied, and may have deceived himself, but he did not deliberately try to deceive others." Another inserted statement read: "For the position of suspicion and disgrace in which I find myself, I blame no one excepting myself. I want it to be understood now that I do not intend to enter into any controversy with Commander Peary, and that my feeling is that Commander Peary deserves the honor of a notable achievement, which was the result of sacrificing life work. I have never questioned Commander Peary's claim to the discovery of the North Pole. I do not now. I did not consciously try to filch an honor which belongs alone to Commander Peary."[10]

In his book Cook expressed his dismay at what *Hampton's* did to him, and there is no reason to doubt his genuine disgust. He blamed a subeditor of *Hampton's* rather than T. Everett Harré (spelled Harry by Cook), who negotiated the magazine arrangement. Kiel, on the other hand, showed congressmen a photograph of Harré, whom she evidently disliked, and insisted that the insertions were dictated to her by Harré: "This is a picture of the noble gentleman," she said. "You can see the intelligence in his face."[11]

Cook did not sue *Hampton's,* and it is quite possible, even reasonable, to believe that he authorized Harré to alter his copy for purposes of creating interest. The editors of *Hampton's* knew they needed something other than a familiar Cook defense. If Cook had not authorized the changes, he would have reason to blame Harré for the final result, and would have been unlikely to accept any excuse from him. Whatever the circumstances, Cook liked Harré enough to hire him as manager of the Polar Publishing Co., a business set up by Cook to publish and sell his book, *My Attainment of the Pole.*

The words of "confession" written by Cook himself in the article, and not attributed by Kiel as editor's insertions, also come close to being a confession: "After mature thought, I confess I do not know absolutely whether I reached the Pole or not. This may come as an amazing statement; but I am willing to startle the world if, by so doing, I can get an opportunity to present my case."[12] In later explaining the use of such language, Cook insisted that all he wished to "confess" was that mathematical uncertainty must always exist as to the precise location of the Pole because absolute determination was impossible.

Cook never made it very clear what his original words had been, nor did he even pinpoint the insertions. His biographers have charitably assumed that his vagueness was the consequence of his not having retained a copy of his original draft. Perhaps he did not, but it would be amazing carelessness for one who had blamed the false reporting of the press for much of his trouble. Well, Cook could be careless. And he could also be vague when it suited him.

Cook's biographers have puzzled over the *Hampton's* affair, seeking "to find some explanation for Cook's incredible simplicity . . . It is difficult to understand why Cook would fling himself at a ravenously sensation-hungry public. Yet that is what he did."[13] Such comments show no understanding of Cook's drive. He had to make a comeback and *try* to create a sensation. He failed to do so, to his and *Hampton's* disappointment. Yet nothing in Cook's case is ever thrown away, and when Cook's friends hoped for help from Congress and Miss Kiel presented herself, the *Hampton's* episode was brought forward once more. It meant as little the second time around as it did when Cook aired it in his book.

Congressman Helgesen of North Dakota used space in *The Congressional Record* in 1915 for Cook's defense. He included a number of newspaper comments favorable to Cook that showed some public support for congressional action.[14]

In Pennsylvania, *The Johnstown Leader* headed an editorial of October 13, 1914, "TIME TO SQUARE IT WITH COOK," and argued that Congress had no good reason for not paying Cook honors "which none denies him except his rival."

The editor of another Pennsylvania paper, *The Altoona Times,* heard Cook lecture and found "it is not possible to come into contact with this great man and not feel that he has been mistreated by his fellow countrymen." In time Cook's sacrifices would be accepted at their real value. "His quiet, unassuming manner invites respect and confidence."

In New York the *Journal* reported on the ill-fated Poindexter resolution to honor Cook in Congress and complained that Congress railroaded through its recognition of Peary "and heaped honors upon him that he did not deserve." Yet Cook had never asked for anything but an investigation and "a square deal."

A Marion, Ohio, lecture audience sympathized with Cook and eagerly signed a petition to Congress, according to *The Marion Tribune* of July 29, 1914.

And in Jackson, Michigan, *The Citizen Press* of December 1, 1913 considered it fair that Peary should answer the challenge of questions Cook propounded in a lecture.

Benton Harbor, Michigan, folks apparently went wild over Cook. His stage appearance was greeted with an ovation and at his conclusion the theater rang with applause, according to *The News Palladium* of November 14, 1913.

In Racine, Wisconsin, the editor of *The Daily Call* stated that "by persistency that is equalled only in his heart-rending dash to the pole, and a sincerity that no man can doubt, Cook is convincing the American people that he actually reached the pole when he said he did." Scientists "now generally" credit Cook, and Congress will surely name him as discoverer, the paper believed.

Fast friends existed in Arlington Heights, Illinois, where the *Review* eagerly awaited the day when Congress and the world would fall into line.

In New Jersey, *The Paterson Press* thought Americans cared not a whit who discovered the Pole, but the paper wanted justice done. Cook's book and lectures shook the faith of the most ardent Peary believer. "Admiral Peary, therefore, needs the official investigation as much as Dr. Cook. What, therefore, stands in the way?"

Another Michigan paper, *The Hartford Day Spring,* declaimed that the world loves a good fighter and that "it is quite incomprehensible that an insincere man could wage the determined fight that Dr. Cook has made." Americans admire courage and determination, and apparently sympathize with Cook, the paper believed.

And in Illinois, *The Rockville Tribune* thundered that "it is a monstrous injustice that the children of the United States should be taught that Peary discovered the Pole." But falsehoods in history rarely survive. "Sooner or later the real historian will get the truth on record." All Americans should call for an investigation, urged the Illinois paper.

Finally, Helgesen quoted *The Des Moines Tribune*: "Whatever else Dr. Cook may be right or wrong about, he is most certainly right about the efforts that are being made to suppress him and his contentions over the North Polar discovery." The Iowa paper had received anti-Cook propaganda from Peary's fans and asked why such an effort should be made to discredit the doctor.

These excerpts disclose that Americans were given plenty of opportunities to consider or reconsider Cook's case. No one was able to suppress Cook. The Peary Arctic Club mailed out propaganda but had no one to stump the country either against Cook or for Peary. Peary himself made very few public appearances, and no one else answering Cook could hope to command sizable audiences. So the battle of propaganda raged between forces that were reasonably even. Cook's disadvantage was in bearing the label of fraud, yet he did appear in small and large towns around the country, and in politics attention to the grass roots may bear fruit.

The evidence does not sustain the glib assertion of Cook fans that conspirators or the Establishment denied Cook's cause a hearing. Cook was heard in 1909, in 1910, and subsequently; others were heard as well. In 1909 the public generally believed he had committed fraud twice. His efforts to reverse public opinion did not succeed, so he turned to other pursuits in 1915.

After a campaign of several years, Cook refused to wait around for a congressional hearing. Congressman Helgesen was shocked that Cook left the country in 1915 "when matters looked as though a hearing might be granted him."[15] Obviously, Cook determined that he would not receive a hearing and left for an Asian journey.

It is unreasonable to believe that Helgesen, a hard foe of Peary and hitherto a friend of Cook's cause, would turn against Cook for this reason alone. Why did Helgesen suddenly attack Cook in September 1916, seemingly reversing his position?[16] What happened in one year? Did Helgesen read *My Attainment of the Pole* and discover that Cook used nasty tactics against Peary? Did he review the whole question and decide that the evidence showed that Cook faked as much as Peary? The answer is buried with Helgesen, who died April 10, 1917.

Perhaps the mysterious Ernest C. Rost, Helgesen's administrative assistant, who may have written all of Helgesen's speeches on the polar controversy, was responsible. Rost did important work as a lobbyist for Cook. He testified in January 1915 before some members of the Committee on Education, and his status as an "expert photographer" capable of labeling Belmore Browne's "false peak" photo as a fake and authenticating Cook's photos was widely proclaimed.

Whether there was any impropriety in a paid congressional aide working as a paid lobbyist for a petitioner to Congress is beside the point. Rost was convinced that he did well by Cook, and he wanted the pay—apparently $3,000 had been agreed upon. Cook's consistency on money obligations was maintained in this instance. He did not pay, and Rost sued him about the time Helgesen blasted Cook in *The Congressional Record*.[17] So ended Cook's congressional route to polar honors.

V

OIL

THE ENTREPRENEUR

*I have never known an explorer
who was not either bankrupt or close to it.*
—Admiral Richard Byrd

In April 1919, at his Washington home Peary celebrated the tenth anniversary of his polar journey. He had been suffering from pernicious anemia for two years and had not many months to live. His last public appearance had been in January when the National Geographic Society honored explorer Vilhjalmur Stefansson.

Friends tried to cheer Peary. Captain Bob Bartlett wrote him a humorous note about a get-rich-quick scheme in Texas, enclosing a newspaper clipping. The clipping was an advertisement for the Texas Eagle Oil and Refining Company. "Get into a sound company," the ad urged. "Dr. Cook, the explorer, and a group of well known substantial men are behind this organization. . . . Deposit your money with us with the same confidence you have in your bank. . . . With the eyes of an eagle we have searched and with claws of an eagle we have gripped the oil fields of mid-Texas."[1]

Whether Peary smiled or not, we don't know. Cook's Texas Eagle Oil and Refining Company lost its grip on "the oil fields of mid-Texas" soon after the ad's publication and went into receivership.[2] The ad indicated that Cook thought his reputation as an explorer possessed sales value. And in equating investment in oil lands with bank deposits, Cook showed his usual flair.

The mystery of Dr. Cook's exploration claims was not clarified by his collision with federal fraud laws. What a consideration of the oil promotion schemes gives us is a more familiar ground for understanding Cook. Exploration is an exotic pursuit that lies outside of the ordinary experience. Business practices, however, are familiar enough; and so are sharp-dealing rogues. Cook turned to business when he required a new field of endeavor. He proved to be a keen opportunist in a rapidly expanding field. His experience in self-promotion carried over from exploration to oil development; in fact, he utilized his fame to promote his companies. With the daring customary to explorers, the skill of a superb salesman, and his complete amorality, he found an excitement and satisfaction in commerce akin to that experienced in exploration.

The dizzy development of oil fields in Texas and elsewhere in the 1920s is a colorful chapter in American history. Houston and Dallas became great cities, huge fortunes were won and lost in land speculation, and money was squandered with enough abandon to mark the era as superlative in luxury, wastefulness, ostentation, prodigality, fraudulence, and all the other aspects of great wealth on the rampage.

Oil drew Frederick Cook and thousands of others to Texas. A bonanza and its prospects attract all kinds, from sober workers hoping for regular wages to cardsharps and con men thirsting to prey on the newly rich.

Cook's talents and experiences as physician and explorer did not equip him remarkably as an oil man, although he professed to "a good working knowledge of geology." Not that deep knowledge of geology mattered when companies were hiring "oil smellers, fortune tellers, wiggle-stick operators, and men claiming X-ray vision."[3] Cook's versatility won him an oil prospector's job in 1916, a fresh start for a fifty-two-year-old man who left a bizarre path behind him. Who could guess that spectacular events would win him fame of sorts again in his new career?

Cook prospected in Wyoming for the New York Oil Company and, according to his own unconfirmed account, discovered important petroleum fields. New York Oil organized the Cook Oil Company, with its namesake as president, but in 1918 Cook sold his stock for $40,000 and headed for Texas and bigger pickings. Near Fort Worth, the headquarters for some 2,000 independent oil companies (a figure that, even if exaggerated, shows the chaotic state of an industry swarming with wildcatters and promoters), Cook acquired leases and organized his own company. A year later his company went into receivership and Cook took up prospecting again, until he conceived the idea of organizing the Petroleum Producers Association in 1922.

Cook was now fifty-seven years old; he wore his gray hair combed back; his eyes were lively as ever; and his manner as pleasant and plausible as in earlier years. He detected a fine opportunity to utilize abandoned oil properties as assets for the financing of development on more promising sites. His intent was not necessarily unscrupulous, yet the scheme, like many others launched during the same period to exploit the gullible, certainly promised a rich field for fraud. Of course, the highly charged, get-rich-quick atmosphere in Fort Worth, and the lack of stringent state or federal regulation, created an environment ripe for all kinds of sharp practices. Many innocent, ignorant investors were fleeced; so many that the situation developed into a national scandal, and urgent cries for reform were heard.

Cook did very well as a businessman. He had great drive. Perhaps, consciously or unconsciously, he longed to achieve a huge fortune so that he might rival the members of the Peary Arctic Club, whom he unfairly blamed for destroying his reputation. We cannot know his true goals, yet we can accept his latest biographer's description of his tremendous effort: "The assault of Mount McKinley had been a charge. The assault of the North Pole had been a charge. Now he was charging oil."[4]

Since Cook's reputation as a swindler had not been forgotten entirely, it is no surprise that the Texas press called attention to a new promoter in the field whose background was questionable. But complaints were not widespread in the hurly-burly of the oil scene. Cook stilled one newspaper by filing a libel suit, and did not attract greater clamor by bringing it to court. After all, Cook had no criminal record. He was only one of many dubious promoters tempted by the oil excitement; and the spirit of caveat emptor prevailed. Promoters liked the oil land situation very much, even if outraged victims and frustrated law enforcers did not. As Cook's biographer put it, with unconscious humor: "As in his previous adventures, he did not attempt to change the environment. He adapted himself to it and became one of the largest, and perhaps the largest oil promoter in Fort Worth."[5] He merged 413 defunct companies into the Petroleum Producers Association (P.P.A.) and hired 83 secretaries. Secretarial services constituted the chief overhead of an enterprise whose product was largely paper—in the form of mailed sales pitches, stock certificates, and assorted tub-thumbing assurances of glittering prosperity. Cook also hired four professional writers of promotional letters, one of whom, S. E. J. Cox, was a known ex-convict. Cox had served time after conviction for oil fraud, yet Cook did not worry about this; he was impressed by Cox's claim to have sold $1.5 million worth of stock for one company. The other major writer was H. O. Stephens.

P.P.A. acquired the oil leases of bankrupt companies and proposed to develop these and other properties. Cook acquired lists of stockholders in the defunct companies and offered these stockholders shares in P.P.A. His attractive offer included that of guaranteed dividends. Usually stockholders received their first contact through letters purporting to be from officers of the defunct company. The writers admitted prospects for profits were bleak and recommended the P.P.A. stock exchange scheme. Actually the letters originated with P.P.A.

Before Cook established P.P.A., promoters had developed a means of keeping within the law by organizing under a "declaration of trust" agreement. The arrangement provided loopholes in existing corporate regulations because an ultimate division of all assets to stockholders was provided for. P.P.A. combined the most appealing features of several companies that were based on trust agreements. Trustees of P.P.A. could operate for twenty years before dividing the assets. Until division they were not limited in their expenditures, and they drew salaries and other emoluments from current earnings.

From March 1922 to January 1923, Cook's letter writers sold $430,818 in stock, most of which, according to Cook, was dispersed for leases and drilling costs. Cook said he concentrated on field exploration during this period, bouncing about Texas and Oklahoma by rail and in an old twin-six Packard, hunting for oil. Alas! He found none.

The year 1923 opened inauspiciously for Frederick Cook. His role as a promoter was singled out by a national organization that was the forerunner of the Better Business Bureau. In January newspapers published the charges of the chairman of the National Vigilance Committee, Herbert S. Houston, that Cook was defrauding investors.

February was a bad month too. Detectives, led by Cook's wife, followed Cook and a woman to a Fort Worth hotel and arrested him for possession of liquor. He denied that the woman in question was with him in the hotel. His wife announced that she was suing for divorce, and she did so successfully.

Cook was in trouble. In February he filed suit for libel against a Fort

Worth newspaper. Other papers disclosed details of the P.P.A. operation in succeeding months, and in April a federal grand jury indicted him for using the mails to defraud.

The federal attorney had been willing to plea-bargain with Cook and other P.P.A. officials. Cook offered to plead guilty if he could avoid a jail sentence. The prosecutor countered with the proposal of recommending a sentence not to exceed two years. Cook refused any compromise that included jail time, which proved to be a terrible mistake on his part.[6]

P.P.A. promotional correspondence and complaints from stockholders had attracted the attention of federal investigators, who presented evidence to the grand jury. In a typical letter to an investor, Cook drew a parallel between his "brain-wracking quest" for ideas to further the interest of stockholders and his past deeds: "It is necessary to be a man of far-vision and direct action to accomplish things of great magnitude, such as I have successfully accomplished in the past, and that was done in most cases for the welfare and good of civilization. Now I am launched on one of the greatest accomplishments and fulfillments of trust that I have ever undertaken in my entire career." One of Cook's oil wells was in the Corsicana field, which had been producing for nineteen years. "That is evidence within itself to sufficiently justify you in believing that this field will be producing oil when you and I have passed into the great beyond."[7]

Another well, in the Vitek field, was "running wild," as a photo enclosed showed. The well is "scattering the liquid gold over the crown block and throwing it to the four winds of the earth, and I might advise you that this company is greatly interested in the profits of this well." P.P.A. plans included drilling such productive wells over a 226-acre tract in the Corsicana field, but "friends must come to my assistance."[8] More money was needed.

Another letter claimed potential earnings of $10 to $20 million for the 226 acres. A "Higher Hand" put oil in the "bosom of Mother Earth" for the use of men of ingenuity. One could rise from poverty to a place of prominence "by making the 'supreme sacrifice' " and investing in good oil securities. The text went on to describe powerful drills biting downward "through the bosom of Mother Earth to that pool of golden liquid which shall soon be released and, with the rush and roar of a raging river, will come spouting heavenward to be turned into the pipe lines and help build for you that permanent cash."[9]

Other Cook letters referred to his more than twenty years of work "devoted exclusively to the upbuilding and extension of civilization." As a continuation of his good work, he wished to lend "a willing hand" in the "recovery of your past losses"[10]

Cook explained his exploration ventures as expressions of his "good will to all men." It was his desire, "in my declining years," to bring pleasure, happiness, and luxury to others. His ambition arose from reflections made while wandering "on the cold, bleak hills around the North Pole, to the wind's sweet seas, and into the noisome pestilence of the tropics."[11] He believed in humanity and the shortness of life, and he felt the responsibility to secure prosperity for those who had confidence in him.

The government investigation also revealed that Cook's promotion of oil stock followed a similar pattern, from his initial entry into the game through his later P.P.A. hustles. His promotion of the Texas Eagle Oil and Refining Company in 1920 stressed opportunity, his own integrity, and other intangible values. Investors would gain "equal profit in a family brotherhood." The company "is organized under the stringent Blue Laws of Texas, assuring each investor a square deal. . . . It is a fair, clean-cut company organized by Cook, who is well known not only as an explorer and scientist, but as a geologist and finder of oil. Every acre has been personally examined and appointed by him." Cook, as "president and world renowned explorer," asserted that "proven acreage is worth more than the entire capital stock issued. . . . This company is as sound as a bank."[12]

Later in 1920 Cook wrote Texas Eagle stockholders that the company had merged with the Revere Oil Company and suggested that stockholders transfer their stock to the new company. A transfer would require a cash investment of 25 percent. One disappointed Texas Eagle stockholder told the government that he wrote Cook explaining that he had no more money and asking him to secure his investment. Cook did not reply.

The investigation of Cook's P.P.A. was part of an extensive federal effort to clean up oil land swindles. A grand jury sat for seven months and indicted 400 individuals. Of all the prosecutions, that of P.P.A. assumed the greatest importance because of the wide scale of its operations and the strength of the government's case. Federal prosecutors believed that a successful case against P.P.A. would highlight the government's determination to end corruption. Smaller con men who had not been indicted would take note and close their shops.

Following federal practice in important prosecutions, the Department of

Justice appointed a special prosecutor, John Pratt of Ohio, and a judge from another jurisdiction, John M. Killits of Ohio. Federal authorities were certain they had a strong case; they subpoenaed 283 witnesses for courtroom appearances.

Cook and the other defendants were defended by a battery of Texas lawyers headed by a former United States Senator from Texas, Joseph W. Bailey, an advocate noted for his oratory and skill.

JUSTICE IN TEXAS

*There is nothing under the sun
more futile than a mere adventurer.*
—Joseph Conrad

The trial opened on October 16, 1923; everyone knew it would be long because of the complexity of the case. And with 22 lawyers, "the greatest assembly of attorneys in a Texas courtroom in years," the press guessed that "legal polytechnics would be the rule not the exception."[1] Yet trials do not usually move at a very exciting pace, and the story moved from front to back pages in Texas newspapers after the first two days' proceedings.

The defense's opening argument was short, unlike the prosecution's. In only twenty-five minutes one of Cook's attorneys laid down the basic defense strategy: The money received from investors was spent honestly, drilling dry hole after dry hole. There was no fraud, he said.

After the second day of the trial, *The Fort Worth Record's* lead story focused on a courtroom reconciliation between Cook and his divorced spouse. She took a seat beside him at the defendant's table, but refused to discuss her divorce with newsmen. Reporters were disappointed in their attempt to learn more about the hotel room episode that apparently caused the divorce. Cook just repeated what he had said at the time: A private detective had framed him. His arrest for possession of whiskey in a hotel room where he had allegedly taken a woman had been a setup. At any rate, any bitterness over the episode and subsequent property settlement had been dissipated. In an out-of-court settlement Marie Cook accepted $15,000 cash and other considerations.

The prosecution told the jury that Cook and his 11 officers were guilty of fraud. P.P.A. had misrepresented its operation to potential stockholders, claiming profitable oil production where none existed. Cook, as a P.P.A. trustee, had knowledge of the misrepresentation and intended to deceive in order to solicit stock subscriptions. If P.P.A. communications deceived stockbuyers, Cook was responsible for the deception of his agents. The government would show that P.P.A. paid dividends from stock sales rather than from profits, which was contrary to law.

To illustrate the use of "sucker lists," the prosecutor quoted from a postcard signed by F.A. Cook that was sent out to stockholders of failed companies: "An important letter which brings a message and documents from a long silent friend—one you have probably misunderstood—should reach you in a few days. Watch for it—I must be certain of its delivery— hence this card. If it does not get to you within a week pen me a note."[2]

From this and other kinds of initial contact, P.P.A. subjected stockbuyers to false assertions of profit potential. The victims of P.P.A. were induced by fraud to purchase stock.

As the government presented its evidence, Cook's operation was exposed in clarifying detail. Like most of the best swindles, Cook's scheme was simple. He started with "sucker lists," the names of disappointed stockholders of defunct oil companies. Other assets might include profitless oil leases and lands drilled with dry holes, but the stockholder list was the single, indisputable treasure to someone shrewd and unscrupulous enough to mine it. With his marvelous understanding of human nature, Cook realized that many such stockholders would be ripe for another fling at the great oil game, assuming that they did not have to risk too much.

And Cook did not ask them to risk anything. On the contrary, he gave them a chance at a fortune in dividends. All they had to do was exchange their worthless stock certificates for an equal number of shares of P.P.A. stock valued at $1 per share. If they would simply dig that old stock out of the trunk or bottom drawer where they had buried it in shame when their company had failed, they could exchange it for a "sure thing" interest in a booming, vigorous, forward-looking company. Well, there was a little catch—if you could call it that. Stockholders had to ante up a little cash, a mere 25 percent of the value of the shares exchanged, but they received full value in more shares for the cash paid in. For example, a man held 500 shares of worthless stock in the Big Bear Oil Company. He received 500 shares of P.P.A. stock for his exchange, paid in $125 in cash, and received another 125 shares in return. How's that for a deal? He got 625 shares in a thriving, progressive, certain-to-prosper enterprise in exchange for $125 and some worthless paper!

It really pained Dr. Cook to hear federal prosecutors hounding him on his brilliant idea. Everyone knew that money was necessary in order to drill and acquire new leases of value. What was wrong with giving frustrated investors another chance to recover their money? Nothing crooked here. Cook would use the money to do what he promised to do—find oil and make everyone rich. So, to hear the prosecutor harp on a claim in P.P.A. literature that "the company was as safe as a bank" and demand the meaning of the assertion was aggravating. But Cook answered cooly that some banks had recently gone to the wall. And when the prosecutor asked whether his puffing of P.P.A. "was pure speculation of future gains," he could answer sharply, "Well, the entire oil industry is speculation." A telling point!

When asked how P.P.A. could promise 10 percent monthly on cash invested and 2 percent monthly on stock invested, "with every chance in the world the dividend would be doubled or tripled," and how it could refer to investors "who were now drawing monthly cash dividend checks" when only one dividend had been paid, Cook could answer justly, "We had paid one, on a theory of a monthly dividend check."[3]

The courtroom grew more uncomfortable for Cook when Prosecutor John Pratt quoted passages from P.P.A. literature that referred to the company's 100 producing wells at a time when P.P.A. had not received "one nickel's worth of oil production."

Pratt: Is it a fact? Not one nickel's worth?
Cook: I don't think that is a fact.

Joseph Bailey, the defense attorney, intervened at this point to protect Cook, but Pratt persisted in questioning Cook and the judge lent his weight as well.

Cook: I don't know.
Pratt: Don't you know you had not received anything?
Cook: I don't know anything of the kind.

Pratt: You heard Matheney's testimony on records of oil production?
Cook: I did.
Pratt: Don't you know—I will ask you again—that you had not received one five-cent piece, or its equivalent?
Cook: The mere fact that . . .
Pratt: Answer the question.
Cook: The mere fact that the money was not in, is not an indication that the oil had not been run to our credit for a long time. We had had oil runs that have been running for years, that we have not got the checks on yet.
Pratt: What was production on the 100 wells?
Cook: I don't know.
Pratt: It was insignificant, wasn't it?
Cook: It was small.
Pratt: It was not nearly enough to pay dividends, was it?
Cook: It was small.
Pratt: It was not enough at any time to pay your office rent, was it?
Cook: Well, I don't think that is—I don't know. We had other sources of income.

John Pratt, the chief prosecutor, wanted to know how much other income, but Cook did not know. Pratt knew.

Pratt: Don't you know it was about $1,070?

Cook replied that he had not regarded the amount as important. He had other accounts, other profits, and oil runs coming later. "Our earnings were all future," he explained.

Pratt established that Cook had paid two dividends of $20,000 each within six weeks, and wondered where the money had come from.

Pratt: You paid them out of money received from the sale of stock, didn't you?

Paying dividends out of stock sales returns was contrary to law, as Cook well knew, hence his evasion.

"I would not say so," he replied. There was other money coming in. He had sold some property and that had helped. "Well," he admitted, "I put in some money from the stock."

Pratt showed that the property sold for income had only yielded a $500 down payment at the time—if indeed, anything at all, since other evidence indicated that the sale was itself illusory and fraudulent.

The income at the time did not matter so much, Cook asserted. They were a "young company" and had high expectations.

> Pratt: It was all a dream of the future, wasn't it, Doctor?
> Cook: Not all. We were a young company, just in the process of developing and had every reason to expect results.

Where did the money to pay dividends come from if it was not from the sale of stock? Pratt wanted an answer to this because he believed that dividends were paid to keep old investors happy and to attract new stockholders. P.P.A. records did not indicate any income from which dividends could otherwise be paid.

Cook's memory often let him down when questions concerning other income came up. He seemed to recall sale of a parcel of land for $15,000. Pratt showed that the buyer only paid a modest down payment and that the deal then fell through because it turned out that it was federal land. Cook grew evasive over the federal land. All he could recall was tendering the purchase money to the government.

There seemed to be no way for Cook to explain paying dividends. Didn't you actually pay dividends from stock sales, Pratt persisted? "We did not regard it that way at all," Cook replied.[4]

Other government witnesses testified on suspicious P.P.A. activities. R. M. Dietrich of Hamburg, N.Y., was urged by a P.P.A. salesman in New York to transfer shares in an inactive company to P.P.A. and was offered a free trip of inspection to Texas. In November 1920 Dietrich met Cook in Fort Worth. An associate of Cook's told him that the wells were too far away for inspection ("it would take a day and night to visit") but that P.P.A. would accept $1,500 cash for his shares.[5] Dietrich refused and returned to New York. Four hours after his return, the P.P.A. salesman contacted him again. Later he saw a P.P.A. letter that implied that Dietrich had recommended a transfer of his shares to fellow stockholders of the failed company. He had not transferred his stock, nor had he made such a recommendation.

Promotional letters sent out by P.P.A., were referred to throughout the trial. When Cook was confronted with the correspondence in his own name, he argued that some of the more blatant claims were not intended to deceive; they were only expressions of optimism. Ultimately, however, his defense consisted of a denial of knowledge. He did not authorize false claims; he had not seen the offending letters that were machine-stamped with his signature.

Cook admitted that he should have watched the output of letter writer H. O. Stephens more carefully: "I frankly admit that." He recalled someone in the office questioning Stephens's grammar, but Cook had told the complainant that the writing lost its forceful character and drawing power when corrected. Besides, the writer got mad when he was edited. And Stephens did more than write. He was a top salesman. "I did not suppose, as we later found out, that there was something wrong with the man's head."[6] He hadn't read Stephens's material, even after hearing complaints.

The government showed that Cook ran P.P.A. without recourse to the nominal board of directors. Prosecutor Pratt pressed Cook hard on the issue of director Ridgell's participation.

Pratt: Did he act?
Cook: We were unable to get a meeting.
Pratt: Did he act? Answer the question.
Cook: I say, we were unable to get a full meeting of the full board.
Pratt: Did Mr. Riley [another listed director] act?
Cook: Mr. Riley was in and out of the office nearly every day.
Pratt: Did he act, as far as the statement is concerned here, in October?
Cook: Well, I talked to Mr. Riley.
Pratt: This board as such, did not hold a meeting, did it?
Cook: We had no meeting, so we gradually changed the whole system.[7]

Pratt pursued the views of directors Turner and Smith when evidence indicated that they had opposed dividends. If they opposed, then granting dividends had been Cook's decision alone.

Pratt: Then your statement that the directors had favored quick returns to investors was not true, was it?
Cook: It certainly was true. . . . We got quick dividends to investors at that particular time.
Pratt: They favored them, but there was not money to pay them; that is a fact, isn't it?

Cook: At that particular time they thought that we had better delay; however, they conceded to it later.[8]

Bailey objected often to the prosecutor's attempts to discover what Cook did for P.P.A. It was a key issue because the defense wished to show Cook's ignorance of any misrepresentations by P.P.A. The judge insisted that Cook must explain his activities, and Cook admitted that he directed the business. He arrived at the office at 6:00 A.M., reviewed the affairs of the previous day, talked to department heads and field heads until 10:00 or 11:00 A.M., then went to the field, working there until 10:00 or 11:00 P.M.

H. B. Matheney, a Department of Justice bank accountant, testified that he had examined the P.P.A. books in November 1922. P.P.A. had been organized the previous March. No regular books had been kept until mid-July; prior records were very incomplete. Cook paid P.P.A. bills with his personal checks.

This government testimony was significant because the defense insisted that Cook received no salary from P.P.A., hence lacked dishonest intent. Yet it appeared that Cook did not distinguish between P.P.A. cash transactions and his personal affairs, a practice indicating an untraceable commingling of money transfers. Corporation laws, of course, prohibited officers from just such an intimate relationship with company business because of the opportunities for a personal rake-off.

One Pratt-Cook exchange bore on the meaning of the "sucker lists" of stockholders of defunct companies, lists which Pratt considered the chief assets of P.P.A. Cook resisted the term "sucker lists." Cook admitted that the term was common phraseology; but Pratt trapped him by referring to a letter of Cook's in which he used the term himself. Then Cook offered the damaging admission that "we didn't use lists as lists, we used them as part of the property of some company."[9]

Spectators in the courtroom looked forward to the closing arguments for the defense and prosecution. A Fort Worth reporter predicted that chief defense counsel Bailey, famous for oratory in the United States Senate, would make the "supreme effort of a lifetime of legal and legislative efforts. When he is done, when the last of the colorful adjectives which will be enunciated with the mellowness of a silver bell" was heard, it would be Zweifel's turn. Henry Zweifel was fiery, although "not given to polished declaration." His presentations followed the lines of political stump oratory—rousing and colorful. Both lawyers were brilliant, and would deliver "sentences that have the snap and speed of a rapier in the hands of an expert."[10]

The judge ordered the defendants' wives to sit behind the courtroom rail for the arguments. Twelve wives were present, and the judge feared the distraction of tears. During the trial the wives had been permitted to sit in front of the courtroom, where they could offer moral support to their husbands. Cook's former wife had been in faithful attendance, but she seemed "apparently unconcerned."[11]

Prosecutor Pratt opened the arguments with a four-hour charge laced with vehement references to the defendants. The other attorneys followed with their own brands of eloquence. All were conscious of the importance of the case. The prosecution culminated the work of Texas's most famous grand jury, a body that considered evidence on various oil swindles from April through mid-October before winding up the investigation.

Defense lawyers denied all the government's charges. Cook and the others were honest businessmen who happened not to be successful. If Cook had drilled successfully in the Corsicana or another P.P.A. field, there would have been no indictment.

In its final argument, the government stressed evidence of fraud. Where fraud occurs, it is no defense to point to the mishap of drilling dry holes.

Judge Killits's charge to the jury was the longest ever heard in a Fort Worth court. He instructed that the actions of Cook's agents were Cook's actions under the declaration of trust agreement that P.P.A. had engaged in with stockholders. It was Cook's duty to see that his agents committed no fraud; he was the sole controller of P.P.A. Killits explained the common law of agency, which had always declared a principal responsible for the acts of his agent.

The judge observed that Cook repudiated his chief promotional letter writer in courtroom testimony. Repudiation, however, was no defense if Cook had engaged in an illegal scheme. Cook bore the responsibility regardless of his knowledge of his agent's work.

The jury retired for deliberation and returned with guilty verdicts on most of the indictments. They had not been impressed by the defense's effort to show that Cook drew no salary from P.P.A. and that he put his own property and funds into the company. They found fraud and responsibility for it with Cook.

After the jury returned with the bad news, Cook remained cheerful. He and the others played checkers in jail. "The hypnotic influence he is supposed to have must help others be cheerful too," a reporter observed.[12]

Cook's conviction was applauded by the local, national, and industrial press. The government prosecutor announced that it seemed possible now to stamp out the threatened epidemic of mail fraud and wildcat promotional schemes. Fleecers were on the run. *Oil Weekly* greeted the decision as a great victory for truth in advertising.

Cook discussed his finances with newsmen, denying the prosecutor's claim that he had squirreled away a good part of the P.P.A. earnings. Prosecutors are inclined to conclude that unaccounted-for money has been hidden, a charge hard to prove and difficult to refute. From the Tarrant County Jail, Cook told newsmen he would appeal if legal costs could be raised: "It seems that an almost impossible burden has been placed upon me. I have no money."[13] Marie Cook, his recently divorced wife, did manage to raise money, some $10,000 for the appeal.

In jail Cook maintained his wonderful poise, the celebrated equanimity that only deserted him once—when he broke down and left the country in 1909 under the terrific pressure. A conviction for fraud does not preclude one from insisting upon one's own innocence. Cook reaffirmed his purity with some panache: "I only had one dream. Call me a visionary if you will, but within me was an abiding desire to find an oil field that would remain a monument to my name and memory, and all the money I received was spent to that end."[14]

There is no reason to doubt Cook's megalomania; it is reasonable that he wished to wipe out his earlier disgraces by creating a prosperous memorial to his name. Yet the law is strict and does not permit men to push forward their dreams by defrauding others, regardless of the essential purity of their motivations.

Cook appealed the decision to the Circuit Court of Appeals without success. Judge Killits was very pleased at his own handling of the trial. The defense did not allege any errors in the judge's interpretation of the law; all seventeen grounds of error involved Killits's disciplining of Cook's chief counsel.

KILLITS'S FURY

The Arctic does not treat men well.
　　　　　—Emil Lengyel

Judge Killits's role in the Cook conviction deserves some attention because of charges that he was influenced adversely by Cook's exploration reputation. Letters written by Killits during the trial do not reveal any bias against Cook, but they show Killits's disgust at the defense tactics.

Cook lost because the evidence of guilt overwhelmed him. His battery of eight lawyers labored through a six-week trial to no avail. The prosecution's case showed his fraud beyond reasonable doubt.

Defense attorney Joseph Bailey tried hard to arouse Texas spirit in the jurors by implying that the federal government's involvement reflected northern interference in Texan matters. Appeals to sectional sentiment failed to distract the jury, but infuriated Killits. The judge kept cool, found occasion to mention before the jury that his wife was a Texan, and avoided errors that might sustain an appeal. Killits privately complained of Bailey's tactics and mannerisms, the drunkenness of several of the defense attorneys, and the general caliber of the Texas bar. But he was satisfied that he conducted the trial fairly.

Before laying a stiff sentence on Cook—fourteen years, nine months, and a $12,000 fine—and comparatively stiff ones on E. J. Cox and other

P.P.A. officials, Killits delivered a scathing denunciation of Cook. Judges often use such occasions to draw moral lessons and to blow off steam accumulated during the tense trial period. Such remarks, made after the jury had delivered its verdict, are not part of the court record and can do no harm to the case. Killits's impassioned diatribe delighted newsmen and has been quoted often by Cook fans who detect personal bias in the judge, and by Cook foes as convincing evidence of his guilt. But Killits's fury was neither of these. He had his chance to grandstand, and probably directed anger at Cook that, in his own jurisdiction, he would have diverted partially toward the defense attorneys, who disregarded the interests of their minor clients. Cook and his lawyers misused the judicial process to cheat the other defendants, and Killits was one judge who hated perversion of the court beyond any other crime.

Killits's statement to Cook deserves quotation in many of its particulars:

> This is one of the times when your peculiar and persuasive hypnotic personality fails you, isn't it? You have at last got to the point where you can't bunco anybody. You have come to the mountain and can't reach the latitude; it's beyond you. First we had Ananias [an early Christian who was struck dead for lying to Peter], then we had Machiavelli; the 20th century produced Frederick A. Cook. Poor Ananias, he is forgotten, and Machiavelli—we have Frederick A. Cook.

Killits declaimed that Cook was "damnably crooked," that his defenders held "their handkerchiefs to their noses" to avoid a "rank smelling to heaven," and asserted that Cook had hidden away the ill-gotten gains taken from widows and orphans, and was too dangerous to run at large:

> Oh God, Cook, haven't you any sense of decency at all, or is your vanity so impervious that you don't respond to what must be calls of decency to you? Aren't you haunted at night? Can you sleep?

Cook remained silent and the judge was incensed:

> What's the use of talking to you? Your effrontery, vanity, and nerve are so monumental, so cold-steel, so impervious, so adamantine to what I have got to say that the only satisfaction I get in saying that is I know I am voicing the feelings of the decent people of Texas.[1]

Among the interesting lessons of the trial is what it showed of Cook's indifference to his employees. The twelve defendants included E.J. Cox, the principal figure in the fraud next to Cook. Cox, a P.P.A. ghostwriter for Cook, received a salary of $30,000 a year, which is some indication of his value. Other defendants were salesmen and superintendents of company divisions.

One salesman, Ambroise Delcambre, possessed the good judgment to retain his own attorney. The others relied upon Cook's attorneys, to their detriment. The salesman Samuel Hess, for example, headed Cook's office in Memphis. He was charged with placing misleading ads in newspapers and sending out deceptive correspondence, all of which originated from P.P.A. headquarters. Hess and five other salesmen told Cook they could not afford a lawyer. Cook explained that there was no need; his attorneys would defend them without charge.

At the opening session of court, Hess and the others asked the judge if they might be excused from attendance. They had new jobs and could not afford to miss work through the long trial. Killits saw no reason why, if they wished to run the risk, they should not be allowed to stay on their jobs. Accordingly, all six men missed the trial, although they appeared as ordered just before the case went to the jury.

According to Killits's private papers, Cook's attorneys did not introduce any evidence on behalf of the absent defendants. The government argued that each was responsible for the ads and letters that misrepresented the truth. Two elements were necessary for conviction: participation in a scheme known by the defendants to have been fraudulent; and intent, through the exercise of their responsibilities, to assist in the fraud. Government evidence reasonably predicated a fraudulent intent; it was up to the individuals to challenge either or both elements of the fraud. Their personal testimony could have offset the government's circumstantial evidence, but none was offered. Delcambre, on the other hand, testified and satisfactorily explained his role. Even the prosecutor was impressed by Delcambre's limited role in P.P.A. and consented to the court's direction of an acquittal.

Hess and the others were convicted. Killits considered their responsibility for fraud to be small and sentenced them to thirteen months in the penitentiary. At the sentencing, the young salesmen, all in their twenties, broke down. They told the court they had depended entirely upon the protection of Cook's counsel. When they had returned to court at the end of proceedings, they were a little worried. Should they take the stand, they asked Bailey? Bailey assured them that the government had failed to make a case against them; they need not bother testifying.

Hess had been prepared to tell the jury that he had never been in Fort Worth while with P.P.A.; that he knew nothing of company assets or its business except what Cook told him; that his ad copy came to him from the head office, and he did not suspect its falsity.

Killits realized that the six salesmen had been duped by Cook and his defense counsel. He ordered a Department of Justice investigation, and assured the young men of his recommendation for a presidential pardon if they were cleared. Eventually the men were pardoned.

Another defendant had headed Cook's correspondence division. He was found guilty and sentenced to seven and one-half years in jail. Like the others, he had requested permission to absent himself from the trial. On his return, he too was told by Bailey that the government could not make a case against him. Killits believed that evidence established his full participation in fraud, yet there were extenuating circumstances. "The most important item of testimony involving him was a very mendacious circulated letter, forged both in composition and signature." Other evidence showed he tried to replace this letter with a genuine letter on the subject covered by the forgery. Because he did not testify, it was assumed he was responsible for the whole event—hence, Killits's tough sentence. In this instance Cook admitted his own responsibility; he had composed the letter and directed its circulation without the other man's consent. Killits acted on Cook's post-trial admission, and the President commuted the company officer's sentence from seven and one-half to two and one-half years.

Belatedly Cook helped one of his codefendants, but not the others. Killits believed that all seven would have gained by separate representation. In examining the situation he determined that the testimony of any one of the seven would have injured Cook's defense. "This explanation would have enhanced the proof of Cook's guilty participation, and for that reason they were deliberately betrayed."

Cook went on the stand, clearly carrying with him the moral obligation to protect the interests of these seven subordinates who were persuaded to trust themselves to the tender mercies of his counsel. Yet in his testimony there wasn't a whisper respecting the interests of any one of the seven. Cook heard the testimony that fully implicated his underlings without batting an eyelash. His direct examination was so skillfully conducted as to leave no opportunity for the district attorney to cross-examine him in any way upon the matters that affected any one of the seven men in question. In the federal practice, a witness can only be cross-examined on subjects upon which he testified in direct examination. Cook's astute counsel limited the direct examination in order to narrow the opportunities for cross-examination.

"This was, to my mind, the most despicable piece of professional misconduct that I have ever witnessed in Court. Had I been trying this case in my own jurisdiction, there would have been an inquiry into professional misconduct, with a sure result of serious consequences to counsel betraying their clients. As it was, the matter was exposed publicly, and left to the conscience of the Judge in charge in whose Court I sat as an assistant, who very conveniently ignored it,"[2] wrote Killits.

In the light of this episode, it is possible to see why Judge Killits was not a Cook fan.

JAIL

He who will tell a lie from idle vanity
will not scruple telling a greater from interest.
—Lord Philip Chesterfield

From the United States Penitentiary in Leavenworth, Kansas, Cook continued to write inspirational works. As editor of *The Leavenworth New Era,* he relived some of his polar experiences in vivid portrayals of his relationship with Arctic animals such as the musk-ox and wolf. He reported accurately on the value of the musk-ox, but his description of the wolf was colored with astonishing statements that caught the attention of his readers: "I have eaten the wolf and he has many times tasted my blood, but as an enemy or as a friend I love him still."[1]

At times Cook appears to be a man ahead of his time in explaining the place of the wolf in natural ecology, and in calling for consideration of the animal's capacity for adaptation. Unfortunately for his credibility as a nature writer, he passes beyond probability to tell of phenomena that no other traveler has ever confirmed: "The wily, cautious and elusive creatures followed us for at least 300 miles" on land.[2] Faithful dogs could hardly do better.

Cook proposed that someone establish wolf farms and market the fur. A fortune was assured to the fur farmer, who could expect $10 each for pelts. Polar bear farms also promised rich benefits to the daring entrepreneur. Bear pelts were immensely valuable, and raising the animals on a suitably located island presented no insurmountable obstacle.

Even more visionary schemes engaged Cook's still-active mind. Polar aviation raised all kinds of possibilities. Planes could carry food stored in frozen state to all parts of the world. The expense of artificial refrigeration would be eliminated.

Jail is not pleasant. By such means and by his hospital work, through which he earned the gratitude of other inmates, Cook passed the time.

Occasionally Cook's editorials hinted at matters touching on his own career. Although his reputation as an explorer exceeded that as a scientist, he apparently had turned against adventure for its own sake. There had been so much scandal over exploration, and "the news vendors of scandal of explorers have spent more in spreading their stories than the total cost of the prodigious undertaking itself." One news agency paid over $300,000 "for a part of the cable dispatches of one icy argument."[3] If only the money had been spent on true exploration rather than scandal: How much better off mankind would be. And so much good could be done when men learned to utilize the regions they explored.

If Cook professed disgust at exploration scandals in 1926, it is not surprising. But, as we will see, the disgust was only a fleeting phase. Cook did not mean to be forgotten, nor to be disregarded as a hoaxer or imposter. At Leavenworth, waiting for parole, he avoided direct discussions of his personal controversies; it was prudent to do so. He had to wait for his vindication. It would come, he was sure. And if it were necessary to wallow in scandal once more in order to achieve vindication, he must be prepared to do it. If we cannot always understand why Cook thought himself a wronged man, we know he burned with the realization of it. Of such stuff zealots are made. They are hard to keep down.

At times comparatively small incidents in exploration history reveal more about the game than major ones. In January 1926 Roald Amundsen, then in the news because of his polar flights, was on an American lecture tour. A newsman in Fort Worth, Texas, queried him on the Peary-Cook dispute after Amundsen's compassionate prison visit to his old Antarctic companion, Cook. Amundsen commented that Cook's claims were just as plausible as Peary's and that he did not think Cook faked his story. From his experience with Eskimos, Amundsen discounted the repudiation of the polar journey by Cook's Eskimo companions. In his experience, Eskimos could be made to say anthing.

When this story reached *The New York Times*, its editors elicited the response of other polar experts. Almost two decades had passed since the

Cook-Peary claims, but a reexamination seemed newsworthy. Donald MacMillan and Matt Henson, members of Peary's team, reaffirmed their faith in their leader. General Adolphus Greely remained convinced that neither man reached the Pole. Anthony Fiala said he believed Peary because Peary was an officer and a gentleman, adding: "Of course, he never presented any scientific proofs of his discovery." Vilhjalmur Stefansson, a staunch friend of Peary's though not of Amundsen's, found Amundsen's statement "extraordinary" and compared "Cook's history of fakery" with Peary's better record.[4]

When the *Times* wired Amundsen to confirm his statements, the Norwegian explorer denied making any commitment to either Cook or Peary. He admitted to a lack of belief in Eskimo testimony and insisted that he would need to study the scientific observations made by both men to form an opinion. The *Times* took Amundsen to task: "It was bad enough for [Amundsen] to seek to rehabilitate Dr. Cook, but it was worse and almost unforgivable for him in the same breath to discredit Peary."[5]

Clearly the partisanship of the *Times* had not diminished over the years. Poor Amundsen needed popularity if his American lectures were to draw, and the *Times* publicity was no help. Despite his disclaimers, Amundsen had raised issues that the *Times* considered "unforgivable." How did Amundsen dare? "This is the first time so far as the record shows that anyone has accused Commander Peary of failing to publish his observations." Peary's records, huffed the *Times*, were published in his book *The North Pole*.[6] Even though the *Times* reproduced Peary's logbook, as published in *The North Pole*, the paper's editors were only continuing an evasion dating back to 1909. No one, it is true, had ever accused Peary of failing to publish any observations, but there had been many calls for publication of reasonable proofs—observations that could have and should have been recorded to substantiate a claim. Congressman Henry T. Helgesen's remarks in Congress ten years earlier reflected doubts about Peary's evidence and the testimony on it. Helgesen and others believed that Peary's statements proved that his claim to the North Pole was without foundation.[7] Amundsen, too, believed that foundation data had not been published.

The Times expected its readers to find that Amundsen was either vindictive or obtuse in suggesting other evidence might be published, and distorted the record to this end. Another strong Peary citadel was aroused by the news stories. The prestigious National Geographic Society canceled a scheduled Amundsen lecture. Its president, Gilbert H. Grosvenor, expressed his indignation at "a statement by Amundsen seriously reflecting on Peary."[8] Oddly enough, no one complained publicly at this violation of free speech. Amundsen, who held the National Geographic Society's highest award, planned to lecture on his own explorations, not on Peary's. On the surface, there should be no reason why his mild and reasonable reservation concerning Peary should bar him from lecturing in Washington, D.C. More than spite was involved, however. The National Geographic Society had verified Peary's claims; Amundsen's comments reflected on the Society's integrity.

In New York, Amundsen denied that he was indignant at Grosvenor's action: "I don't want to get into any controversy. . . . I am rather amused than otherwise at the childishness of things. Maybe they will grow up some day."[9]

The Amundsen episode reflects sadly on the pettiness of Peary fans toward a distinguished man who did not share their biases. An equally disturbing example of partisan nastiness occurred when Cook became eligible for parole. William H. Hobbs, a University of Michigan geologist and later Peary's boigrapher, wrote to a number of individuals asking that they protest against Cook's parole. The hostility of Hobbs, and those who joined him, had nothing to do with the oil swindle. Hobbs despised Cook because of the polar controversy. Peary had been dead for ten years, but the spirit of vengeance raged on among his family and some friends.

One recipient of Hobbs's letters was the great polar explorer, Vilhjalmur Stefansson. Stefansson was a friend of Peary's and a doughty defender of the Admiral's reputation, but he was also humane and sensitive. Such vindictiveness as Hobbs represented appalled him. He tried to respond tactfully to Hobbs: "It seems to me that as friends of Peary's we are interested in Dr. Cook's moral branding as an untruthful person, not his physical incarceration." Wasn't the conviction enough, Stefansson asked? It showed that Cook's word could not be trusted on any subject. Stefansson refused to join Hobbs's campaign: "I am sure that even if you may not personally agree with it, you will understand sympathetically this distinction which I make between Dr. Cook as a human being and as a candidate for a position among explorers."[10]

Hobbs did not understand; he was incapable of such subtle distinctions. His was a nasty case of frenzied loyalty. Subsequently he attacked fiercely any writer who cast doubt on Peary and gloated to friends when such foes became ill or died. Cook's release from Leavenworth fell on March 8, 1930. He was sixty-five years old. A reporter interviewed him on his prospects, which Cook admitted were slim. Cook took pleasure in telling the newsman that a magazine had offered him $20,000 for his confession, while he was in prison. "To a man in prison, $20,000 is a lot of money. It was indeed fortune to me, since I am without funds."[11]

It seems unlikely that any Cook story might command a $20,000 offer in 1930. *Hampton's* had paid only $4,000 twenty years before when the polar issue was much hotter. At any rate, Cook was not ready to confess: He had not given up.

A few years later, his parole period ended, he opened a new attack with great spirit. He was seventy-one, he admitted to a friend, but "I am on the way for 90 years." The main thing was "to fire ambition and keep it in line for specific action."[12]

In a two-pronged attack, Cook demanded consideration from the American Geographical Society and the courts. The American Geographical Society turned him down without undue anxiety. A new investigation of such a stale, potentially embarrassing matter did not lure the Society. And why should it? Cook had his day earlier. Yes, his partisans could charge that the Society's indifference showed a Peary partisanship, that its membership feared a searching scrutiny of the truth, but it was not enough to cry out at injustice. Cook had nothing to offer as a basis for reopening a case that, after all, had never been the official concern of the American Geographical Society. He might better have appealed to the Explorers Club, where his Mount McKinley's claim had been officially demolished. But he had no new evidence to justify a reconsideration of either Mount McKinley or the Pole. Most geography fans were long since weary with Cook and not a little bitter over the disgrace he brought to their manly cause.

Cook's excitement and expectations were caused in part by favorable, hard-hitting articles by Ted Leitzell in *Real America*, a popular magazine. Leitzell was neither the first nor the last to discover the dramatic "truths" that Peary lied and Cook told the truth, and such affirmations heartened old Cook. With the utter implausibility of the diehard, Cook found "a tremendous effect" in Europe from the articles, and this despite the fact that the press paid little attention.[13]

Cook planned to sally forth to New York City from Buffalo from time to time to marshal his forces and "encourage those who have the issue there under fire."[14] A writer, Andrew Freeman, was working on a book that would present Cook's case. A septuagenarian feeling his oats may be forgiven for exaggerating his striking power and boasting of the "boreal thunder" he was unleashing against his detractors. All unsuspectingly, the world went about its work: Cook's thunder resounded only in the small circle of polar buffs who worried over Peary's reputation. Some of its members resembled Cook in tenacity and neuroticism and matched him in nastiness.

Cook's suit against Viking Press, Houghton-Mifflin, *The Encyclopaedia Britannica,* author Jeannette Mirsky, and explorers Donald MacMillan and Vilhjalmur Stefansson over libels in *To the North,* a well-written history of polar exploration written by Mirsky and introduced by Stefansson, provided a sharp issue for his pretensions. Cook had no case for libel. A court cannot judge between the truth of conflicting narratives of events. The suit could only be a harassment, a reminder that Cook still had teeth, that "boreal thunder" might yet issue forth.

In preparing defenses to Cook's suits, the publishers, Stefansson, and the others were put to the trouble of gathering rebuttal evidence. Someone, probably W. H. Hobbs, compiled "Material for Rebuttal . . . at the Cook-MacMillan Trial," focusing on authorities cited in support of Cook in Leitzell's *Real America* articles. Of the ten authorities cited by Leitzell, who got his list from Cook, only three had not repudiated Cook, according to Hobbs. The list included Roald Amundsen, Dr. Georges Le Cointe, Otto Sverdrup, Anthony Fiala, W. S. Schley, Professor W. H. Brewer, Evelyn Briggs Baldwin, Dr. Otto Nordenskjold, J. E. Bernier, and Edwin Swift Balch. Two ardent defenders stand out on the list: Balch, "a rabid defender of Cook even after the Copenhagen verdict"; and Rear Admiral Winfield Scott Schley, "a rather difficult subject, very bitter over the court-martial and reprimand of him by the Dewey Board of the Navy for his behavior at the battle of Santiago, and an alcoholic subject frequently intoxicated on the streets of Washington."[15]

Poor Schley, and poor other witnesses called from the shades to hold up Cook's standard in 1936. All were dead by that time except Anthony Fiala, a former explorer and owner of a New York sporting goods store. Fiala defended Cook and prepared the homecoming banquet at the Waldorf-Astoria in 1909, yet served on the Explorers Club committee investigating the Mount McKinley climb and voted against acceptance of Cook's account. Fiala accepted the verdict of Copenhagen but remained a warm friend of Cook's.

Quite a mound of documentation was raised by defenders against Cook's suit. Nothing new, of course. All it meant was a renewal of titillation and anxiety, a rehashing of old matters, a summoning of ghosts as witnesses once more. Cook lost his suit, as was inevitable.

Late in 1939 *Time* magazine interviewed Cook in Pelham, N.Y. The occasion was a meeting between Sir Hubert Wilkins, a younger, less controversial polar explorer, and the seventy-four-year-old Cook. Much of Cook's "old ebullience was gone," but he still talked of exploration, the outbreak of war in Europe, and held his white head high. "Most of all we have got to explore this area here—that lies back of the eyes and between the ears. When that cranial sphere is fully explored men will have no reason to fight wars."[16]

A few months later he was cheered by news of a presidential pardon for his fraud conviction. Ralph Shainwald von Ahlefeldt, a wealthy manufacturer and an old friend, had induced someone in President Franklin D. Roosevelt's executive office to grant mercy to a dying man. Shainwald's friendship with Cook went back to the 1903 Mount McKinley expedition, which preceded the controversial expedition of 1906.

In thanking Roosevelt, Shainwald could not resist the opportunity to ask the President to reopen the congressional investigation of 1915. He cited Lillian Kiel's testimony before Congress on *Hampton's* magazine and her recent telegram to the President arguing that President Wilson had intended to investigate but for his ultimely death.[17]

Less than three months later, Cook died. *The New York Times* and other newspapers published lengthy obituaries, summarizing his stormy career. His old antagonist, Peary, had been dead for twenty years. Exploration was not such a popular topic as it had been, but the great controversy was remembered by many people.

VI

Need for
Reexamination?

THE PHILADELPHIA
LAWYER

The truth that survives is the lie
that is pleasantest to believe.
—H.L. Mencken

S hainwald's loyalty to Cook was echoed by others. By all accounts
Cook was an attractive and compelling personality. Aside from
personal friends, his case attracted a number of individuals who
published articles and books in defense of his cause. Edwin Swift Balch
wrote books on the Mount McKinley and North Pole disputes and
appeared personally before a congressional committee on Cook's behalf.
Captain Thomas F. Hall, a New England mariner, published *Has the
North Pole Been Discovered?* in 1917. Hall, a sincere man and knowledgeable navigator, was apparently not a personal friend of Cook's but preferred the latter's evidence over Peary's. Hall's book is difficult to digest. He
did not write well and did not have great knowledge of polar conditions.

Another supporter was William E. Shea, an assistant to Mark Sullivan,
the author of *Our Times*, that great and lively historical narrative published
in the 1930s. Shea objected to Peary's claims, but Sullivan was not interested in reviewing the controversy in *Our Times*. Shea wrote the first draft
of a book in defense of Cook, but it was never completed for publication.

Most of the writing on Cook has been marred by various authors'
antipathy for Peary. The issues and evidence are confusing enough if one
examines either case; when both cases are lumped together, as is usual, the
confusion easily overwhelms the reader.

In reexamining Cook's case, it is also better to separate the issues of Mount McKinley, the North Pole, the oil fraud, and the Yahgan diction-ary. It seems better, too, to focus on more recent works, since their authors would have had access to any recently discovered facts on the contro-versies.

Of the earlier writers, it may be worthwhile to examine Edwin Swift Balch, because he treated the mountain and the Pole and because Cook made much of his authority.

Edwin Swift Balch, born in 1856 to a wealthy, socially prominent Philadelphia family, was something of a Renaissance man. He painted, climbed mountains, and wrote solid books on glaciers, art, exploration, and other subjects. His *Glaciers or Freezing Caverns* is considered a classic in the field and was reprinted in 1970. As an early advocate of submarines, he was ahead of his time, and he was considered an expert on Antarctic discovery and on other cultural, biographical, and linguistic subjects. The "precision, clarity, and single-mindedness of his writings" has been praised, yet these lawyer's virtues owed nothing to professional practice. He did not actually practice law, but traveled widely and lived as a wealthy, cultured gentleman.[1] His amateur pursuits sufficiently occupied his time.

Why Balch added Cook's career to his hobbies is unknown, but Balch's championship damaged his reputation in some circles. It is not difficult to see why. For all Balch's pretensions to science and scholarship, his profes-sional training was only in law, and whatever his accomplishments in the several fields he dabbled in, his contribution to the Cook controversy bordered on the ridiculous. He published two thin, handsome volumes concerned with Cook in 1913 and 1914, neither of which do credit to his power of advocacy.[2] The books show his commitment to Cook and are not difficult to read, resembling well-written briefs of a nontechnical nature. One could not ask the impossible, but what Cook needed were technical and scientific arguments.

A long article in *The New York Tribune* heralded Balch's *North Pole and Bradley Land*. It gave a good, concise summary of the book and indicated that the *Herald* welcomed a reopening of the controversy. It also lauded the author's credentials: "The intrepid defender—and it takes real bravery to take such a stand today in the scientific world—the intrepid defender of Cook is Edwin Swift Balch, fellow of the Association for the Advancement of Science, member of the Wyoming Historical and Geolog-ical Society, the Franklin Institute, American Philosophical Association, American Geographical and Royal Georgraphical Societies, writer on arctic, anatarctic, geographical, and ethnological topics for the learned societies of the world."[3]

Balch was a legitimate expert on glaciers, yet his book, *Mount McKinley and Mountain Climbers' Proofs*, puts forward arguments for Cook that are ridiculous on their face. Belmore Browne's notes on Balch's Mount McKinley book fix the weakness of the arguments:

1. *Shortness of breath, cold, and dark sky.* Cook's allusions to these phenomena, which Balch cites as proof of Cook's having been high up on Mount McKinley, are of no importance, as these are commonplaces, well known not only to mountaineers, but to all students of mountaineering literature.

2. *Ice blink over Saint Elias and Wrangell glaciers.* Even assuming that there be such an ice blink and that it be visible at such a distance, Cook could not have seen it from an altitude of 18,400 feet on Mount McKinley, because at that elevation he would have been in the Upper Basin or on the northern slopes of the South Peak, and the view to the south would have been hidden by the South Peak itself.

3. *Photographs of Cook's (or Fake) Peak.* A careful comparison of Cook's photos and the Parker-Browne photos of this peak and its surroundings must be absolutely convincing that the peak shown in Cook's "Top of the Continent" photo and that shown in the Parker-Browne "Fake Peak" photos are identical.

4. *Other Photographs.* A comparison of other photos in Cook's book with Parker-Browne photos shows:
   a. How Cook misnamed various views.
   b. How far Cook went (about the end of the "Great Gorge").
   c. How impossible it was for Cook to reach the North East ridge from Ruth Glacier.

5. *Cook's selection of the North East ridge and his story of its climb and of his ascent of the South Peak.* Cook could very easily guess that the North East ridge was the best (if not the only) approach to the Summit, from his general knowledge of this mountain and of mountaineering literature. He made various mistakes, however, among which are:
   a. Summit rocky, whereas it is perpetual ice and snow.
   b. When passing from North East ridge to Upper Basin, he says he turned to *east*. This would take him off into space. The real turn is to the *west* or *northwest*.
   c. Grade of 60° on backbone of ridge itself. No such slope except on side of ridge.

6. Balch makes various errors of location, among which are:

a. He says Cook reached a point on the glacier at altitude of 8,000 feet, *northeast* of summit. There is no such point on Ruth Glacier.

b. He says that three parties (Lloyd's, Parker-Browne's and Stuck's) approached from the *Northwest*, and that one (Cook) approached from the *Northeast*. On the contrary, the above three parties approached from the *Northeast,* and Cook from the *South and Southeast*.[4]

One of the great mysteries of the Cook controversy is Balch's amazingly uncritical support of the Mount McKinley and polar claims. Years after writing his silly books, Balch continued to feel good about his arguments for Cook. Writing to author Henshaw Ward in 1926, he noted that "you don't go for Cook yet" without expressing any rancor. Although Ward was not pro-Cook, he was definitely anti-Peary, and this was enough for Balch. The Philadelphian saw hope for Ward's conversion; Cook's claims were "provable in the future from his own observations and with the next explorer"; and with the advent of the air age, more confirming evidence would be forthcoming.[5]

Belmore Browne, a member of Cook's Mount McKinley expedition, had published his book, *The Conquest of Mount McKinley*, a few months before Balch's book appeared. Like other zealots, Browne hoped for an opportunity to enlighten Balch, or at least, to provoke a fruitful discussion.

Browne seems to have been a frank, noncontentious man, so we can accept the humility of his approach without jaundice. He regretted that the greater part of disproving Cook's claims fell on him, and found that "the task of attacking a former comrade was . . . distasteful"; he always kept his arguments short and regarded them "as an invitation for further study, rather than a final statement."[6] If Balch cared to visit Browne in New York and to bring any friends, Browne would be happy to share material he had not utilized in print.

Balch responded, saying he was surprised that Browne held evidence not used in his "big book," and suggested it be published at once for its interest.[7]

It does seem odd that Browne would withhold evidence against Cook when his book related an expedition organized for the purpose of refuting Cook. In another letter, Browne tried to explain: The material was voluminous and no publisher would entertain the publication of all the photos Browne had. Besides, publishers told him that the Cook controversy was dead, that the public was "tired of the controversy."[8]

Browne tried to clarify his position. He had been forced to cut his own narrative to include the Cook matter and still meet his publisher's limitations. But for space limitations, he would have directed more evidence to Cook's climb. Balch told Browne that the matter was public property and would be analyzed by mountaineers and geographers in the years to come; "It is almost certain that it will be further examined into by the Congress . . . next winter."[9] Thus Browne should present his proofs publicly "to all geographers and mountaineers." How this presentation could be made without publication or a possible invitation from Congress, Balch did not say.

And Browne did not understand Balch's apparent indifference to an opportunity to study material "that has an important bearing on the future standing of your book."[10] How could Balch insist upon publication after Browne explained that no one would publish his material and that he could not afford to underwrite the costs?

The tone of this letter was too sharp for Balch, who evidently was not curious about material gathered by a foe of Cook. Balch wrote angrily: "I am tired of your nonsense. You are certainly in a hole." Balch sarcastically advised Browne: "Because you cut up the northeast ridge on slopes of 60° and because you painted the frontispiece of Mount McKinley," call on Senator Miles Poindexter or Cook himself and "tell them the truth, the whole truth, and nothing but the truth. Probably in the long run you will fare better than by sticking to those who put upon you 'the greater part of the burden of disproving Dr. Cook's claims.' "[11]

This squabble between rival fans illustrates the entire controversy. Neither of the partisans liked the other's "truth," or cared to give it objective scrutiny. Things had gone too far. Balch had already written two books dismissing Cook's critics and had appeared before Congress. Browne had written his book and climbed the mountain.

Balch's book, *North Pole and Bradley Land*, did not add any evidence or perception to Cook's own defense. He relied upon future explorations that would confirm the existence of Cook's Bradley Land. Of course, later explorations proved that Bradley Land didn't exist.

Balch made much of Peary's descriptions of physical conditions at the Pole. It seemed striking to him that both explorers described conditions similarly. This notion is not unlike his Mount McKinley argument and, in fact, means little, since polar conditions do not differ appreciably over a region of many thousands of square miles. Each explorer could have described the Pole equally well on the basis of earlier experience in the Arctic. Even some Cook supporters like William Shea could not see any sense in this part of Balch's argument.

Balch's other contribution consisted of a historical perspective: He discussed the travelers of the past whose discoveries were denied at first. "And this should make it clear how inaccurate and valueless any preliminary popular or even scientific denial of the claims of explorers is apt to be." Herodotus questioned the ancient Phoenician sailors who voyaged into the southern Atlantic Ocean. The great Marco Polo's book had been described as a clumsily compiled fraud. Amerigo Vespucci had been accused of trying to cheat Columbus of fame by renaming the latter's discoveries. Fernando Pinto became famed as a travel liar—yet he was not. And, as for polar exploration, the exploits of the American seamen Nathaniel B. Palmer, who first sighted Antarctica, and James Weddell, who made major land discoveries, had been ignored or derided. Balch quoted the airy dismissal by geographer Clements Markham of any but British endeavors in Antarctic discovery: "Several private expeditions were started, Belgian, German, Swedish, Scottish, French, but none of them were of any use as regards Antarctic discovery."[12]

Balch had plenty of other examples of carping critics who tried to diminish the credibility of explorers. James Bruce, discoverer of the sources of the Blue Nile, was labeled a liar and, in fact, inspired the creation of the character Baron Munchhausen. Cries of derision greeted the German missionaries who reported snowcapped mountains on the equator in Central Africa in 1849. Paul Du Chaillur's description of baboons raised a chorus of hecklers from "Africa experts." And so it went through history. Doubters were commonplace. "What has happened in the past will doubtless happen again in the future." Advocate Balch was certain that critics of Cook would have to eat crow some day. "Historical precedent points to historical geographers recognizing Dr. Cook as the discoverer of the North Pole, with Admiral Peary as a close second."[13]

To the *New York Tribune* review of Balch's book which Cook included in *My Attainment of the Pole,* Cook also appended a note from a letter to him from the faithful Balch: "I have tried to look at it as if this were the year 2013, and all of us in heaven. . . . It is only a question of time till Dr. Cook is recognized as the discoverer of the North Pole."[14]

Balch's view from A.D. 2013 comforted him. Not too scientific—or even lawyerlike—a perspective, but it is not for us to question his need. It worked for him; it gave him patience with Cook's detractors.

TESTING
MOUNT McKINLEY

The explorer is the poet of action and
exploring is the poetry of deeds.
  —*Vilhjalmur Stefansson*

M ountains do not move, and if anyone wishes to test Cook's claim to Mount McKinley's peak, he need only follow his route. Once at the top, he could trumpet to the world that, in tracing Cook's footsteps, he proved Cook told the truth. No one has managed to do this, and it has not been for lack of effort. The Mazama Club party, intent on defending Cook's good name, failed in 1910, concluding that the route Cook indicated was impossible. Since that time scores of parties have assaulted Mount McKinley, some with success on various routes, and the mountain is much better known today than it was in 1906. Traffic was particularly heavy in 1976, the Bicentennial year, and some lives were lost despite improvements in equipment, techniques, and knowledge of the mountain over the years. Climbing Mount McKinley demands great skill and daring, and even the most dedicated and experienced climbers can be defeated.

In 1956 Walter Gonnason, a Seattle climber sponsored by Cook's daughter, Mrs. Helene Cook Vetter, tried to follow Cook's route and was forced to turn back. Bad weather had slowed him and fallen snow cornices had blocked his path; he gave up at 11,500 feet.

Mrs. Vetter waited anxiously at Talkeetna, a small community in the foothills, hoping for a vindication of her father. Gonnason returned with the bad news, but promised to try again the next year. Mrs. Vetter, as persistent as her father, refused to acknowledge anything beyond a temporary setback: "If the route is possible and my father claims he went up, no one can prove or disprove that he did not get to the top."[1] Hope still lives, but the route has not yet proved possible.

The drama of Gonnason's return was heightened by the presence of *Life* magazine photographers and other climbers, led by Bradford Washburn, whose purpose was to show conclusively that Cook faked his climb and his evidence. Washburn, director of the Museum of Science in Boston, knew Mount McKinley better than anyone and believed that the photographs he had taken in 1955, and on other occasions, confirmed the Herschel Parker-Belmore Browne evidence presented decades earlier. Washburn acted from a scientific interest in truth and to protect the reputation of Parker and Browne. Cook and his fans had dismissed the Parker-Browne photographs as forgeries and insisted that Peary fans had corrupted them.

Photographic evidence gathered by Washburn showing the fake peak Cook passed off as the summit even convinced Hugh Eames, author of *Winner Lose All*, the most recent book-length defense of Cook. It was not a grave fraud, says Eames, yet clearly a misrepresentation; "it was cutting a corner," an effort to please magazine readers and lecture audiences. "He had made that one small, miserably slight slip that, in large affairs, is sometimes fatal."[2] And Eames still defended Cook's Mount McKinley claim, relying on the same nonsense Edwin Balch had put forward in 1913 based on Cook's observations of physical conditions and estimate of height.

Eames admits that "Washburn's photographs demonstrate what he contends they do: that Cook did photograph the fake peak and present it as a picture of McKinley"; but then Eames tries to explain away the deception.[3] Cook fans might be better off if they conceded the entire fakery of Mount McKinley and explained it as a desperate gambit to win money and recognition in support of the polar quest, and if they insisted that the mountain fakery is no evidence of polar fakery.

Eames explains Cook's fraudulent use of photographs of Mount McKinley in unconvincing fashion. Explorers were sportsmen rather than scientists and had to be showmen to support expeditions. Cook's actual photos of the peak probably did not turn out, but luckily he had suspected the possibility and took "insurance" photos of lesser peaks so as to avoid disappointing lecture audiences. "Although it was a foolish action, it cannot be regarded as the sort of deed that is described as 'a grave fraud on the American people.' " Eames imagined Cook's frame of mind: "Perhaps he reasoned that a picture of a mountain is only a picture. Just as a picture of a lovely woman is only a picture, by no means the real thing, so he may have believed that extreme accuracy was unnecessary."[4]

Someone might appreciate Eames's conjecture of Cook's mental processes, but it does not reconcile well with Cook's presentation of himself as a scientist and a truthful man.

Writing in 1958 in *The American Alpine Journal,* a publication of the American Alpine Club, of which Cook was a founding member until dropped in 1910, Washburn devastates Cook's case through analysis of his narrative and photographs. It does not take any particular knowledge of mountaineering to understand the inconsistency of Cook's narrative. Cook partisans have made much of the consistency of his polar narrative but avoid such a reference with the Mount McKinley account. It is one thing to try to reconstruct Cook's alleged polar dash over shifting sea ice and quite another to observe descriptions of the little-changing ground of McKinley.

Cook's ascent is described so vaguely and confusingly that it is impossible to follow him, and he spared only eighteen words in describing his descent from the peak. Essentially, climbing a mountain for the first time is a discovery. One does not discover the peak, which has been seen often from a distance, but the mysterious route that leads to it. If a discoverer does not record his route in plain enough terms so that others following him can see it, what is the meaning? Finding the route is the key, the ultimate joy and reward of the venture, yet no one, friend or foe, in the last seventy years, has been able to find a logical, possible route by which Cook could have ascended.

Cook confused his climb marvelously by starting on the southeast side of the mountain, then describing his 12,000-foot camp on the northeast side while preparing to climb the north arête. Washburn argued that "it is humanly impossible" to have made such a traverse as Cook claims because of precipices, icefalls, and buttresses.[5]

Washburn's long article contains ample refutation of Cook's claim. In point after point he demonstrated the implausibility of Cook's report. Of course it did not convince Eames, and need not convince anyone who has no knowledge of Mount McKinley. Topographical evidence is much easier to brush aside when it concerns something that seems as remote as Mars. It is easy enough to go on arguing that Cook got to the top. Faith can move mountains, and it is not necessary to climb them. It is significant that Cook has no believers among those who have climbed Mount McKinley by any route. Virtually all defenses have been written by those who have never seen the great mountain and have never climbed mountains anywhere. As Washburn puts it: "They are exercises in reshuffling or re-editing the statements made by others over the years without an *iota* of near factual data to support what is said."[6]

It is impossible to prove Cook did not climb Mount McKinley if you reject the circumstantial and eyewitness evidence against him. This is one last refuge of Cook partisans, the bastion of mountain-moving faith. Yet it is possible to prove that Cook faked his evidence, and while this may be explained by all the ingenuity and imagination possible, it does not remove the fraud. Anyone who can believe, despite eyewitness testimony and overwhelming circumstantial evidence to the contrary, that Cook did what he claimed and committed fraud only in compiling evidence, shows a very moving faith in the man. But this kind of faith, or mischief, or unreason is unsettling. An unreasonable defense of a lie is an attack on reason.

Cook's biographers show irritation with the Mount McKinley dispute because of the impact it had in 1909—and still must have—on belief in any of his claims. In *The Big Nail*, Theon Wright describes the argument made in Congress to refute Hudson Stuck's refutation of Cook after Stuck reached the summit in 1913. Senator Miles Poindexter, using material provided by Cook, employed a familiar argument: Stuck's description of the summit resembled Cook's, thus Stuck's narrative corroborated Cook's claim.

The only importance of such wholly disputable testimony is in what Wright does with it. Quoting Poindexter's conclusion—"It is difficult to explain Dr. Cook's previously published accurate description of these things, the first ever given, except by admitting his actual ascent of the mountain summit"—Wright professes to believe that such a conclusion settled matters. "This might seem to have closed the McKinley controversy," Wright says, "but it did not."[8]

No, indeed, it did not, and for good reason. That Wright, writing in 1970, tries to throw this past his readers is appalling. Wright knows that the *Congressional Record* statement had no genuine authority as an objective analysis and that it was substantially a published handout prepared by Cook, yet he dares to cite it as the last word on McKinley, the ultimate conclusion that "settled matters."

Wright passes over Cook's faked photos quickly with a breezy reference to Cook's need for color to support his narrative. Then, with an astounding leap, Wright concludes that Mount McKinley's "ultimate significance" is in showing the "implacable determination" of Peary fans to destroy Cook. Such strained logic is the reason we are still asked to validate Cook's claims. Wright's reasoning is idiotic, but defending Cook on Mount McKinley drives men out of their wits.

Mount McKinley, majestically indifferent to all the squabbling, stood waiting for confirmation of Cook's claims. In a short season Cook might have scrambled over his previous route and given the lie to his detractors. He was perhaps in no condition to do this in 1910 yet might have done so in 1911 or afterward. Under pressure in 1909 he declared plans to climb, then never mentioned the possibility again.

Rather than driving his foes to the corner with an unanswerable field performance, he chose to stonewall the Mount McKinley question, concentrate on his North Pole claims, and raise what doubts he could to confuse the public.

In the 1913 edition of *My Attainment of the Pole*, Cook added a lie to the pile of Mount McKinley untruths and, characteristically, it was a bold one. He cited *The Los Angeles Tribune* of February 13, 1913, as quoting one R.C. Bates, a mine engineer and inspector, United States revenue officer, explorer, and mountaineer, who supported Cook's claim, confirmed that Parker and Browne were being paid $5,000 to refute Cook, and denied Parker's assertion that Cook's northeast ridge was unsurmountable. "I, with a party of two," said Bates, "explored the mountain in 1911 and selected the north-east ridge as the only feasible route to the top."[9] Bates allegedly went on to say that Parker contradicted himself after learning of Bates's climb and now says that the northeast ridge is the best route.

Cook quoted Bates further to strengthen his charges against Parker: "In a personal interview Mr. Bates made the very grave charge that one of the leaders of the very expedition [the Parker-Browne Explorers Club expedition, presumably] sent out to discredit me, had offered him a bribe to swear falsely to certain assessment work on claims which had not been done. The Peary-Parker-Browne movement is therefore from many sources a proven propaganda of bribery, conspiracy and perjury."[10]

Parker and Browne did do some mineral prospecting in 1910-11, and this activity apparently attracted Cook as one through which further discredit could be laid on his enemies. To measure Cook's flamboyance under assault, we have only to reflect upon the indignation he was capable of expressing: "That such men can escape the doom of prison cells is a parody upon human decency, and yet such are the men who are responsible for the distrust which has been thrown on my work."[11]

Parker and Browne lived a long time after 1913, escaped "the doom of prison cells," and, in fact, remained well-respected individuals. Cook, who marveled on more than one occasion that his foes escaped jail, did not do as well.

But these accusations against Parker and Browne, as nasty and unwarranted as they were, only touch the tip of Cook's impudence in his page-long updating of the Mount McKinley scandal for the revised edition of *My Attainment of the Pole*. What really highlights his daring is the fact that there exists no evidence of a 1911 Bates expedition nor of *The Los Angeles Tribune* article Cook quoted so extensively. Cook must have created the whole story from his imagination, since the zeal of Dr. Terris Moore, the historian of Mount McKinley climbs, has not turned up anything else on Bates's expedition aside from Cook's reference. "Nevertheless," Moore observes, "some later writers accept as fact Dr. Cook's original assertion about Bates' supposed expedition."[12]

It seems more than passing strange that the three doughty defenders of Cook's Mount McKinley claims, authors Wright, Freeman, and Eames, make no mention of Bates or his alleged expedition. In their hard-driven quest for confirmation of their hero, they have preferred to ignore Cook's testimony on the Bates expedition. Obviously their researches did not turn up anything on Bates. But instead of confronting Cook's big lie, they suppressed it. Yet all three biographers go along with Cook's bribery charges against Parker and Browne.

In *My Attainment of the Pole*, Cook's explanation of the Mount McKinley affair consists chiefly of a diatribe against the Peary cabal for bribing Edward Barrill. Cook treated Barrill rather gently as a "good-natured and hard-working packer" who, in his ignorance, allowed himself to be used by Peary and Parker. There is really no way of refuting the only witness of a shared deed, except by insisting on perjury and corruption. Unfortunately, there is a great deal of evidence that Barrill had consistently denied that the climb had been made. Cook ignored such evidence and, without explaining how he gained the knowledge, claimed that Barrill often bragged about the climb. "He went from house to house boastfully, with my book under his arm, telling and retelling the story of the ascent of Mount McKinley." This simply was not true; the evidence shows that Barrill joked about the book and made clear to friends that a fraud had been committed by Cook. Barrill wrote nothing and gave no public interviews in support of the claim. He was just the packer. Yet Cook argued that because of Barrill's previous support of the climb, he had become a perjurer: "That anyone should now believe the affidavit, secured and printed for Peary, did not to me seem reasonable."[13]

Whether Barrill ever did say he conquered the summit with Cook is a matter of interest, because a finding that he reversed himself would make his affidavit less convincing and a bribery charge much more convincing. Here was the only other man who could know with certainty whether Cook lied, and he appears to have said invariably that Cook lied. Both recent biographers of Cook rely entirely upon Cook's unsupported assertion that Barrill boasted of the successful climb, and, in doing so, these writers show how important it was to discredit the only witness. Out of necessity they depended upon Cook's bribery theory, because a superficial examination of its truth would bring the whole of Mount McKinley tumbling down over Cook's ears. Both biographers emphasize the confrontation between Cook and Barrill in the packer's hometown, the opera house meeting that made it abundantly clear that the hometown man's version of the climb was believed rather than Cook's. Barrill was no folk hero in Hamilton, Montana, but a relatively obscure figure, while Cook was a man of wider reputation and an appealing public speaker. But Barrill was more believable than Dr. Cook.

The Cook apologists do some disservice to history by failing to note a newspaper story of October 17, 1909, in which the opinion of people in Hamilton was sounded by a reporter: The consensus there was that Barrill had denied the climb's success for years.[14] The biographers might explain away this news story as a *New York Times* fabrication, but a failure to cite it, combined with a failure to question Cook's unsupported story of Barrill's switch, is suspect. It amounts to an uncritical acceptance of Cook's desperate defamation of Barrill. Poor Barrill, a man who would lie for $5,000, "ignorant, poor, good-natured, but weak"—and irresistibly tempted. But no one in 1909 or since has shown evidence that Barrill ever lied or was bribed. Evidence of Cook's lies abounds.

Quite deliberately Cook sets out to offset Parker's damaging testimony by ridiculing his physical ability and courage, and, more dubiously, by hinting that the initial efforts to climb the summit were canceled because of such shortcomings. Parker was disgruntled, suffered from ill health, inexperience, and inefficiency. It took two men to help Parker onto a horse. He was a quitter: "climbing a little peak forty miles from the great mountain . . . he had pronounced Mount McKinley unclimbable." Both Parker and Browne balked at the first large glacier ("an insignificant ice-wall") before the mountain.[15]

Thus Cook implies that he turned back at first attempts because of the fears of his detractors. If this was his opinion in 1913, it does not square with what he wrote in 1906-07 in *To the Top of the Continent*: "The combined result of this reconnaissance proved to us finally the hopelessness of further mountaineering from any point of attack which could be reached before the coming winter closed the gates to the upper world."[16] And he goes on to describe the descent, the dispersal of his party, and his accidental discovery of a summit route when he and Barrill were unencumbered by the presence of knowledgeable companions.

Cook also claimed in *My Attainment of the Pole* that, after he returned from Alaska "and Parker learned the details, he publicly and privately credited my ascent of Mount McKinley."[17] If this had been true, it would imply that Parker reversed himself again after the polar claim, which would indicate that he had been influenced by later events. Actually there is no record of Parker's public or private abandonment of his original doubts of Cook. Cook's biographers have not cited any either; instead they note Parker's presence at a geographers' dinner at which Cook told of his climb and allow readers to assume that such presence was assent to Cook's claim. Since the dinner in question involved more than a Cook testimonial, the presence of Parker and Browne meant no such thing; and their silence meant nothing. Should they have shouted down Cook after his talk? That would not have been very good form.

In truth Parker and Browne never accepted Cook's fraud. Parker tried hard to impeach Cook in New York and was unsuccessful. It was necessary then to wait for Cook's book, but when it appeared Cook had already left for the North. Browne observed that the book gave them irrefutable proof of "countless misstatements" that he and Parker could challenge: "Many of the misstatements we knew to be downright falsehoods." Yet, influenced by ideas of fair play, "we refrained from publishing anything derogatory to the Doctor's character while he was absent, and unable to defend himself."[18]

After Cook returned in 1909, Parker and Browne took their evidence before the Explorers Club, with results devastating to Cook. Whether they would have remained silent had not Cook claimed the Pole cannot be known. Browne affirms that the polar controversy "put an entirely new light on our claims against Cook," which "were really more or less private and personal," a matter of "mountaineering ethics," as distinguished from the "international importance" of the polar matter. Certainly the polar controversy provided a more receptive hearing at the Explorers Club than Parker was able to get in 1906, but whatever Browne's feelings, I suspect that Parker would not have allowed the Mount McKinley matter to rest indefinitely. True sportsmen cannot abide a fraud, and Parker showed earlier how much he cared about setting the record straight.

Neither Cook nor his defenders have ever been able to explain the Explorers Club's rejection of his Mount McKinley claim, except in terms of Peary's influence. Their explanation does not make sense for a number of reasons. Cook's friends served on the investigation committee and voted with the majority against him. Most Club members had no reason for undue bias against the Club's former president, a man who had been well liked and respected. To blame Peary's influence is begging the question. The issue was one of proof. If strain prohibited Cook from coming forward with evidence in 1909, as agreed, he could have done it subsequently. From 1910 through 1916 he spoke and wrote a good deal, but he had nothing substantial to offer on his mysterious ascent.

LOYALTY

Something which everyone accepts as
the gospel truth is inevitably false.
                    —H.L. Mencken

A small group of people gathered together on September 21, 1975 at Hurleyville, N.Y., near Cook's birthplace in Sullivan County, to dedicate a bronze bust of the explorer. The ceremony and a commemorative biographical pamphlet published for the occasion originated with the Dr. Frederick A. Cook Society. While the pamphlet writer desired to stress Cook's achievements rather than to revive "any unfortunate controversy," he treats "Cook's priority at the Pole as an historic fact."[1]

It would be good if Cook were honored as a pioneer explorer, recognized for undisputed contributions to knowledge and unquestioned demonstrations of daring, yet it cannot be—and his fans do not really want to avoid "any unfortunate controversy." Cook's reputation in history must rise or remain as it is in the shadow of the mountain and the Pole.

The honest believers insist that "Cook's own story of the polar journey is virtually unassailable" (i.e., the book *My Attainment of the Pole*). "To this," writes a fan in *Arctic* magazine, "has now been added powerful *ex post facto* evidence concerning ocean currents and ice islands."[2]

Actually what we have learned about the Arctic since 1909, including currents and ice islands, bears very little on Cook's case. And what we have learned about human psychology since that time does not help our understanding much either. We will probably always have Cook believers who discern confirming evidence that others assess differently, and who believe that truth has been obscured by the duplicity of Peary partisans. Our culturally diverse society can stand dissent. When Cook partisans seek too much, however, they are rebuffed, as in their centenary drive for a proclamation of an official Centennial Day approved by the New York legislature, which Governor Nelson Rockefeller refused to sign. Naturally they saw the forces of the old conspiracy at work in this refusal; Donald MacMillan, a survivor of Peary's expedition, had protested. To zealots, the protest and refusal "brings into focus the unrelenting attacks Peary's adherents continued to make on Cook."[3] So anyone who remains puzzled at their meaningless attempts to win some kind of official approval of Cook seemingly is either part of the conspiracy or a dupe of it.

At the centenary ceremony, plans for establishing a Cook Memorial Library at an eastern university were discussed. The nucleus of the collection now held by Cook's daughter, Helene Cook Vetter, includes "all original records, charts, manuscripts," and the polar diary. "Probably little of the primary material in Mrs. Vetter's collection has ever been examined by a professional historian," we were told in 1966.[4] The implication was that historians would find this material valuable in restoring Cook's image. If such was the belief, then why the delay in making available such pertinent evidence? Fifteen years after the library announcement the material still rests in the family's possession. Since 1965 two pro-Cook books have been published, and while neither is convincing, it is interesting that Theon Wright's *The Big Nail* (1970), written without the Vetter papers, is a better book than Hugh Eames's *Winner Lose All*. Eames used the Vetter papers to some extent, although he does not say whether he had unrestricted use or only utilized what was given to him. Whether despite the undisclosed papers or because of them, Eames's book offers more unsupported inferences and defies credulity more than Wright's or *The Case for Doctor Cook*, by Andrew A. Freeman, an earlier work that is in many ways the best of the pro-Cook books. No doubt others will follow Eames with future defenses of Cook; the trail is well marked, yet it does not lead where his defenders want to take it. Not yet revealed secrets of the Arctic or alpine environment are likely to change this; and it is futile to dream of documents, now hidden somewhere, that will be found to vindicate Cook.

What the historic record proves is that Cook cannot be vindicated—or even understood—better now than in 1909. All we get out of pro-Cook labors is a further exposure of the Peary Arctic Club's work against Cook. Yet there is nothing in the Club's record that shows dishonest tactics, or in the newspaper coverage either. Cook fans complain of packets of propaganda dispatched around the country to editors and others, yet they directed similar propaganda efforts.

John Euler, a Cook supporter, writing in *Arctic* in 1964, spoke for "a small number of skeptics who seek a true verdict in place of what some feel was a decision forced by newspaper propaganda."[5] But, unfortunately for the skeptics, it is clear that the newspapers reported fully and accurately on events as they occurred. The events influenced public opinion against Cook; it could not be otherwise. Cook wooed the public as well as he could, lied in press interviews and lectures, and failed to convince the majority.

Euler tells *Arctic* readers that justice to Cook can only be done if we reject "hearsay, pseudo-scientific testimonials, and evidence not directly related to the case." All can go along with him in this, and certainly he is right in saying that hundreds of thousands of words in the published literature fall into the three categories list above. Euler defines seven arguments in support of the probability of Cook's polar success:

1. Feasibility of method.
2. Proven ability.
3. Original descriptions.
4. Unknown westerly drift.
5. Ice islands.
6. Bradley Land.
7. A consistent narrative.

What Euler asks is that we accept these agruments and ignore all the other evidence of Cook's fraud. Even this acceptance of such an implausible basis for re-examination would not take us in the direction of truth.

However, let's assume that arguments one through six are valid and, further, that they are incorporated in the seventh argument, "a consistent narrative." After all, the book does hold all the other arguments and the consistent narrative argument was a favorite of Cook's. Euler says that Cook's book has never been "seriously refuted on the basis of internal evidence."[6] Does Euler mean that Cook's book fails as evidence if any inconsistency is exposed? If so, Euler's argument fails, because inconsistencies do exist in the book.

But why all the emphasis on "a consistent narrative"? Liars can be consistent, too! Many authors have written fiction in the form of factual narratives that hold together consistently; Jules Verne's *A Winter Amid the Ice* and Daniel Defoe's *Robinson Crusoe* are only two of many such works. There is no great trick to such a task; and, after all, no one has accused Cook of writing a complete fabrication or fantasy. He traveled in the Arctic with Eskimos and dogs and described with accuracy much that he experienced. On the other hand, Jules Verne and Daniel Defoe used their inventive powers to supplement facts in their narrative novels. It just does not make sense to claim that "a consistent narrative" is of great significance in establishing the full truth of Cook's journey. A soundly constructed narrative helps, and detailed scientific observations help. But if scientists can expose the implausibility of Cook's scientific proofs, such exposure ravages the "internal evidence" that Cook offers. Dennis Rawlins, using data from *My Attainment of the Pole*, shows that while Cook assumed such data placed him within one mile of the Pole, that actually it indicates "that he must have hovered for that period [twenty-four hours] four miles sunward of the Pole, while the Earth spun just beneath his feet."[7]

But, such "hard" evidence aside, is Cook's story of his disposal of his data at Etah plausible or consistent? If consistent in anything, it is in evasion and inexplicable conduct—or stupidity.

And what of the conflict between his grandiose feelings of personal achievement in reaching the Pole, his questionable assertion that he had striven for the goal for years, his statement that the object obsessed him; and his professed surprise that Copenhagen crowds found his venture remarkable?

Cook was consistent as a liar and in blaming a pro-Peary conspiracy for exposures of his lies.

It is possible to go on interminably analyzing the defenses of Cook and his more recent supporters, but it is tedious. A couple of points may be selected to illustrate some of the problems.

Consider Dunkle and Loose, who swore that Cook hired them to fake his North Pole reckonings. No one has been very comfortable with these two characters. They could have been bribed by Peary or his friends, but I think it more likely than not that Dunkle and Loose told the truth. But, whatever their integrity, the episode tells as much about tactics and polemics as anything else: Cook's red herring tactics and his biographer's polemics.

Hugh Eames has no light to shed on Dunkle and Loose. He handles the serious charges by intimating that the two rogues were hirelings of the Peary Arctic Club. He does not give a shred of evidence linking the Peary men with Dunkle and Loose. It is the kind of inference that disgraces the writer who indulges in it, the conduct of a desperate advocate. One may surmise, but good conscience requires some care in accusing men—whose only proven fault (if it was a fault) was an aggressive concern for Peary's protection—of being thorough crooks who bribed dishonest men to swear to lies.

Eames's work in this instance is appalling. He writes that "the episode . . . remains a collector's item for students of the diabolic." He equates Dunkle and Loose with Barrill as "self-confessed participants in an attempt to defraud" and observes that all three inferred that Cook was a very stupid man. Dunkle and Loose, Eames insists, did not act independently; "there was a ruling mind behind the episode"; and as the only support for his conclusion, Eames points up the timing of the rogues' affidavits. The story was planted to bully the Danes into rejecting Cook. "One way or another, the club was determined to be present at the examination of Cook's report, and mounted atop Dunkle and Loose, it arrived in the lowest possible style."[8]

The handling of the episode by Wright and Eames, both of whom had access to Cook's private papers still held by his family, seems to confirm the valuelessness of the papers to a reevaluation.

Cook's greatest defense of his North Pole claims has nothing to do with the exploration venture at all. But in presenting himself as an underdog unjustly abused by Peary's forces, he struck a chord that has resounded since 1909. Much of the sympathy generated for Cook for more than seventy years derives from the underdog theme. People should not really believe Cook or disbelieve Peary because Cook was the underdog, but it happens. It happens, and it is understandable that we feel sympathy for underdogs. What is amusing, and little understood, is that Cook was not really an underdog.

Cook made much of the unlimited resources of the Peary Arctic Club that supposedly were devoted to crushing him. Yet the Club did not need to spend large sums of money to nail Cook. The Mount McKinley exposure and the publicity emanating from Peary and other critics of the polar claim damaged Cook's reputation initially, and then the University of Copenhagen delivered the coup de grace. Even if the Club had bribed the Mount McKinley critics—Barrill, Prinz, Miller, Browne, Parker, and others—the costs would not have been high. Barrill received travel expense money and perhaps more; Prinz may have been offered $1,000 for his affidavit; but no substantial money was involved. If Professor Parker could have been bribed—as Cook charged—why was it necessary, when he had publicly doubted Cook before Cook returned from Alaska, three years before the polar controversy?

Cook's underdog status cannot rest on the Club's spending or its manipulation of the press. *The New York Times* fervently supported Peary and did some loose reporting and article captioning, but its influence on the nation's press was slight. Cook made news; Peary made news; and anyone of note having anything to say about either of them made news. There was no newspaper conspiracy, and the *Times* praised Cook's *To the Top of the Continent* on its publication, despite Parker's charges, which it had published in 1906, and only turned against Cook after investing in Peary's polar story.

Cook was firmly established as a pillar of the exploration community before the polar controversy. As president of the Explorers Club in 1907, elected after the doubts raised by Parker, he stood at the top of the exploration Establishment. He was generally, one could say universally, respected for his past adventures, his personal manner, and all else. He only became an underdog after being disgraced.

Although he commanded some sympathy in lectures by appealing to his audience as a little fellow like themselves who had been wronged and suppressed by the mighty and prestigious, his adherents were limited. Lecture audiences fell off, and he had to find other ways to earn a living. Perhaps there were too many underdogs in the world just then.

Every idea has its time, and nothing prevents zealots from refurbishing an old idea to suit new social developments. Cook had gone to his reward long before, when Americans were again swept up in emotional frenzy over a new version of the put-upon underdog theme. That was the nation of the "perfidious Establishment," which radicalized youth of the 1960s claimed to have discovered. In the spirit of the times, historians dug into the past to resuscitate characters who suffered neglect or infamy because of their "anti-Establishment" stances.

And, of course, poor old Cook filled the bill nicely for writers better attuned to the new mood than to the time-consuming work of historical research. Farley Mowat, a Canadian writer, allowed his enthusiasm to carry him far beyond the facts and to an unsober reassessment of Cook. Mowat decided that as a naval officer Peary formed part of the Establishment and appreciated its value, and that he thus ingratiated himself with men of influence and fortune in the furtherance of his exploration career. Of course Peary associated with rich and powerful men, as did every other explorer who wanted someone else to foot the bills. But the designation of Establishment and non-Establishment figures is fraught with complexity, as a look beyond the simplistic reveals in Peary's case. Peary suffered the agonies of any aspiring outcast when he and his backers tried to hustle a promotion for him from Congress over the remonstrances of the naval command. Peary won his battle over the naval Establishment, but it took all the political pressure his powerful civilian friends and a few naval backers could master.

But in treating Cook, Mowat draws a wholly implausible portrait, a caricature tailored to fit his non-Establishment theory. "Cook lived his life outside the Establishment," we are told, and was viewed with contempt by it. As a medical doctor and an explorer honored by European and American pillars of the geographic Establishment, Cook hardly meets this description. Mowat gushes on: "He would have fitted into the Establishment about as readily as a Zen Buddhist would fit into the Mafia. He was essentially a pariah in his own time."[9]

"Not only did Cook lack Peary's no-nonsense practicality, he seemed to choose deliberately to flaunt his addiction to the idealistic way of life." He persisted in volunteering for other men's expeditions, did not use other men as pawns, and even treated the Eskimos fairly. He even liked small birds, lemmings, old stories, moss, and clouds in a distant mirage. "One of the most frequent and telling criticisms of him is that his book, *My Attainment of the Pole*, is full of extraneous details about man, his thoughts, and the world he lives in. Such trivia found no place in the business-like communiques issued by Robert Peary."

Mowat strains our tolerance in contrasting Cook with Peary, particularly in forcing a distinction between their methods, finding in Cook an attunement with nature that accords with our contemporary benevolence toward natural ecology, while exposing Peary as an exponent of brute force, wasteful wealth, and machines. In truth both men used the same methods. Both exploited Eskimos and killed dogs for food, yet only Peary is faulted, because "as far as he was concerned Eskimos and dogs were mere machines."

Several ideas rushed through Mowat's mind as he sketched the rival explorers, and he used Cook as an ill-suited vehicle for them. His concern with depicting Peary in unflattering terms is unimportant; others have done this more convincingly by confining themselves to facts. In distinct ways Cook and Peary are equally grotesque or pathetic, depending upon the faults chosen for emphasis. Mowat's novelty is in his restructuring of contemporary national stereotypes and applying them to characters in an old story, and in freshening up the characters, he gives new meaning to past events.

It certainly is a heartwarming story. In view of the odds, Cook should not have won. "He represented no great body of savants and no consortium of wealthy interests; his methods were insultingly simple; he represented the wrong set of values." Mowat's Cook emerges as the old Horatio Alger hero, reinforced with ecological concern, and contempt for the Establishment and America's industrial might.

Mowat strains the tolerance of alert readers when he patronizes and insults them for continuing to be misled "by the discredited and discreditable attempts to destroy Cook, his work and his character." He is so sure. "Presumably these blind adherents to the verdict of the Establishment remain unaware that modern scientific investigations have established beyond reasonable doubt that if Frederick Cook did not reach the top of the world, he at least came as close to that elusive goal as any other man, including Peary, and he properly deserves (for whatever it may be worth) the title of discoverer of that peculiarly non-objective yet passionately desired Holy Grail of so many men—the North Pole."

If Mowat singled out elements of the anti-Cook attacks that were discreditable (and some were), and if he could show that such discreditable attacks brought about Cook's fall from grace, his general position would become stronger. Rather he assumes unfairness and complains that people today have not reversed history's opinion of Cook. Aside from his vague allusion to "modern scientific investigation" (no references given), he gives no reason why his generation should be keen to refurbish Cook's image. Calling Peary bad names is hardly a justification for raising Cook's status. What Mowat should do is convince us that people were mistaken in 1909-10, either because facts were not known or because people were deceived. He cannot do this.

Mowat's vilification of Peary's friends and their works does not explain why Cook's original supporters turned away from him. Cook did have friends, good friends who knew something about exploration, and he saddened most of them by his lies and disgusted them by his persistence. Such friends were not poisoned by Cook's enemies, and to intimate it is ridiculous. There were a few friends who stood by him out of personal loyalty—which is different from belief in his claims. Anthony Fiala was one and he had been an explorer, but he did not defend Cook's claims.

26

OIL SCAM

Ah, who shall soothe these feverish children?
Who justify their restless exploration?
    —Walt Whitman

Apologists for Dr. Cook who yearn for his acceptance as an honorable man should avoid all but the briefest mention of his oil stock swindles. They might reasonably argue that the criminal prosecution did not have anything to do with mountaineering or exploration, and leave it at that. Others might resist such a disclaimer, arguing that whenever a man's veracity is at issue, it is germane to consider whether he was convicted of fraud.

Earlier writers showed some wisdom in restricting their discussion of the oil stock affair. They did echo Cook's post jail declaration that some of the fields he had been accused of misrepresenting had since become big producers. They also suggested that the Peary forces' conspiracy against Cook brought about the federal prosecution, although they could present no evidence of this.

But recently, writers Farley Mowat and Hugh Eames have treated the problem of Cook's credibility with more boldness. Mowat's audacity exceeds that of Eames. He dismisses the whole trial as a sham, without troubling to examine any of the court records. Cook "was convicted," Mowat writes, "against all the evidence."[1] In writing so positively, Mowat does not show much regard for the Anglo-American legal tradition, but it enables him to sweep away a troublesome matter with a certain style.

Hugh Eames is the only one of the Cook apologists who bothered to look at the trial records. He accepts Cook's version of events, although it is not clear whether he saw the records held by the family or the entire five-box collection in the Federal Record Center at Fort Worth.

If one wishes to determine whether Cook was justly tried and convicted, the trial record and a consideration of the appeals made to higher federal courts would be reasonably convincing evidence that our venerable judicial process in criminal cases was followed. The record holds the arguments and evidence offered by both sides. Jury and appeal courts rejected Cook's arguments. The jury may have erred in deciding that Cook was one of the greatest cheaters in Texas history, but they did sit through the lengthy trial while the lawyers battled. And they observed Cook's behavior on the stand. Even Cook never charged the jury with accepting bribes to find him guilty, and certainly there is no evidence of such a crime. Taking all this into consideration, a writer would be sensible to accept the jury's verdict as plausible, unless he could turn up better evidence than the zealous lawyers could find at the time.

Of course, no one can convince Cook apologists that the man was what the courts found him to be. They must find ways to explain it away. They insist that there was no real fraud. So did Cook's lawyers. They insist that Cook's oil fields turned out to be productive years after the so-called misrepresentation, although neither Cook nor anyone has ever precisely identified a producing field as one of those which Cook held at the time of his indictment. Not that the argument of subsequent yield makes any sense in a fraud case anyway. The jury found that Cook misrepresented the present state of the fields in which he sold stock.

Eames does his best with the same defense that failed Cook under the stricter standards of federal procedure. He obviously feels that the government's prosecution of Cook bears some relation to the North Pole affair, although he offers no support for this beyond the opinion of a contemporary newsman. He also has severe reservations concerning the judge's impartiality. He does not accuse Judge Killits of corruption or of accepting bribes, but for some reason he reports on controversial incidents in the judge's career, and on the fact that the judge's wife's estate was larger than that of the judge. Perhaps Eames means to hint at some chicanery, but he is very cautious.

Cook broke the law and paid accordingly. There do not seem to be any sensible grounds for disputing the truth of this.

27

LITTLE LIES

I think nothing of the world and the public. They cheer you one
minute and howl you down the next.
                            —Sir Ernest Shackleton

Cook dazzled us with big lies, but the little lies reveal as much. Why would a professional man, a physician, identify himself as an ethnologist and doctor of anthropology? Cook dabbled a little in such subjects and was entitled "ethnologist" on the Belgian Anatarctic expedition and by Peary, but he did not meet professional standards in training or experience. Why did he pretend he knew Eskimo and other native languages?

Expedition leaders encouraged Cook's little deceits, since the deceits helped them. Cook was a doctor for the Belgian Antarctic Expedition and was needed for his professional qualifications. A trained ethnologist willing to labor without salary on a perilous voyage might have been found, but the Belgians did not really need one, since ethnography was not a serious goal of the expedition. And earlier, Peary, whose interest in Eskimos was narrow, praised Cook's ethnological accomplishments in the Arctic, although they were minimal. In doing this, Peary was just applauding his own team. The world cared about exploration results—not about ethnographic study. Who cared when Cook published the fascinating blunder that Eskimo women only gave birth in the spring? Amusing enough, and illustrative of the low standard set for any exploration goal except that of making a geographic record.

In his book, *Through the First Antarctic Night*, Cook included a chapter describing Fuegians and their customs, crediting Thomas Bridges, a resident missionary, for his information. This was standard travel-book practice, and it would be as foolish to praise Cook's contribution lavishly—as has been done—as it would be to censure it.

The transaction that concerns us, however, involved Bridges's Yahgan Indian dictionary. In 1910 it was claimed that Cook had tried to steal the lifework of the scholarly parson and pass it off as his own. What actually happened is fairly involved, and the circumstances would have discredited a reputable ethnologist or an honest amateur.

Cook met missionary Thomas Bridges in Punta Arenas, Chile, and learned much from him about the region's natives. He recognized the value of Bridges's extensive vocabulary of Yahgan words and offered to secure its publication. Bridges trusted the amicable and appreciative explorer and agreed to entrust his manuscript to him after the *Belgica* returned from Antarctica. On the return voyage Cook reaffirmed his devotion to the scholarly cause to Bridges's family and was given the manuscript. The missionary had died in the interval between the *Belgica*'s calls. It was kind of Cook to take the trouble, yet in a sense the acquisition swelled the scientific results of the expedition, so the gain was mutual.

In June 1899 Cook, back in New York, discussed his Antarctic experiences with newsmen. Modestly and accurately, Cook told his story, stressing the success of the venture, its fine scientific accomplishments, and the good quality of the personnel. Although the *Belgica* men did not actually attain their goals, it was good form to emphasize the positive aspects. Cook believed they had done well enough and need not cower in shame merely because ice barred the ship's passage to the polar continent.

Cook included in his account of the expedition's scientific accomplishments his acquisition of Bridges's vocabulary, and clearly designated its origin: "A missionary named Thomas Bridges has compiled a Yahgan vocabulary of 30,000 words. This compilation is the result of nearly 30 years' work."[1] Whatever intent he might have developed later, Cook intended no misrepresentation and gave full credit to Bridges.

Among the authorities Cook consulted concerning publication of the dictionary was the distinguished American anthropologist, Franz Boas. Later Boas recalled that "Dr. Cook intimated at the time that it was largely his work."[2]

Publication of the dictionary was long delayed. Bridges's son inquired of friends and eventually visited Belgium and saw the title page of his father's work. The title page credited Cook, a "Doctor of Anthropology," with authorship. Below this credit, in small type, the Reverend Thomas Bridges received acknowledgment as "instrumental in collecting the words."[3] Only part of the book had been printed at this time. Young Bridges had the credits reversed.

Cook's version of the incident appears in *My Attainment of the Pole* and does not affirm or deny that he claimed authorship. His reluctance to deny such a claim is significant; he could not have known the original title page would be lost. Or perhaps he considered his place on the title page as author deserved because "working on this material for one year without pay, I changed it to ordinary English orthography, but made few other alterations." To transcribe the manuscript from Bridges's "old Ellis system of orthography, which is not generally understood," to a standard penmanship might have seemed a great labor to Cook.[4] Claiming authorship, however, was beyond his just deserts. Cook thought it worthwhile to gain credit for a dead scholar's work.

In *My Attainment of the Pole*, Cook professed his innocence and assailed his exposers. He sharply questioned the veracity of Charles H. Townsend, director of the New York Aquarium, who publicized the fraud in 1910.[5] Townsend, "who, like Mr. Peary, was drawing a salary from the taxpayers while his energies were spent in another mission," lied, and *The New York Times* and other pro-Peary papers "printed columns of absolute lies in what purported to be interviews with Townsend."[6] Cook was always concerned by attacks from men who cheated their employers (i.e., men like Townsend, Herschel Parker, and Peary). To be insulted by men who stole time was too much! Cook was incensed that Townsend, Frederick Dellenbaugh of the Explorers Club, and others did not expend a postage stamp to learn the truth. All they could learn, is that Cook's name had been credited as author on the title page of Bridges's book. And that is what they had complained about.

How do recent apologists for Cook handle the exposure? As usual, they do not improve upon Cook's arguments. Eames does a disservice to his hero by referring to *The New York Times* story of 1897 on Cook's return from Antarctica as if it accused Cook of cheating, when, in fact, it exculpated him of any fraudulence at the time. Andrew A. Freeman doubts that Cook would make such a misrepresentation because specialists knew Bridges's reputation. Theon Wright follows the same line: "Cook, as a reputable ethnologist, would hardly have appropriated the missionary's work of thirty years, after spending only a few weeks with the natives."[7]

Eames raises similar defenses, yet does concede the possibility of Cook's cheating: "Perhaps the resourceful doctor imagined that a time would come when having a reputation as an authority on the Yahgan language would be handy."[8]

An examination of Cook's books, *To the Top of the Continent* and *My Attainment of the Pole*, could endlessly occupy a literary-psychological sleuth. For an example of a tall tale so much at odds with the common practice of explorers and Eskimos, consider the chapter, "The Moonlight Quest of the Walrus," from the latter book.

To pass the time and gather much-needed meat, Cook made a winter walrus hunt, an "Eskimo sport . . . of a most engaging and exciting order."[9] Never mind that Eskimos did not hunt in darkness and did not hunt for sporting reasons, let's just enjoy the story.

The trek begins with Cook in feverish heat, as usual when he undertakes some daring thing. "Its very danger lent an indescribable thrill, for success now meant more to me than perhaps hunting had ever meant to any man." In November the Arctic day is short and dim, and soon after the hunters harness their dog teams and speed south, darkness falls. There is no thought of camping for the night, because the night is long. Whatever is done must be done in the dark. For 40 miles over broken sea ice, "surrounded on every side by a blackness so thick that it was almost palpable," the men sped on. Traveling over sea ice by daylight had cost some men their lives, and in darkness it would require extraordinary spirit. "As I now recall that mad race, I marvel how we escaped smashing sledges, breaking our limbs, crushing our heads," Cook wrote. "We tumbled and jumped in a frantic race over one broken, irregular pack-in from Annoatok to Cape Alexander."

When the ice became thin the hunters drove overland, "over the frozen Greenland mountains . . . through murky clouds, a route of twisting detours, gashed glaciers, upturned barriers of rock and ice, swept by blinding winds, unmarked by any trail." How did they dare the initial barrier —"a vast glacier rising precipitously, like a gigantic wall, thousands of feet above you, and creeping tortuously up . . . formed by the piling of one glacial formation upon the other . . . blocked here and there by apparently impassable impediments, pausing at almost unscalable, frozen cliffs"?

Fleetingly the moon glimmered on this awesome obstacle and left the men with "despair, fear and hope" tugging at their hearts. "Some of these misty shapes seemed to threaten, others shook their rag-like arms beckoning forward." The beckoning must have overcome despair and fear: "I realized that the frightful ascent must be made. The goal of my single aim suddenly robbed the climb of its terrors." Somehow in Cook's fevered imagination this sporting journey elevated itself beyond ancillary needs, which he subordinated to his primary polar quest, so 50 dogs pulling sleds were driven upward, climbing like cats and taking "long leaps over the serried battlements." How far can harnessed dogs leap in coordinated rhythm? Far enough, apparently, because they made it. Sled travelers have often praised their dogs; here explicit praise is hardly necessary because Cook followed the animals' "unfailing instinct," while realizing "that a misstep might plunge me to a horrible death in the ice abyss below." Such a climb was especially remarkable because the dogs were harnessed fan-style rather than in linked pairs.

At the heights an enchanted scene, familiar to Cook heretofore only in his dreams, greeted the travelers. As the moon "poured liquid silver," they viewed a spectacle both awesome in delight and terrifying: "The eyes ran over fields of night-blackened blue, gashed and broken by bottomless canyons which twisted like purple serpents in every direction." Of all the explorers' narratives, only Cook's had a palette that held tints equal to such scenic impressions. What a visual guide he was! And, although for untold reasons he seemed to be in a fearful rush to complete this trip, he took time for brief reveries induced by the thrill of "the magical spectacle" and the justly felt terror of the scene.

But there was time for only a brief pause, and then "we leaped forward into the purple-gashed sea, with its blinding sheets of silver. I seemed carried through a world such as the old Norsemen sang of in the sagas." Amid such perilous labors, Cook felt carried along, a spectator and dreamer, sensitive to impressions only known before in reading tales of wanderings through "the nether region of the dead." "Only now did I have a faint glimmering of the terror (with its certain, exultant intoxication) which lost souls must feel when they wander in a darkness beset with invisible horrors." The literary impressions Cook recalled were probably romantic rather than Norse. Shades of Coleridge's *Rime of the Ancient Mariner* and other such pictures jumbling awful beauty and shrieking terror were dancing in his head.

But this was not the journey's climax. They fled on behind dogs "veiled in the argent, tremulous mists"—that is to say, virtually invisible. And at burning speed. Why the speed? And how is it maintained when the drivers cool off occasionally by riding in the sleds? They are hot because of heavy furs, though the temperature is about -40° F. Well, in the rush, Cook admits he felt detached: "The ice sped under me; I was no longer conscious of an earthly footing; I might have been soaring in space."

At last, after shooting down the mountain, checking the headlong pace of the marvelous dogs by their savage strength in manipulating the sleds, the men bivouacked and rested for twenty-four hours. Apparently, this was their first respite in a dash of 87 miles over sea ice, then up, over, and down a towering glacier.

Now there seemed to be no hurry. The men visited various Eskimo dwellings and passed the time until December, when they started for the walrus-hunting grounds, an open space of water some 10 miles south of Cape Alexander. Out on the ice the Eskimos harpooned walruses in the water, held them by the harpoon lines until they died, then hauled them up on the ice. Hauling 2,000-to-3,000-pound mammals onto an unstable ice floe must have been an agony of effort, although Cook made no point of it. Time is an element of art in Cook's narrative, and one of wondrous flexibility. It took two hours to battle the first walrus as he thrashed in the icy sea, diving and then emerging to the surface to receive the thrust of Eskimo spears and Cook's rifle bullets. After this victory an indeterminate number of other mammals were slain, butchered, and loaded, until seven sleds were full and great piles of flesh were left for later loading. All this took only several hours.

Nature contributed other bits of drama: There were distant icebergs crashing together and flashing like lighthouses because teeming germ life on their surfaces flashed in the moonlight. "The effect was indescribably weird." A storm smashed the ice and carried an Eskimo igloo to sea, and a wind even picked up an old man and tossed him into the water. Cook uses this last tragedy to illustrate the common hazards of Eskimo life. Very effective too. In such circumstances it is incredible that Eskimos survived at all. And Cook, after describing the procession of Eskimos bearing the dying man back to his village as "long shadows, like spectral mourners, robed in purple" (always Cook's favorite color), marvels "upon the lure of this eerily, weirdly beautiful land."

Somehow this journey of twice 500 miles, or a round trip of 1,000 miles, proved logistically feasible, although Cook says nothing of the return trip to Annoatok. Perhaps a number of trips were made. The labor seemed not to matter because indefinite numbers of Eskimos helped out. Many a travel narrative has failed in literary effect because the writer larded in too many practical details. Cook did not make that mistake.

THE OTHER
CLAIMANT

We must explore our own dominion. It is a fine heritage.
                                    —*Isaac Hayes*

obert E. Peary's name is enshrined in the record books as the discoverer of the North Pole, an honor held only because Cook's trek a year earlier has been generally disputed. Peary, a hard-eyed, dour man sporting a luxurious mustache, seems the prototype of the polar explorer. His toughness, endurance, and grim determination can be read in every portrait, and those showing him in 1909 reveal the effects of age and long struggle. In 1909 he was only fifty-four years old, but looked much older. He was one of those ambitious individuals who determine early on a strange goal and drive toward it relentlessly, regardless of any other circumstances. No explorer has ever matched his tenacity of purpose, his egotistical craving for the fame heralding a single accomplishment. He was a zealot who allowed nothing to stand in his chosen path.

Quite unwillingly, indeed to his disgust and chagrin, Peary became linked with Cook in the contemporary public eye and in history. To Peary, the North Pole was everything, yet his victory was besmirched by a man he termed "a cowardly dog of a sordid imposter."[1] It seemed grotesquely unjust, a devilishly bizarre circumstance, that an unworthy challenger threatened to undo Peary's lifework. To Peary's loyal friends, Cook's pretensions appeared tragic rather than farcical. Some contended that Cook drove Peary to an early grave. Whether it was true or not, as Peary

241

lived out the few years left to him after his epic voyage, he was a very unhappy man. The fame, sought with unceasing ambition for so long, gave small satisfaction. And this was because of Cook's perfidy, said Peary's friends. No, said others who did share their admiration, it was because he knew that he had not reached the Pole, despite his claim, and his failure had nothing to do with Frederick Cook.

Most literature on the polar controversy is marked by the authors' strident advocacy. While defending one's favorite makes sense, attacking his rival does not. Cook, if he reached the Pole, did not do so because Peary failed. Conversely, if Cook defrauded the public, that fact does not sustain Peary's claim to have achieved his goal.

Cook's most ardent recent defenders, Andrew Freeman in *The Case for Doctor Cook* and Hugh Eames in *Winner Lose All*, base too much of their argument for Cook's success on Peary's failure. Thus Freeman's index has 34 lines of text references to Peary, with 5 more lines of references to the Peary Arctic Club, and only 48 lines to Cook; similarly, in Eames's index Peary rates 2½ columns to Cook's 3½. Why the emphasis on Peary in a defense of Cook? No one ever questioned Cook's priority in reaching the Pole. If he got there at all, he was first, and, consequently, his record could not be upset whether or not Peary ever got there at all. In stating the obvious—that the proofs of the two explorers stand entirely on their individual qualities—there is no room for questioning the point. Yet the record is ridden with confusion because of the obfuscation of this elementary distinction.

The ferocious vehemence of William Herbert Hobbs, a Peary biographer, toward Cook is understandable given his insistence on linking the two explorers. In his preface to *Peary*, Hobbs praises his subject as probably the greatest of polar explorers, a man whose career was unique in its success and in the unwelcome prominence of an extraordinary controversy: "The 'Cook affair' of necessity loomed large in the later career of Peary, and the full acclaim that was his due was not alone delayed, but . . . had repercussions which endured and saddened the later years of his life."[2]

In another part of the book, Hobbs quotes with approval a magazine's comment after the University of Copenhagen's decision not to accept Cook's proofs: "As for Peary himself, he has been defrauded of something which can never be restored to him. . . . False as it has been proved, the claim has dimmed the lustre of his true discoverer's achievements.

He will receive the full acknowledgment that his work merits, in the form of recognition from scientific and other bodies and of a sure place in history; but the joy of the acclaim that should have greeted him at the triumphant close of his twenty-three years' quest can never be his."[3]

Hobbs is correct, but Peary caused some of his own problems with the public. Peary blundered in publicly dismissing Cook's claim before either man had the opportunity to bring forward his evidence. His reaction was fully understandable, but it created an awkward situation. Peary's telegrams to the United Press came within a few days of Cook's news: "Cook's story shouldn't be taken too seriously. Two Eskimos who accompanied him say he went no distance north and not out of sight of land. Other tribesmen corroborate." And to *The New York Times*: "Do not trouble about Cook's story as attempt to explain any discrepancies in his installments. The affair will settle itself."[4]

"He has not been to the Pole on April 21, 1908, or at any other time. He has simply handed the public a gold brick. These statements are made advisedly and I have proof of them. When he makes a full statement of his journey over his signature to some geographical society or other respectable body, if that statement contains the claim that he has reached the Pole, I shall be in a position to furnish material that may prove distinctly interesting reading for the public."[5]

When Peary's denunciations hit the newsstands, Americans had been reading about the acclaim given Cook in Copenhagen and had been thrilled by his exploits and nationalistic sentiments. Now they read dismaying news that, in effect, accused them of being conned. No one cared much for the "gold brick" metaphor. Peary's language and the circumstances created some suspicion and ill will; his denunciation offended many as unsporting. The code among explorers and other sportsmen has never been firmly promulgated, yet a gentlemanly manner and reservation of criticism were, like modesty, expected attributes.

So some newspapers and authorities criticized Peary's behavior. The publicity hurt his public image somewhat. Peary biographer John Edward Weems cries that "the reaction of American newspaper readers was an almost universal denunciation of Peary, whose unfairness appeared to be despotic." An adverse press reaction infuriated Peary, and his "arrogant manner and his fierceness" further antagonized the public "and, in fact, surprised his friends."[6]

Weems overstates the press criticism. Peary biographers, like Peary

himself, are too sensitive to any criticism. There were some critical press
stories and letters to the editor deriding Peary. Cook did win some newspaper public-opinion polls. Yet it is understandable that it would take some
time for the tide to turn in Peary's favor. He had been the second to
announce success and had claimed a later date of reaching the Pole. Why
should he be so outraged that the public would not dismiss Cook as
summarily as he did? The answer is easy: Most explorers were men of
towering ego and were acutely sensitive to scorn in a game that depended
upon popular acceptance. For Peary the matter seemed crystal clear. Cook
was a fraud. Peary exposed him. Now Americans were blackguarding him
"because I attempted to warn them and keep them from making damned
fools of themselves."[7]

Contrary to Weems's assertion, Peary received a great deal of support.
Even *The New York Herald*, which published Cook's series on his journey,
did not aggressively support Cook or deride Peary. Peary's strong defenders included *The New York Times*, which heavily and aggressively committed itself to Peary's cause and actively questioned Cook's merits. Two men
who were leading supporters of Peary and pillars of the Peary Arctic Club
influenced *The New York Globe* and *The Brooklyn Standard Union*.
Thomas Hubbard was part owner of *The Globe*, and Herbert Bridgman
was business manager of the *Standard Union*. Peary had strong support in
Europe, particularly in England, because press lord Alfred Harmsworth
believed in him, as did the prestigious Royal Geographical Society.

Note should be taken of the time involved in the first stage of the dispute.
Only one month elapsed between Peary's return to America and the
heaviest blow to Cook's reputation, the evidence of the Mount McKinley
fraud. Quite naturally, opinion in America on the rivals had been mixed
during that month, but after the October 14 Mount McKinley story broke,
Peary swept forward in public favor.

Peary's biographers may have misstated the intensity of public disbelief
in him because Peary himself felt mortified by any doubts expressed. Or
perhaps they have done so to highlight the infamy of Cook. Peary was the
kind of character who would have been unnerved and outraged by any
dissent, whether Cook existed or not.

Partisans of both men have misinterpreted the press and public reaction
in 1909. Cook argued that the world generally acclaimed him until the
Peary men conspired and committed fraud to destroy him. Peary fans have

seen any doubt or ridicule of their favorite as unjust and unreasonable. Both sides bid for sympathy on the grounds that public opinion was wrong and had been misdirected. Both exaggerate the shifts in public opinion, yet such shifts adhered closely to the relative plausibility of the two explorers over the 1909-10 period. In neither Cook's nor Peary's case could it be said objectively that the explorer was unfairly victimized by an aggressively hostile press or public.

Peary and Cook did not have very much in common, but both resented the press's treatment of them. Yet their passion, however deeply felt, should not confuse their biographers into a belief that their grievances were justified. Each man reached for fame and approbation; if neither of them was equipped with conclusive means of diverting criticisms, it was each man's own fault.

Eventually Peary won his promotion, but in the process suffered through an examination that revealed his evasiveness and the inadequacy of his evidence. His testimony exposed the fact that his situation was like Cook's at the University of Copenhagen: He had not compiled a data record that supported his contention of attaining the Pole. Only two subcommittee members realized that Peary's revelations amounted to an admission of "no evidence." Congress finally voted on the basis of Peary's reputation and the acceptance of this polar claim by the National Georgraphic Society. There was no immediate harm to Peary, yet he had added vital matter to the record that raised far more questions than it answered.

Dennis Rawlins' controversial book, *Peary at the North Pole: Fact or Fiction?*, details how Peary exposed his weak position as a polar claimant by pushing for promotion. Peary, like Cook, claimed something he could not prove. This does not mean that Peary was a fraud; it simply means that he was unable to demonstrate his journey in scientific terms. If one believes that Peary reached the Pole, or got close enough so that some error hardly matters, one must do so on the basis of circumstantial evidence. Unfortunately, when one moves from objective measurement to circumstantial evidence, the door opens to all such evidence, and some of it suggests the possibility of fraud.

Any anti-Peary feeling among the public was more than set off by a resentment against Cook for robbing Peary of honors that the latter appeared to have richly deserved. An understanding of this view of a "robbery" is essential to divining the virulence of some of the distaste for

Cook. Cook cheated the public at large, not just Peary, and it is difficult to see Peary's plight as clearly as he himself saw it, particularly when questions about his own pretensions remained unanswered.

Most insiders to the exploration world felt the personal impact on Peary very keenly, excepting those who had reasons for disliking him. The situation brought into contention two conflicting sources of sympathy, the loyalty to the proven champion versus the approval of the new challenger. In all sports the public divides its affection between champion and challenger to a varying degree, depending upon the personal appeal of each. In the polar contest Cook had the advantage of a pleasant personality that enhanced his appeal. Had Cook's claim been less obviously spurious, the public would have found little difficulty in giving him its full devotion. Of course, some individuals would have resented Cook's challenge. They would have found Cook's conduct unsportsmanlike for a number of reasons: His secret preparations and his reliance upon much that Peary had accomplished before would be enough for condemnation. But such resentment would have had little voice in the long run. There is no advantage greater in achieving general esteem than being a clear winner.

Cook was not a clear winner by any means, so it is no wonder that his claim was particularly abrasive to those inclined to favor the champion over any challenger. One expression of this sentiment can be seen in the attitude of polar explorer Vilhjalmur Stefansson, who was in the North when the dispute erupted, and thus isolated from the heat of contention. His isolation did not make him neutral, because he was strongly influenced by a previously formed belief that Cook's Mount McKinley feat had been a fraud.

In the spring of 1910 Stefansson read a magazine article on the controversy and laid out his views in his diary, views that did not change in essence after he returned to civilization and could hear all aspects of the argument. Stefansson was among those who had warned Peary personally that Cook's Mount McKinley claim might be a prelude to a polar fraud. "Hardly anyone doubted Cook would come back claiming the Pole," Stefansson reflected.[8] Stefansson had worried about the possibility beforehand, although there was nothing that anyone could do about it after Herschel Parker's vigorous attack on Cook failed so abysmally and Cook gained the honor of the Explorers Club presidency. Stefansson's reference to "hardly anyone" doubting Cook's intent to defraud does not square with Cook's elevation in the Club. Apparently most of the membership were not tuned in to the Seattle and Alaskan sources that influenced Stefansson's bias.

Stefansson knew Peary only slightly, but liked him. He did not know Cook at all, but heard derogatory things that made him suspicious. But Stefansson's bias was not based on his like or dislike of the claimants; rather he regretted "that a man of worth and much accomplished good should be placed in Peary's position." If Cook actually did what he claimed, Stefansson thought that the accomplishment "was not much more than 'stealing a march' on Peary." Stefansson's argument merits attention because he was always somewhat contemptuous of the sporting nature of the polar quest. Achieving the North Pole would not have satisfied him, because he was more a scientist than an adventurer. What Stefansson respected in Peary was his "consistency and persistence over a quarter century of hard labor under trying circumstances." What credit did Cook deserve? Stefansson asked, since if he reached the Pole it was because he waited "till just the right moment to step in and snatch deftly the wages of another man's toil when that man's work was done and his payday had at last come."[9]

Others shared this opinion of the relative merits of the two claimants, but Stefansson's particular outlook was important because it made him impervious to the doubts raised about Peary's journey. Quite simply, it did not matter to Stefansson whether Peary did precisely what he said, since he deserved honors for his long labors. If Peary fell short of the goal, it meant nothing. He had gotten close enough, had developed the techniques by which it could be done, and had persisted.

Stefansson's viewpoint infuriated some Peary detractors. It appeared to them that Stefansson was begging the question. The attainment of the Pole could be demonstrated scientifically; Peary had not done this, and should be condemned for claiming what he could not prove.

Stefansson argued that the purists among Peary partisans missed the important point, which was that Peary had earned the Pole, whether he had stood at it precisely or not, and should be honored. The purists did Peary a disservice by allowing Cook, a cheater, to rob him of glory on a technicality.

While a roll call of doubters of an explorer's claims tells no more about the truth than a listing of believers, their reasons for doubt should be examined. Peary's supporters found it convenient to write off all complaints as ill-founded carping emanating from Cook's camp. Another thrust was to cry that the doubts of men like Shackleton, Nansen, Sverdrup, Amundsen, and Markham reflected a jealousy of American supremacy.

Yet a cooler scrutiny of the situation indicated plenty of reason for suspicion. Suspicion is not enough to beget full exposure of duplicity, however, if a forum is denied or a quasi-official investigation is prevented. Peary's supporters acted sensibly to gain approval for him by arranging the superficial examination of records conducted by a National Geographic Society committee, a body without genuine official standing. But, of course, there existed no such thing as an established body of judges for exploration feats. Peary did not tax the United States Navy, or any domestic or foreign universities, or other geographic societies, to look at his documentation—and none of these, except the navy, could make demands. It was none of their business, and requesting their involvement would only create bad feelings. The few Peary critics in Congress were overwhelmed by a majority of their colleagues, who waved the flag furiously over a national exploit and had no real reason to come to grips with what seemed a highly technical and, possibly, an embarrassing issue. Finally, it was easy to ignore some querulous articles and a few books of small circulation.

Dennis Rawlins has pointed out the facts that experts might have considered with profit. Peary went to the Pole unaccompanied by anyone who knew navigation. His sextant readings of the sun's attitude at the key point were unshared with anyone, though Matt Henson could use a sextant. This failure to compare observations with Henson was critical, because the figures alone could be calculated anywhere at a later date.

Rawlins argues that Peary's astronomical data consequently lacked value, but "his stated means of navigation *to* the goal are simply incredible." A whole string of journey observations would have been hard to fake. "Peary simply produced no data enroute beyond the genuine shots by Marvin and Bartlett . . . so he never even *claimed* to have found his way to the Pole by observations."[10]

The North Pole is not easily discovered. Peary told congressmen that in traveling hundreds of miles over the unpredictably drifting pack ice, he had never planned a single sextant check for aim. A desert traveler would experience difficulty adhering to a 413-mile-long beeline to a fixed point. Imagine compounding this task by traveling over a moving, jagged surface that demanded detours! And for the last 135 miles he did not even check his forward motion to the Pole. "He opined he was about there, and then pulled out his sextant to check—and, sure enough, he was!" Quite amazing accuracy! "By all odds the most astounding dead-reckoning feat in the history of exploring. Yet, curiously, Peary—who was not known for his modesty—had to have the admission of this nonpareil achievement dragged out of him by skeptical inquisitors."[11]

Would a skillful, vastly experienced explorer depend upon such luck to keep him from veering or overshooting his mark, when his life depended upon precise calculation? Anyone who believed this would believe anything. Every other traveler over rough, moving ice—including Peary on other journeys—found direct-line movement impossible. Periodic sextant determinations to prevent veering were essential.

Peary relied entirely on his compass, yet its "variation" from true north increased approximately 13° between his starting point and the Pole. Compass variation in this region was greater than 90°—that is, the compass pointed somewhat nearer south than north. Precise knowledge and frequent rechecking of this variation depended upon solar observation, and such information was necessary for accurate steering. Yet Peary produced no compass figures. Peary told the congressmen vaguely that the compass needle pointed near the magnetic pole. "We now know," Rawlins says, "that in 1909 the compass needle at the North Geographic Pole pointed over 30° to the right of the North Magnetic Pole."[12]

Such sloppy navigation appears uncharacteristic of a serious traveler. Peary knew he was racing Cook and should have understood that rivalries create controversies that only hard evidence can settle. He also knew that magnetic observations constituted the most valuable scientific gain of his trip. Yet he offered no such evidence. As Rawlins puts it: "The sum total of Peary's claim to the North Pole is: no witnesses, no specific scientific yield, and a 'method' of aiming which no one familiar with Arctic Ocean ice conditions could possibly take seriously."[13]

There were other intriguing questions, such as Peary's reticence about his discovery on his return trip and even after reaching his ship. Critics argue that his behavior indicated Peary had not yet made up his mind whether to make a polar claim. But such circumstantial matters, however suspicious, need not have been reviewed. An earnest inquiry into the lack of navigational data would have been enough to show that Peary had not substantiated his claim. If one must fall back on a belief in his integrity in the absence of evidence, then the introduction of countering circumstantial matter becomes reasonable. Such an opening also lets in unsavory and irrelevant incidents, such as Cook and others dredged up. And this type of slander naturally outraged Peary and his friends. Not that their rage needed such fuel. Most of his partisans showed their colors at Cook's initial challenge. On faith they accepted Peary's triumph in the greatest polar game. In defense and vindictiveness they savaged all critics and robbed the polar game of what respectability it held. Their conduct could be compared to that of gamblers who bribe ballplayers or prizefighters. Presumably such characters call themselves sportsmen. Peary's leading partisans did not think they dishonored themselves as geographers, scientists, or rational men. They believed—they believed.

Peary prevailed because the exploration Establishment in America respected his past work. Peary deserved their respect and all the gold medals various geographic societies of the United States, England, Scotland, and France granted him. He was a great explorer—of that there could be no question. His reputation would have suffered had his earlier journeys been investigated as critically before his polar claim as after. Not that his earlier claims compared with Cook's Mount McKinley fraud, but his mistaken identifications in Greenland and other places show him to have been capable of serious mistakes and fierce ambition. But he had demonstrated qualities of greatness often enough. Unfortunately, he had always played for the ultimate exploration prize. There were honors for the farthest-north achievement, but time was running out for the surpassing honor. Thanks to his work and to the contributions of others, the world sensed that victory was near. Whose victory? Well, who deserved it most? A wholly rational man would answer: Whoever clearly won it. But partisans lean toward their champion. They are devoted adherents lacking in detachment.

Looking again at the doubters and defenders of Peary, we might conclude that the English and Scandinavian questioners found it easier to be detached. Not that all foreigners withheld criticism. The British explorer George Nares criticized Cook's record marches, yet accepted Peary's claim before learning of the details, because of his "well-known Arctic veracity." Such a response exhibited courtesy and a gentleman's grace. There were many men like Nares who may have felt a withholding of acceptance to be boorish, small-spirited act. In this instance, we see an example of a choice of priorities: Good will prevailed over geographic curiosity.

Other individuals indicated a more curious balancing of priorities. George Melville, of *Jeannette* fame, rejected Cook's speed of 14 miles per day, yet accepted Peary's 25-mile average for the last five days to the Pole. What does this tell us about Melville?

The National Geographic Society committee's judges were Henry Gannett and Admiral Colby Chester—two good friends of Peary—and Otto Tittmann, who later said he left the matter to the others because of work pressure. Even for his friends, Peary delayed a good while before submitting his fragmentary, inconclusive evidence. The committee's approval pleased him. And for all his real agony over criticism, and in spite of the call of Admiral Winfield S. Schley for a submission of Peary's documents to the University of Copenhagen tribunal that was judging Cook, Peary did not seek any more resounding approval than his friends gave him.

Obviously, the Peary-Cook affair had many strange aspects. But the behavior of all parties to it is much more understandable if the intensity of the contest is remembered. The event seemed to culminate four hundred years of aspiration and, for this and other reasons, it was significant. The episode's interest for us will not vanish with time. The attainment of the pole was thought to be an illustrious incident in civilization's advance. An adventure that resulted from inordinate ambition and led to startling frauds on the public is certainly not without value. At the very least, we gain by learning something of human nature under stress. And in this instance the shock waves of stress vibrated widely.

29

TRUTH AND ZEAL

*Truth is not a science, it is an art, and a man
succeeds in it only by imagination.*
                        —*Anatole France*

Was Frederick Cook one of those irrepressible characters, a Fal-
staff or a Willy Sutton, whom we cannot help admiring despite
their affronts to society, one of the class of lovable rogues?
Popular appreciation of rogues is a study in itself. For reasons peculiar to
each case, we have elevated some rogues to esteem, while others, responsible for similar villainies, have been condemned.

In considering a possible misrepresentation of Cook, we are confronted
with the question of historical revisionism. Our contemporaries who are
trying to restore Cook's standing are reflecting a new wisdom or bias of our
times. They have reexamined the evidence in the light of viewpoints of the
1960s and 70s and have proposed a reassessment. They may not be right,
but the fact that they feel compelled to reassess does show us something.
What it shows is not easy to say. It is not satisfactory to conclude that Cook
can still con individuals today as he fooled them in the early years of the
century. We must find out what sustains the revival of Cook.

In November and December 1976, Russell W. Gibbons, a Philadelphia
journalist and editor, whose zeal for Cook's cause dates back some twenty
years, read a paper before two different groups interested in exploration.
The Bicentennial consciousness, he thought, might stimulate "a new tolerance level for revisionist schools when they came to bat for the so-called

'poor person's' candidates for historical attainment." And Gibbons urged his audiences to believe "that Cook may well have been the victim of a pre-World War I 'Icegate.'"[1]

Good for Gibbons! He gives us such freshness, with his appeals to the Bicentennial and Watergate. Memories of founding fathers and recent political rogueries are summoned in behalf of old Cook. Once more we are being manipulated, this time in the name of historical consciousness. That is not what historical consciousness is supposed to do. We should not have to defend our veneration for history by standing ready to revise settled interpretations, regardless of evidence that would make a new view plausible.

History belongs to everyone, and no law forbids each man from making his own or trying to swing others his way. Gibbons tries. He shows us how gentle, unselfish, and kind Cook was, and explains his undoing by other wicked men. He finds that Cook's character provides the key to the question, and that Cook's character was good. Testimony of others supports this, as does Cook's stubbornness in refusing to write a journalistic confession, despite offers of high fees.

Gibbons's sometimes lofty tone in reviewing events can be understood. He sees a man's honor besmirched by others respected as honorable men. In his telling, it is a sad story and one wonders how such evident goodness as Cook personified could have been so thoroughly besmirched.

What is even sadder than Gibbons's story is his inability to grasp Cook's real character. Having decided that Cook had been wronged by others, Gibbons loses his chance to understand Cook. I do not want to make light of someone who has pondered over Cook's case off and on for twenty years, but the Cook story as he presents it makes no sense. Nor does he report it accurately.

Why cannot Gibbons and others believe that Cook often lied? His lies are as well documented as those of any liar in history. Many of his lies were unmasked and he was denounced. Why blame a group of pro-Peary conspirators for undoing Cook, when the record shows that the exposure of his lies did him in?

Recognizing Cook as a liar does not prevent an admirer from praising his other sterling qualities, but the failure to recognize the obvious will lead an advocate to corruption. There is no way to advocate Cook's cause satisfactorily without slandering others on the slightest of evidence—and all Cook's fans are too eager to do this. Quite simply, they are corrupted by this determination to defend lies. None of Cook's defenders has dealt with the biggest lie of all, which involved the public at large, in a reasonable or scholarly manner. They insist that the public was fooled in 1909-1910 by Cook's enemies, when, in fact, the public followed the exposure of lie after lie and reached the only conclusions possible.

We can live with the knowledge that great liars have existed throughout history. Lying has been commonplace. Cook's defenders resist the exposure of his lies with all the tenacity of last-ditch warriors willing to lay down their lives. Civilization will not crumble if they acknowledge Cook as a liar, yet they dread lies too much to entertain their possibility.

Recently we have learned much about liars and the public's reaction to them from Richard Nixon, former President of the United States. What the Nixon case shows clearly is that even sophisticated, cynical, political-minded people return again and again to repugnant lies, as if hypnotized by their enormity. Why? People lie all the time. Why keep going back over wearisomely familiar ground to inquire anew—with, I assume, fresh confidence—about lying?

We know why Nixon lied; there is no mystery. So maybe we return to the question to satisfy a different psychological need: the hope that the liar, confronted once more with closed roads of evasion, will finally give us the balm we are seeking and admit he is a damn liar. But men like Nixon and Cook cannot do that naturally, and there is no reason why they should feel the impulse to let us off the hook. If we feel tarnished as human beings because of their lies and misdeeds, they might well reflect, "That's your problem." And it is. We should just praise or blame our great liars for their works and get on with our business. As a means to higher knowledge of humanity, trying to make a fine liar confess is about as useless as studying alchemy.

No wonder the Cooks and Nixons feel badgered as the press rides them, as the same old accusations are cast up in various forms. It is badgering— and to no purpose. Here we demand the ultimate from the liars and offer nothing in return. With a deal like that who can blame the liars for being resentful? Those suffering for truth must find some softer way of alleviating their pains than demanding that scoundrels recant. Truth cannot be purchased so cheaply.

This sense of harassment explains the indignation that was roaring in Cook's heart as he wrote *My Attainment of the Pole.* He raged in several places in the text at all the lies told against him. No one in history, he believed, had been lied about as extensively. He admitted that he made mistakes. And he admitted that his claim may always be questioned. He could, seemingly, accept that. What he could not accept were the lies told about him. And, in the confusion and heat of passion over his lies, others did misstate, exaggerate, jump to unwarranted conclusions—yes, lie— about Cook. It pained him; liars bleed too.

Another point of interest is Cook's admission that the lies told about him eventually made him indifferent. Indifference is a defensive posture he unconsciously took against lies directed at himself. Although he did not analyze this further, it would be reasonable for him to state that but for his indifference, he would have become paranoid. The evidence sustains Cook's indifferent attitude, if we judge by the little unnecessary lies he told in *My Attainment of the Pole* and elsewhere over the years. And nothing indicates that he became paranoid as time passed. Even the oil scandal and the intensification of slander did not unhinge him. Like the storm-beaten but still-tough forest oak, he did not bow to fresh storms.

So why not a little truth in Cook's case? Liars are not so mysterious when we understand the reasons for their lies. Lying is part of our national and international tradition. Once we learn to appreciate great liars like Cook, we can gain some value from their experience. Don't disband the Frederick A. Cook Society, you friends of Cook, just broaden your charter a little.

As for the personal as distinguished from the public Cook, what do we know? The right questions were posed by historian L.P. Kirwan:

"What led Cook to indulge in such an elaborate fraud has never been discovered. Was it pure chicanery? Was it from some distorted, cynical sense of humour? Or was it perhaps sheer malice against Peary, guessing as indeed turned out to be the case, that in the absence of independent and reliable white witnesses on both sides, he, an experienced and quite reputable explorer, had at least as good a chance as Peary of being believed. There is still an interesting psychological problem to be solved in the strange case of Dr. Frederick A. Cook."[2]

Kirwan's book, *The White Road: A History of Polar Exploration*, explains the emphasis of some of his questions. He did not treat Mount McKinley, the oil fraud, or the Yaghan dictionary affairs. Considering this, we can perhaps reject Kirwan's questions concerning Cook's malice toward Peary as a prime motivation of his polar fraud. Malice may have existed, but Cook set a pattern for fraud with the dictionary and his Mount McKinley claims. The North Pole was a glittering prize; Cook's ambitions directed him to it regardless of Peary. As for Kirwan's question concerning a distorted sense of humor as a motivation, there is little evidence of humor in Cook. He was a very serious man.

There is an interesting psychological problem in Cook's case. It is beyond my capacity to assess it, but a recent examination of Edmund Backhouse is suggestive. Historian Hugh Trevor-Roper investigated Backhouse, a hermit, brilliant scholar, pornographer, calligrapher, linguist, and expert on Chinese history, who fabricated a book, *China Under the Empress Dowager*, from imaginary sources.

Backhouse was peculiar yet sane, in Trevor-Roper's view. Backhouse lived in a world of fantasy and was inclined to self-glorification. His world, "created by romantic vanity, suspended between distant points of truth, and yet internally coherent and rational, was more real to him than the objective, external world." When the external world collided with the fantasy, the former was made to yield: "It yielded intellectually, in the victory of fantasy over fact. It yielded physically in the actual forgery of such documents as might be necessary to sustain the illusion." Backhouse may not have even been aware of the conflict. "Even when he was physically forging documents, he may have been unconscious of the fraud involved."[3]

Perhaps Cook was like Backhouse. His fantasy would explain his frauds and lies: He may not have been aware of the distinction between truth and lies. We can't be sure of the certainty of any explanation of Cook's psychology. But it does seem safe to conclude that, for whatever reason, he was a damn liar.

APPENDIX

(Letter from Peter Freuchen to Vilhjalmur Stefansson, November 16, 1934)

I beg to give you a few notices about the subjects you wrote me about, but I ask you to look at them as they are; not scientific proven statements but to some extent biological reactions to people not in contact with politics of any kind or having any interest for or against.

I am in the following spelling the Eskimo names as I am used to according to the Eskimoic language used in the schools in Greenland.

I met Itukusuk and Apilak first time in 1910 when I first came to Smith Sound. Itukusuk married our servant and stayed in our house more than two years, he is a very capable hunter and has since that time travelled lots with MacMillan and others, a very reliable man. Apilak was at this time a strong man, always on his toes and nervous. Both of them told me about the trip with Doctor Cook though they do not like to talk about it, they are looked a little down at compared with the boys that joined Admiral Peary. This of course most because of their minor economical result also because the men chosen by Peary forever had a reputation in the tribe.

The two men traveled with Doctor Cook from Etah. At that time nobody had been muskoxhunting for long time, and they had no muskox garments at all. Special Itukusuk would not have had such because he was at that time married to Aranluak who was young and unable to sew such things as muskox kamipaks. Now when they went away they left early in the year and took the course right across Grant's Land—a good trip as trip

259

concerned—and during that journey they alright got some muskoxen. But the temperature was of course rather low, so nothing in the kind of tanning skins and dry them and sew them could be done in that time of the year. Specially as they were going on the whole time.

Itukusuk therefore at once paid attention to the fact, that he in the picture book given out by Dr. Cook and indicating "the conquering of the North Pole" is standing boasting a pair of muskox kamipaks. These—he said—were made by him the summer they stayed at Cape Sparbo in North Devon. There he made these footgear as he had rather poor boots his wife being young and unexperienced to sew. You will see the kamipaks not too nice but Itukusuk was son of Panigpak—well known from Peary's books— and a rather ill tempered woman who often refused to sew for the family. Therefore, the husband and the two sons had to make their own garments often, as she would not do it. That made it possible for him to make those kamipaks, still in a magnifying glass you can see they are different. The two Eskimos state that they never were out of sight of land. The two small islands related to as Bradley Land in Cook's book are situated close to Grant's Land on the northwest side. I have taken photos of them and so has McMillan on the Crocker Land Expedition.

The Eskimos tell that when they came a little north of Grant's Land the ice became heavy and rough, so Cook decided to go south and they drove down through Eureka Sound. They made good time and never hurried. They asked Dr. Cook several times why they should not traverse Ellesmeres Land and go home, but he refused. They talked about it with themselves and understood, that he was afraid of the terrible wind on the glacier in Ellesmeres Land. This was before we found the wonderful way from Flagler Fjord east til Bay Fjord west that allows you to go across Ellesmeres Land in two days and also have good going and usually good weather and rabbits the whole way enough to feed the dogs.

Before this route was explored people went across by the glacier west of Cape Isabella and had a heavy job getting the sledges up on the glacier and dogs and everything had to be hoisted up in lines (I have never been there myself, but Knud Rasmussen has).

As the party went south, they had plenty of game and never were without food. Got several bears and all kinds of muskoxen.

At Hellgate, which is a place where the current always keeps the ice open, they had some difficulties getting across. But they managed to do it on icepans, and Dr. Cook told them to leave their dogs behind. They dared not to disobey him, but felt very sorry and they told him about shooting the poor animals left alone.

But he refused and the dogs were left howling at the edge of the ice. They went to Cape Sparbo across the Jones Sound and made there a house for the summer and a tent out of sealskins. Dr. Cook was very acceptable for a fellow and spent most of his time walking inland and looked for animals and plants. But he never collected anything as the scientist with Peary used to do.

After the summer had gone, and the new ice was formed, Dr. Cook wanted to start back; but they told him the ice would not cover the sound between Ellesmere Land and Etah before late in the year, and they, therefore, stayed at Cape Sparbo during the winter having enough of food as they had splendid catch on muskoxen and big seals and bears. They missed their dogs lots, but managed to go along. Dr. Cook put much attention to cooking, they tell.

On their way home to Etah in the spring they suffered from the well known deep and soft snow along the east coast of the southern part of Ellesmeres land. They made short days, and they travelled slowly. Still, they had plenty of ammunitions, and they always tell about themselves going and wasting the cartridges shooting target practice after seals on the ice. Dr. Cook encouraged them to do that "as he wanted to come back without ammunition."

After they were back at Etah, they learned that Franke—a German steward from Hamburg that came up on board Bradley's boat and stayed with Dr. Cook, had sold all the stuff for foxes that Dr. Cook had promised them for joining him on the trip. They only received each two boxes of matches.

When, therefore, Dr. Cook going south left his sextant and a hand medicine box at Etah, they regarded it proper justice that they took that because he had given them too little.

When I came next year to Etah I found the sextant in care of Itukusuk and bought it from him for an alarm clock. But he kept the box for the sextant as a toolbox and had that in several years on his sledge for ammunition, matches, and so on.

The medicine rack contained some poison so I thought it was very bad to leave that in care of Eskimos that could not read.

I poured it out and gave the glasses to the natives. The sextant I sent home to *Politiken*, my newspaper, and made them sell it for charity purposes, the money came to poor children. I never heard who bought it. I had sealed it and written statement that it was the very instrument from Dr. Cook. I did this to get Dr. Cook to sue me and thereby be caused to tell how badly he paid his natives.

But not a word was said by Dr. Cook to his two men, that they had been at the Pole. They would have denied it as they from the many expeditions of Peary's knew that the Pole could not be reached in such a way.

I hereby want to put the attention to the fact, that nothing was said to Admiral Peary when he came down with his Eskimos about the Pole having been reached. They certainly would had told him, as they both of them saw the admiral when he came from the north. Admiral Peary asked them about their trip and they told him.

Dr. Cook meantime had gone south across the Melville Bay by sledges. But none of the four or five men that took him down to the colonized Greenland heard about the Pole.

They had special good going and they wanted to hurry, as they were not sure, Peary would like them to bring the man down; they knew from his own telling, that he and Admiral Peary were on no friendly terms. Later they got all means of regretting going as it was just in the very best season of the year to hunt for seals on the ice, and Dr. Cook who had no provisions but depended on their skill as hunters, paid them very badly. He left them at the northernmost settlement and took a sledge from this place, Ituisalik. He told the Smith Sound natives to wait for their payment, and drove to Tassiussak with the best hunter at the place by name Simon called Itue. From Tassiussak he send a piece of canvas to each of them used for sealhunting on the ice to hide back, when the seal is asleep. It cost 22 re or almost six cents a piece, which shows that the doctor is a special economic man.

In Tassiussak he was taken in by Mr. Dahl, Danish trader at the place (now in Copenhagen working at Frihavnen, the Free Harbour, at that time employed in Greenland).

Mr. Dahl has told me that Dr. Cook did never mention the North Pole at all during his stay here.

From there Dr. Cook was taken to Upernivik the northernmost colony in Greenland. He talked very freely with the two drivers that took him down; in the middle of the day they came to Qassiussaq, where they had coffee by Mr. Bistrup, now dead. He never talked about the Pole here either, the same with the natives dog-drivers.

They arrived to Upernivik very early in the morning. The manager at that time was the late Mr. Kraul, a very intelligent man, but affected by his many years in the Arctic.

When Dr. Cook came about two o'clock in the morning, the natives wakened up Mr. Kraul and told him that a stranger has arrived. Mr. Kraul went up and saw the American walking outside in the bright night.

He thought it was a run-away from a whaling ship, in any way he went to bed again and slept until his usual hour to get up.

Dr. Cook meanwhile walked forth and back between the house and the flagstaff in Upernivik and waited for the Danes to get up. About eight o'clock, Mr. Kraul came out and greeted Dr. Cook:

"How do you do? Where do you come from?"

"Oh, I merely come from the North Pole," was the answer.

"What do you say? From the North Pole? Hey, Miss Larsen, here is a man from the North Pole." And Miss Larsen, now Mrs. Jespersen in Ronne, Bronkolm, Denmark married to the former priest Erik Jespersen in Greenland, came hurrying out. At the same time came the minister at the place, the late Mr. Knud Balle, out from his house.

Mr. Kraul shouted out for him to tell that the North Pole has been explored, and the minister came over. The last bottle of wine in the colony was opened and a celebration as they are in the far north took place.

It is my opinion, that Dr. Cook just happened to say his stuff about the Pole at this very moment just as a saying or joke. But before the first breakfast was over, an express sledge was send south to boast the news and a message was send to the inspector of North Greenland—now director Daugaard-Jensen of Greenland.

Later on Dr. Cook became the hero in the entire Greenland until he could go home with the SS *Hans Egede* to Copenhagen.

He went south to Jakobshavn and stayed by Dr. Holger Kier, who later on told me that he invited Dr. Cook to go with him to look at the sick people in town; but this did not interest the doctor at all, though he was a colleague and he proved not to be a very smart physician either to the Greenland doctor.

On his way home, Dr. Cook was a passenger together with several Danish people including the late Professor Steensby and Thomas Thomsen, inspector at the Museum in Copenhagen. They told me later that Dr. Cook had formed his story by this time, but he had no real understanding of what he was up against. He also at this boat trip on the way to

Denmark tried to pull more over the head of the Danes, he told them he had found a new and unknown animal or two. But as the scientist examined him, he gave it up as they informed him that this was too much and they agreed upon it being an ermine, which he stated he did not know until he saw such a one at Cape Sparbo.

Nevertheless, the Danish scientists came to Copenhagen believers on him. So did most of the people down there. What had taken them is a mystery up to this day. He had no proof at all; he did not show any observations, only the astronomical professor at the University of Copenhagen found out that Dr. Cook understood so little about astronomy that it would be impossible for him to fake observations and make them false.

But I have heard several times from Itukusuk and Apilak that Dr. Cook never used his sextant during the expedition and they never were out of such places as the natives know by heart.

As to use this as a proof may be too much. It is only a statement, but it gives a true picture of the unhappy Dr. Cook which respond wonderful with that of him obtained from every place where he has been. He is always recognized as untruthful and not able to tell the facts or the truth. Neverless he is well liked. His Norwegian friends told me he had done several dirty things during his trip with Captain Gerlache, still they liked him. Amundsen told me about him; they stuck together during that expedition where the days not always went too peaceful of.

He betrayed the natives in Greenland, too. He left his house at Etah in charge of a certain German Rudolf Franke, a cook and steward on Bradley's boat. He went crazy during his stay there; the Eskimos tell about him that he was scared of them shooting him.

But he sold all the stuff Dr. Cook had promised the two boys that went with him. He also, the natives tell, helped himself from the caches left by Admiral Peary at Etah. I have forgotten the detail though told to me several times.

Later on Rudolf Franke was taken back to American on Peary's ship and the natives told about him, that as soon he was on board he would not allow them to come in the cabin where he roomed together with the crew on board—because "he could not stand their smell" having depended on them for that long time. He knew nothing about Cook's case. We had him up in Denmark sometime to examine him. But he proved to be a common cook and not knowing a thing about his master's work.

Dr. Cook never tried to stick to his promise and send anything up to his two boys; in all he has always shown himself dishonest, as when he took the only keroseen left from Dr. Knud Rasmussen during his absense, left by Knud Rasmussen as reserve for his home trip. At the same time he took Rasmussen's new sleeping bag and left his own full of lice.

The fact that Knud Rasmussen disliked him personally made him take a more favorable stand towards him when it came to bring out the news about the Pole, but he never went in for him as often told.

According to the foolish accusal against Peary done by Gordon Hayes, I kind of find it funny that anybody cares what he says.

I know from the stories of the natives, that Peary reached the point he told them was the Pole in excellent condition. He was favored by many things: Good going, good dogs, the very best natives and exceptional good weather. Furthermore he had during his many years developed such a technique as a traveler, that is far beyond the understanding of Gordon Hayes. He had his system of travelling completed from many unsuccessful expeditions. The natives say that he had his men trained from childhood like you break in dogs from young to get them to understand you. They all wanted to do what he wished; it was not only employer and his men, they were *friends.*

Only one of them is left now; the oldest, Odark. The three others are dead; Iggianguark, Ukujark, Sigdlu (as we spell them in Greenland). They have told me time after time about it.

On their way home they had the advantage of the igloos built on the way up. But they did not use them all. They passed during the day at least one igloo because they did not use them, and here is a thing an Eskimo never forgets to notice. That is, that they left so much behind them of the supplies laid out for them by supporting sledges on the way up.

Ukujak told me that Peary allowed them to eat what they could when they passed a house, but not to take anything along. They went home with practically empty sledges. That is why they could do it.

They could have travelled much longer, they always like to tell, but they were at the very spot and Peary showed his happiness so evident that everyone could understand he was where he wanted to be during the many years.

This alone is enough to tell that Peary himself believed to be at the Pole and the explanation about bad observations do not count at all. First Admiral Peary was a very experienced explorer, had made observations during many years. They never failed. Second, should any place in the world be called easy to determin, it must be the Pole where you never have to think of the longitude what always was our trouble before the radio made it easy. He only had to look out for the latitude, and up there he could do it not only at noon but any time of the day.

The natives also have told me the sun was on the sky when they were there.

Furthermore, we have the statement of Captain Bartlett's and McMillan's and the late George Borup's and Professor Marvin's. If one will check up on their statements it is easy to find out how fast they went and the fact is, that the last division: the admiral, Matt Henson and the four natives, went on. Never had Peary laid down doing nothing, why should he have done it this time, where he was so determined to do the Pole, and when he had the best natural condition ever seen during his many years?

I happen to live in the very district where Admiral Peary spent so many years. I have been on expeditions where his records have been found and brought back. I took myself his record at Navy Cliff. Never has any of the admiral's statements failed, never has he ever been found out telling anything but the truth.

He has been loyal all his life to his work, and it seems to me like an insult that I shall sit here and defend Admiral Peary against Mr. Gordon Hayes. If this gentleman only has the speed of the dogs to hang his hat on, it is because he never saw how Greenland Eskimos can travel. And if he sees Greenland Eskimos travel, he may not understand how they would do it when they have a leader as Robert Peary to do the command.

I dare say that a man like Admiral Peary only was able to accomplish what he did because of his helpers. That includes the white and the Eskimoic. But he could only get them because they believed in him and they would like to work the life out of themselves for his sake. People never raise such an affection for a man unless they trust every word he says. Peary is known for never having given a promise to an Eskimo unless he kept it. They tell about him, that he was unable to tell a lie. That is the secret back of the wonderful discipline he infected upon the Eskimos.

Such a man never comes back and fakes results from an expedition. If that had been in his mind, he could have done that years ago; but he never was afraid for anything in the world. He would not have been afraid of telling about a defeat either.

Dear Dr. Stefansson, this is what I can write down in a hurry without having notebooks along with me. But if you can have use for it, I will only feel happy, therefore.

Sincerely yours as ever
(signed: Peter Freuchen)

NOTES*

Chapter 1

1. Cook, *My Attainment of the Pole*, pp. 286–287.
2. *Ibid.*, p. 287.

Chapter 2

1. Cook, *My Attainment of the Pole*, p. 42; p. 43.
2. *Ibid.*, p. 43.
3. *Ibid.*
4. Eames, *Winner Lose All: Dr. Cook and the Theft of the North Pole*, p. 13.
5. Weems, *Peary: The Explorer and the Man*, p. 124.
6. Cook, *Through the First Antarctic Night*, p. 186.
7. *Ibid.*, p. 197.
8. *Ibid.*, p. 399.
9. Amundsen, *My Life as an Explorer*, p. 28.

---

*Archival sources listed with parenthetical abbrevistions in these notes are identified in the bibliography.

10. Dunn, *The Shameless Diary of an Explorer,* p. 93; p. 86; p. 95.
11. *Ibid.,* p. 101.
12. Cook, *To the Top of the Continent,* p. 41.
13. *Ibid.*
14. *Ibid.*
15. *Ibid.,* pp. 41–42.

Chapter 3

1. Cook, *To the Top of the Continent,* p. 205.
2. *Ibid.,* p. 207.
3. *Ibid.,* p. 215.
4. *Ibid.,* p. 218.
5. *Ibid.,* p. 231.
6. *Ibid.,* pp. 231–232.
7. *Seattle Post-Intelligencer,* June 9, 1903.
8. *Ibid.,* November 8, 1906.
9. *Ibid.*
10. *Ibid.*
11. *New York Times,* October 7, 1906.
12. *Ibid.*
13. *Ibid.*
14. *Ibid.*
15. *Ibid.,* October 31, 1906.
16. *Ibid.* November 10, 1906.
17. Browne, *The Conquest of Mount McKinley,* p. 70.

Chapter 4

1. Cook, *My Attainment of the Pole,* p. 113.
Other quotes from *Attainment* are at pp. 206, 229, 235, 238, 242, 257, 258–259, 259, 262, 272, and 284.

Chapter 5

1. A de Quervain and A. Stolberg, *Durch Gronlands Eiswüte.* English translation made for W. H. Hobbs; copy in Cook-Peary Collection (SC)
2. Cook, *My Attainment of the Pole,* p. 467.

3. *Ibid.,* p. 469.

4. *New York Times,* September 5, 1909.

5. *Ibid.*

6. *Ibid.*

7. Cook, *My Attainment of the Pole,* p. 467.

8. Freeman, *The Case for Doctor Cook,* pp. 145–146.

9. *New York Times,* September 8, 1909.

10. *Ibid.*

11. Eames, *Winner Lose All,* p. 117.

12. *Ibid.,* p. 118.

13. *Ibid.,* p. 119.

14. Freeman, *The Case for Doctor Cook,* p. 152; Cook, *My Attainment of the Pole,* p. 474.

Chapter 6

1. Peary, *The North Pole,* p. 270. Other Peary quotes in this chapter are from pages 275, 281, 284, 287–289, 296, and 299–300. Peary's physical condition on the last drive has been a matter of controversy. Henson said that Peary had to ride in the sledge. Peary denied this vehemently. There is no way to settle the question, but it has little bearing on whether Peary made the Pole. Certainly Henson did not have any doubt that they had reached their goal.

2. Freeman, *The Case for Doctor Cook,* p. 157.

3. *New York Times,* September 11, 1909.

Chapter 7

1. *New York Times,* September 24, 1909; Eames, *Winner Lose All,* p. 141.

2. These and other related events were recounted in the *Times* and are summarized in *The New York Times Index.*

Chapter 8

1. Villarejo, *Dr. Kane's Voyage to the Polar Lands,* p. 54.

2. *Ibid.,* p. 64.

3. Kane, *Arctic Explorations,* vol. I, p. 171.

4. Greely, *True Tales,* pp. 93–94.

5. Nansen, *Farthest North,* vol. I, p. 232.

6. Elder, *Biography of Elisha Kent Kane, passim.*
7. Loomis *Weird and Tragic Shores,* p. 79, paperback edition.
8. *Ibid.,* p. 222, paperback edition.
9. *Nome Nugget,* February 28, 1903.
10. *Ibid.*
11. Loomis, *op. cit.,* p. 342.

Chapter 9

1. Melville, *In the Lena Delta,* p. 15.
2. *Ibid.,* p. 43.
3. *Ibid.,* p. 335.
4. *Ibid.,* p. 368.
5. *Ibid.*
6. *Ibid.,* p. 370.
7. *Ibid.*
8. *Ibid.,* p. 458.
9. DeLong, *Voyage of the Jeannette,* p. 893.
10. Hoehling, *Jeannette Expedition,* p. 190.
11. *Ibid.,* p. 181; pp. 196–197.
12. *Ibid.,* p. 205.
13. Newcomb, *Our Lost Explorers,* p. 476.
14. *Ibid.,* p. 477; p. iii; p. 479.
15. Tyson, *Arctic Experiences,* p. 67.
16. *Ibid.*
17. *History of the Adventurous Voyage and Terrible Shipwreck of the U.S. Steamer Jeannette,* p. 86.
18. *Ibid.,* p. 89; p. 90.
19. *New York Times,* September 18, 1882.
20. Hoehling, *op. cit.,* p. 148.

Chapter 10

1. Kirwan, *The White Road: A History of Polar Exploration,* p. 188.
2. Greely, *Three Years of Arctic Service,* vol. I, p. 85.
3. Brainard, *The Outpost of the Lost,* p. 160.
4. *Ibid.,* pp. 289–290.
5. Greely, *Reminiscences of Adventure and Service,* p. 146.
6. Brainard, *op. cit.,* p. 291.

7. Todd, *Abandoned: Story of the Greely Arctic Expedition 1881–1884*, p. 116.
8. Ellis, "The Greely Expedition: The Last Days," *Beaver*, Spring 1974, p. 33.
9. *Proceedings of the "Proteus" Court of Inquiry*, p. 276.
10. Schley, *The Rescue of Greely*, p. 223.
11. Todd, *op. cit.*, p. 284.
12. *Ibid.*, p. 286; p. 287.
13. *Ibid.*, p. xv.
14. Barclay, *The Greely Arctic Expedition*, p. 51.
15. *Ibid.*
16. *Ibid.*, p. 62.
17. *Ibid.*, p. 67.
18. *Ibid.*
19. Todd, *op. cit.*, p. 294.
20. *London Daily Chronicle*, November 2, 1900, press cutting (SPRI).
21. *Windsor Magazine*, December, 1901, press cutting (SPRI).
22. *Natal Mercury*, September 23, 1902, press cutting, (SPRI).
23. Fiala, *Fighting the Polar Ice*, p. 4.
24. *Ibid.*, p. 7.
25. *Polar Times*, June 1969, p. 28.
26. *Ibid.*

Chapter 11

1. This and other following quotes concerning Barrill's exposures are from *New York Globe and Commercial Advertiser*, October 14, 15, and 16; and *New York Times*, October 17, 1909.
2. *Literary Digest*, January 1, 1910.
3. Whitney to Greely, October 5, 1909 (SC).
4. Greely to Whitney, October 15, 1909 (SC).
5. Abstract of the September 29, 1909 Explorers Club Board of Governors' report. Typescript in the Stefansson Collection, Baker Library, Dartmouth College (SC); also *New York Times*, December 25, 1909.

Chapter 12

1. *New York Times*, December 9, 1909, has this and following quotes on the affair.
2. Cook, *My Attainment of the Pole*, pp. 535–536; p. 537. Quotes following are on pp. 538 and 539.

Chapter 13

1. Peary to Hubbard, October 19, 1909 (NA).
2. *Ibid.* Peary's "Yellow Paper" reference was probably to *New York Herald* and as usual was unfair and exaggerated. *Herald* was not notably zealous in defending Cook.
3. *Ibid.*
4. Peary to Bridgman, October 13, 1909 (NA).
5. *Ibid.,* October 26, 1909 (NA).
6. *Ibid.*
7. Peary to Bridgman, October 27, 1909 (NA).
8. Cook, *My Attainment of the Pole,* p. 496. Quotes following this are from pp. 495, 500, 501, 502, 503–504, 504, and 504–505.

Chapter 14

1. Until indicated by another note reference, all the quotes given are from *The New York Times,* December 22, 1909.
2. *Literary Digest,* January 1, 1910.
3. Remaining quotes in this chapter from *The New York Times,* December 27, 1909.

Chapter 15

1. Peary to Bridgman, October 5, 1910 (NA).
2. Peary to Hubbard, February 13, 1910; December 24, 1910 (NA).
3. Hobbs, *Peary,* pp. 406-407.
4. *Ibid.,* p. 407.
5. Peary to Stokes, February 21, 1910; July 12, 1910 (NA).
6. *New York Times,* May 21, 1910.
7. Moore, *Mount McKinley: The Pioneer Climbs,* p. 83.
8. *Ibid.,* p. 85.
9. *Ibid.*

Chapter 16

1. Cook lecture transcript in Cook-Peary papers (SC).
2. *Ibid.*

3. Stenographer's transcript in Alexander-Peary letters (NA).
4. Cook, *My Attainment of the Pole,* pp. 436–438.
5. *Hamilton Journal,* July 30, 1914; transcript in Alexander-Peary letters (NA).
6. *Athens Herald,* August 15, 1914; *Grass Valley Morning Union,* August 14, 1914; *Saint Louis Globe Democrat,* September 25, 1914; *Grand Rapids Press,* June 3, 1914; *San Antonio Light,* August 31, 1914; all transcripts in Alexander-Peary letters, 1914 (NA).

Chapter 17

1. Cook, *My Attainment of the Pole,* p. 8. Other quotes from *Attainment* are on pp. 8, 9, 506, 508, 509, 510, 511, 515, 519, 519–520, 520 (the photograph is at p. 493), 578, 583, and 593.
2. High to Baldwin, January 4, 1914 (UV). For this and two following quotes.
3. Peck to High, January 6, 1914 (UV).
4. High to Peck, February 9, 1914 (UV).

Chapter 18

1. *New York Sun* transcript, undated, in Alexander-Peary letters, 1914 (NA).
2. Keltie to Peary, April 9, 1914 (NA).
3. Alexander to Hubbard, April 9, 1915 (NA).
4. *Ibid.*
5. Weems, *Peary: The Explorer and the Man,* p. 311.
6. "The Attack on Dr. Frederick A. Cook," Speech of Hon. T. H. Caraway (Ark.), H.R., March 4, 1915, Wash.: GPO, 1915, p. 8.
7. *Ibid.*
8. "The Attack," *op. cit.,* p. 17.
9. *Ibid.*
10. *Ibid.,* pp. 22–23.
11. *Ibid.,* p. 22.
12. Wright, *The Big Nail: The Story of the Cook-Peary Feud,* p. 247.
13. *Ibid.,* p. 250.
14. Helgesen, "Extension of Remarks," *Congressional Record,* 64th Congress, 1st session, pp. 2–16, March 4, 1915.
15. Eames, *Winner Lose All,* p. 285.
16. Thomas F. Hall, *Has the North Pole Been Discovered?,* pp. 439–464, gives a rather odd scrutiny to Helgesen's speech.
17. Weems, *Peary,* p. 347, cites the *Lancaster Gazette,* October 7, 1916.

Chapter 19

1. Weems, *Peary,* p. 323, cites *Wichita Falls Times,* May 19, 1919.
2. Eames, *Winner Lose All,* p. 290. Information on Cook's first years in oil is from Eames, who seems to have relied entirely on Cook's statements, which are always subject to question.
3. *Ibid.,* p. 287.
4. *Ibid.,* p. 292.
5. *Ibid.*
6. Cook's defense counsel questioned the prosecutor on the stand at the trial's end. The defense hoped to show that Cook had refused to plea bargain on any terms that would require a guilty plea and any punishment. The prosecutor insisted that Cook's bottom line was imprisonment: He would have accepted a guilty plea and a fine.
7. Cook to Cornhauser, February 6, 1923 (FW).
8. *Ibid.*
9. Trial record in Government Exhibit No. 882, vol. 26, p. 101 (FW).
10. Cook to Grace Couchman, January 29, 1923, in Box 1 (FW).
11. *Ibid.*
12. Trial record in Government Exhibit No. 873 (FW).

Chapter 20

1. *Fort Worth Record,* October 16, 1923.
2. Trial record, grand jury indictment (FW).
3. All of this exchange is in trial record, vol. 26, pp. 39–41 (FW).
4. *Ibid.,* p. 78.
5. Trial record in Government Exhibit No. 876 (FW).
6. Trial record, vol. 26, p. 111 (FW).
7. *Ibid.,* pp. 26–27.
8. *Ibid.*
9. *Ibid.,* p. 67.
10. *Fort Worth Record,* November 20, 1923.
11. *Ibid.*
12. *Ibid.,* November 23, 1923.
13. Eames, *Winner Lose All,* p. 303.
14. *Ibid.,* p. 292.

Chapter 21

1. Eames, *Winner Lose All,* pp. 301–302.
2. Killits's summary of this episode is an undated memo in Cook-Peary papers (SC). Probably it was given to William Hobbs in the 1930s, and Hobbs sent a copy to Stefansson.

Chapter 22

1. *Leavenworth New Era,* vol. XIII, no. 5 (June 1926), p. 1.
2. *Ibid.*
3. *Ibid.,* no. 8 (September 1926), p. 1. An amazing price! Cook gave no other information on the particular expedition.
4. *New York Times,* January 25, 1926.
5. *Ibid.*
6. *Ibid.*
7. Rawlins, *Peary at the North Pole, Fact or Fiction?,* p. 268.
8. *Ibid.,* p. 252.
9. *Ibid.,* March 4, 1926.
10. Stefansson to Hobbs, January 20, 1930 (in response to Hobbs to Stefansson of January 15, 1930) (SC).
11. Eames, *Winner Lose All,* p. 307.
12. Cook to William Shea, August 22, 1936 (NA).
13. *Ibid.;* Leitzell's articles appeared in October 1935 and January 1936 in *Real America.*
14. *Ibid.*
15. "Material for Rebuttal . . . Cook-MacMillan Trial," 1936 (SC).
16. *Time,* December 4, 1939.
17. Shainwald von Ahlefeldt to F. D. Roosevelt, May 20, 1940, copy in Cook-Peary papers (SC).

Chapter 23

1. Balch, *Glaciers or Freezing Caverns,* p. v.
2. Balch, *Mount McKinley and Mountain Climbers' Proofs;* Balch, *North Pole and Bradley Land.* As a young lad, Balch met explorer Henry M. Stanley in Paris and spent much time with him. It could be conjectured that this

association conditioned Balch to a defense of Cook. Stanley had been treated harshly by some critics after his great African journeys.

3. *New York Tribune,* April 14, 1913. Reprinted in Cook, *Attainment,* pp. 594–599.
4. Browne papers (SC).
5. Balch to Ward, November 24, 1925, in Ward Collection (NA).
6. Browne to Balch, March 17, 1915 (SC).
7. Balch to Browne, March 19, 1915 (SC).
8. Browne to Balch, March 21, 1915 (SC).
9. Balch to Browne, March 25, 1915 (SC).
10. Browne to Balch, March 29, 1915 (SC).
11. Balch to Browne, April 1, 1915 (SC).
12. Balch, *North Pole and Bradley Land,* p. 16; p. 19.
13. *Ibid.,* p. 25.
14. Cook, *My Attainment of the Pole,* p. 599.

Chapter 24

1. *Life,* August 20, 1956.
2. Eames, *Winner Lose All,* p. 67.
3. *Ibid.,* p. 63.
4. *Ibid.,* p. 65.
5. Washburn to author, April 6, 1977. And see Washburn, "Doctor Cook and Mount McKinley," *American Alpine Journal,* vol. II, no. 1, issue 32 (1958), pp. 1–30, for a convincing analysis of photographic evidence.
6. *Ibid.*
7. Wright, *The Big Nail,* p. 241.
8. *Ibid.*
9. Cook, *My Attainment of the Pole,* p. 534.
10. *Ibid.*
11. *Ibid.*
12. Moore, *Mount McKinley: The Pioneer Climbs,* p. 107.
13. Cook, *op. cit.,* p. 526.
14. *New York Times,* October 17, 1909.
15. Cook, *op. cit.,* p. 524.
16. Cook, *To the Top of the Continent,* p. 173.
17. Cook, *My Attainment of the Pole,* p. 524.
18. Browne, *The Conquest of Mount McKinley,* p. 72.

Chapter 25

1. *Newsletter,* Cook Society, December 1975.
2. Euler, "Pioneer American Explorer," *Arctic,* p. 209.
3. Wright, *The Big Nail,* p. 281. Mrs. Vetter has since died and the papers are held by her daughter.
4. Euler, *op. cit.,* p. 210.
5. *Ibid.,* p. 219.
6. *Ibid.*
7. Rawlins, *Peary at the North Pole,* p. 86.
8. Eames, *Winner Lose All,* p. 230.
9. Mowat, *The Polar Passion,* p. 237. Other Mowat quotes are from pp. 237 and 238.

Chapter 26

1. Mowat, *The Polar Passion,* p. 340.

Chapter 27

1. *New York Times,* June 24, 1899.
2. Boas to Hobbs, March 6, 1916 (SC).
3. Eames, *Winner Lose All,* p. 258; *New York Times,* May 21, 1910.
4. Cook, *My Attainment of the Pole,* p. 498.
5. *New York Times,* May 21, 1910. Others helped too, see Charles Fulong to Louis Milhau, April 24, 1962 (SC).
6. Cook, *op. cit.,* p. 497. Actually the exposure created little interest and I found no follow-up to the initial middle-page story in *New York Times,* May 21, 1910.
7. Eames, *Winner Lose All,* p. 259; Freeman, *The Case for Dr. Cook,* pp. 213–214; Wright, *The Big Nail,* p. 243.
8. Eames, *op. cit.*
9. Cook, *My Attainment of the Pole,* p. 116. Other *Attainment* quotes are from pp. 116–117, 117, 117–118, 119, 120, 121, 125, 126, 129.

Chapter 28

1. Weems, *Peary,* p. 284.

2. Hobbs, *Peary,* p. v.
3. *Ibid.,* p. 426.
4. *Ibid.,* p. 375.
5. *Ibid.*
6. Weems, *op. cit.,* pp. 281; 282.
7. *Ibid.,* p. 284.
8. Stefansson diary, June 6, 1910 (SC).
9. *Ibid.*
10. Rawlins, "A Retrospective Critique," p. 30.
11. *Ibid.,* p. 31.
12. *Ibid.,* p. 36.
13. *Ibid.,* pp. 38–39.

Chapter 29

1. Gibbons, Russell W. "Frederick Cook and the North Pole: The Unmaking of a Discoverer." A paper read at the 1976 Annual meeting of the Society for the History of Discoveries, November 5, 1976; also in *The Arctic Circular,* March 1977, pp. 1–11.
2. Kirwan, *The White Road: A History of Polar Exploration,* p. 263.
3. Trevor-Roper, *Hermit of Peking,* p. 275.

BIBLIOGRAPHY

I. ARCHIVES

Depositories are cited by initials in the reference notes.

(FW)   Fort Worth Record Center
           United States v. Cook Trial Records

(LC)   Library of Congress
           Baldwin Collection
           Greely Collection

(NA)   National Archives—Center for Polar Archives
           Cook Collection
           Peary Collection
           Stafford Collection
           Ward Collection

(SPRI)   Scott Polar Research Institute
           Polar Press Cuttings

(SC)   Stefansson Collection, Baker Library, Dartmouth College
           Correspondence
           Cook-Peary Collection

(UA)   University of Alaska
           Brooks Collection

(USC)   University of Santa Clara
           Hubbard Collection

(UV)   University of Virginia
           Balch Collection

II. PERIODICALS

Arctic, passim.

Arctic Circular, passim.

Leavenworth New Era, 1926–1927, *passim.*

Newsletter, Dr. Frederick A. Cook Society.

Polar Notes, passim.

Polar Record, passim.

Polar Times, passim.

Ellis, Richard N. "The Greely Expedition: The Last Days." *Beaver,* Spring 1974, p. 33.

Euler, John. "Pioneer American Explorer." *Arctic,* June 1961.

Rawlins, Dennis. "Evaluating Claims of North Polar Priority." *Norse Geogr. Tidsik* 26:135–40.

Rawlins, Dennis. "A Retrospective Critique of Peary's North Pole Claim." *Polar Notes.* October, 1970.

Washburn, Bradford. "Doctor Cook and Mount McKinley." *American Alpine Journal,* vol. II, no. 1, issue 32 (1958), pp. 1–30.

Press cuttings: Artic Exploration (SPRI). *London Daily Chronicle: Windsor Magazine; Natal Mercury, et. al.*

III. BOOKS

Amundsen, Roald. *My Life as an Explorer.* New York: Doubleday, Doran, 1928.

Anderson, J.R.L. *The Ulysses Factor.* London: Hodder & Stoughton, 1970.

Balch, Edwin Swift. *Glaciers or Freezing Caverns.* New York: Johnson Reprint, 1970.

Balch, Edwin Swift. *Mount McKinley and Mountain Climbers' Proofs.* Philadelphia: Campion, 1914.

Balch, Edwin Swift. *North Pole and Bradley Land.* Philadelphia: Campion, 1913.

Barclay, George Lippart. *The Greely Arctic Expedition.* Philadelphia: Barclay, 1884.

Brainard, David L. *The Outpost of the Lost.* Indianapolis: Bobbs-Merrill, 1929.

Browne, Belmore. *The Conquest of Mount McKinley.* New York: Putnam's, 1913; New edition, Boston: Houghton Mifflin, 1956.

Bridges, Esteban Lucas. *Uttermost Part of the Earth.* New York: Dutton, 1948.

Caswell, John E. *Arctic Frontiers.* Norman: University of Oklahoma, 1956.

Cook, Frederick A. *My Attainment of the Pole.* New York: Polar, 1911.

Cook, Frederick A. *Return from the Pole.* New York: Pellegrini & Cudahy, 1951.

Cook, Frederick A. *Through the First Antarctic Night.* New York: Doubleday & McClure, 1900.

Cook, Frederick A. *To the Top of the Continent.* New York: Doubleday, Page, 1908.

Davis, Elmer. *The History of the New York Times 1851–1921.* New York: Greenwood, 1969.

DeLong, George W. *Voyage of the Jeannette.* Boston: Houghton Mifflin, 1884.

Dunn, Robert. *The Shameless Diary of an Explorer.* New York: Outing, 1907.

Eames, Hugh. *Winner Lose All: Dr. Cook and the Theft of the North Pole.* Boston: Little, Brown, 1973.

Elder, William. *Biography of Elisha Kent Kane.* Philadelphia: Childs & Peterson, 1858.

Fiala, Anthony. *Fighting the Polar Ice.* New York: Doubleday, Page, 1906.

Freeman, Andrew A. *The Case for Dr. Cook.* New York: Coward-McCann, 1961.

Freuchen, Peter. *Arctic Adventure.* New York: Farrar and Rinehart, 1935.

Gibbons, Russell W. *An Historical Evaluation of the Cook-Peary Controversy.* (Typescript, Ohio Northern University, 1956.)

Greely, Adolphus W. *Reminiscences of Adventure and Service.* New York: Scribner's, 1927.

Greely, Adolphus W. *Three Years of Arctic Service.* New York: Scribner's, 1886.

Greely, Adolphus W. *True Tales of Arctic Heroism in the New World.* New York: Scribner's, 1912.

Hall, Thomas F. *Has the North Pole Been Discovered?* Boston: Badger, 1917.

Hayes, J. Gordon. *Robert Edwin Peary.* London: G. Richards & H. Toulmin, 1929.

History of the Adventurous Voyage and Terrible Shipwreck of the U.S. Steamer Jeannette. New York: DeWitt, 1882.

Hobbs, William Herbert. *Peary.* New York: MacMillan, 1931.

Hoehling, A. A. *Jeannette Expedition.* London: Abelard-Schuman, 1967.

Huntford, Roland. *Scott & Amundsen.* New York: Putnam, 1980.

Kane, Elisha Kent. *Arctic Explorations.* Philadelphia: Childs & Peterson, 1856.

Kirwan, L. P. *The White Road: A History of Polar Exploration*. London: Hollis & Carter, 1959.

Lewin, W. Henry. *The Great North Pole Fraud*. London: Daniel, 1935.

Loomis, Chauncey. *Weird and Tragic Shores*. New York: Knopf, 1971.

MacMillan, Donald B. *How Peary Reached the Pole*. Boston: Houghton Mifflin, 1934.

Melville, George. *In the Lena Delta*. Boston: Houghton Mifflin, 1884.

Mirsky, Jeannette. *To the Arctic!* New York: Knopf, 1948.

Moore, Terris. *Mount McKinley: The Pioneer Climbs*. College: University of Alaska, 1967.

Mowat, Farley. *The Polar Passion*. Toronto: McClelland & Stewart, 1967.

Nansen, Fridtjof. *Farthest North*. London: Newnes, 1898.

Neatby, L. H. *Conquest of the Last Frontier*. Athens: Ohio University, 1966.

Newcomb, Raymond Lee. *Our Lost Explorers*. San Francisco: Bancroft, 1882.

Noyce, Wilfrid. *Springs of Adventure*. London: Murray, 1958.

Peary, Robert E. *Nearest the Pole*. New York: Doubleday, 1907.

Peary, Robert E. *The North Pole*. New York: Stokes, 1910.

Peary, Robert E. *Northward Over the "Great Ice."* New York: Stokes, 1898.

Peary, Robert E. *Secrets of Polar Travel*. New York: Century, 1917.

Proceedings of the "Proteus" Court of Inquiry on the Greely Relief Expedition of 1883. Washington: Government Printing Office, 1884.

Rasky, Frank. *North Pole or Bust*. Toronto: McGraw-Hill, Ryerson, 1977.

Rasky, Frank. *The Polar Voyages*. Toronto: McGraw-Hill, Ryerson, 1976.

Rawlins, Dennis. *Peary at the North Pole, Fact or Fiction?* New York: Luce, 1973.

Schley, Winfield S. *The Rescue of Greely*. New York: Scribner's, 1885.

Stefansson, Vilhjalmur. *Discovery*. New York: McGraw-Hill, 1964.

Stefansson, Vilhjalmur. *The Friendly Arctic*. New York: MacMillan, 1943.

Stefansson, Vilhjalmur. *The Problem of Meighen Island*. New York: Explorers Club, 1939.

Stuck, Hudson. *The Ascent of Denali*. New York: Scribner's, 1914.

Todd, A. L. *Abandoned: The Story of the Greely Arctic Expedition 1881–1884*. New York: McGraw-Hill, 1961.

Trevor-Roper, Hugh. *Hermit of Peking*. New York: Knopf, 1977.

Tyson, George. *Arctic Experiences*. Edited by E. Vale Blake. New York: Harper, 1874.

Victor, Paul-Emile. *Man and the Conquest of the Poles*. New York: Simon & Schuster, 1963.

Villarejo, Oscar M. *Dr. Kane's Voyage to the Polar Lands.* Philadelphia: University of Pennsylvania, 1965.

Washburn, Bradford. *Mount McKinley and the Alaska Range.* Boston: Museum of Science, 1951.

Weems, John Edward. *Race for the Pole.* New York: Holt, 1960.

Weems, John Edward. *Peary: The Explorer and the Man.* London: Eyret & Spottiswoode, 1967.

Wright, Theon. *The Big Nail: The Story of the Cook-Peary Feud.* New York: John Day, 1970.

INDEX

285